PRACTICE TEACHING

A REFLECTIVE APPROACH

Jack C. Richards
Thomas S.C. Farrell

CAMBRIDGE
UNIVERSITY PRESS

CAMBRIDGE UNIVERSITY PRESS
Cambridge, New York, Melbourne, Madrid, Cape Town,
Singapore, São Paulo, Delhi, Tokyo, Mexico City

Cambridge University Press
32 Avenue of the Americas, New York, NY 10013-2473, USA

www.cambridge.org
Information on this title: www.cambridge.org/9780521186223

First published 2011

Printed in the United States of America

A catalog record for this publication is available from the British Library.

Library of Congress Cataloging in Publication data

Richards, Jack C.
Practice teaching : a reflective approach / Jack C. Richards, Thomas S. C. Farrell.
    p.   cm.
Includes bibliographical references and index.
ISBN 978-0-521-18622-3 (alk. paper) – ISBN 978-1-107-00644-7 (alk. paper)
1. Language teachers – Training of.   I. Farrell, Thomas S. C. (Thomas Sylvester Charles)   II. Title.
P53.85.R533   2010
418.0071′1–dc22   2010036413

ISBN 978-1-107-00644-7 Hardback
ISBN 978-0-521-18622-3 Paperback

CONTENTS

INTRODUCTION

To the Student Teacher

This book is designed to provide support and guidance for student teachers who are practice teaching as a component of a teacher education course, either at diploma, undergraduate, or graduate level. Throughout the book we invite you to examine your beliefs and understandings of language teaching and your knowledge and skills as a learner of language teaching as you plan, teach, and reflect on lessons you teach during your teaching practice, as well as those you observe taught by other teachers. The book sets out to help you better understand what to expect from your teaching practice, how to prepare for it, how to work with those who will be arranging and supervising your teaching practice, and how to plan, teach, and learn from your teaching practice experiences. Throughout the book we present accounts by student teachers, cooperating teachers, and supervisors that will enable you to compare your experiences with others involved in practice teaching.

To the Supervisor and Cooperating Teacher

In this book we adopt a "reflective approach" to teaching practice. By this we mean one in which student teachers are shown how to explore and reflect on the nature of language teaching and their own approaches to teaching through their experience of practice teaching. Rather than presenting prescriptions on how to teach, the book is built around core chapters that describe a contemporary perspective on the nature of second language teaching and teacher learning; other chapters examine the issues involved in working in a cooperating teacher's classroom and developing teaching skills through observation and supervised practice.

Throughout this book, in most cases, we speak directly to student teachers, since we want the book to provide them with a basis for planning, learning, and understanding different aspects of language teaching. However, the book is also designed to be used by

Instructors as the core component of a practice-teaching course. Some chapters will most usefully be employed before teaching practice commences (e.g., Chapters 1 to 4) but can also be returned to during practice teaching. The remaining chapters can be used in the sequence that best suits your needs. We suggest that you come back to the issues the various chapters raise throughout your practicum. Some discussion questions and activities can be assigned after your student teachers have completed a chapter; others can be used some time later.

TERMS USED IN THE BOOK

We have adopted the following terms throughout the book:

- *Practice teaching* and *teaching practice:* We use these terms throughout as synonymous with the term *practicum*, which is also used in the literature.
- *ESOL:* This general term stands for *English for Speakers of Other Languages*. It applies to situations that are sometimes referred to as *ESL (English as a Second Language), EFL (English as a Foreign Language)*, ESP (*English for Special Purposes*), or *TESOL (Teaching English to Speakers of Other Languages)*.
- *The student teacher*: This term refers to the person completing a practice-teaching experience.
- *The cooperating teacher*: This is the classroom teacher in whose class the student teacher is carrying out his or her teaching experience. This person is referred to as a *master teacher* or *mentor teacher* in some schools.
- *The supervisor*: This is the faculty member or teacher trainer in charge of the practice-teaching course.
- *The host school or institution:* This is the school where the practice teaching takes place.

ACKNOWLEDGMENTS

This book reflects our experiences working with student teachers, teachers, cooperating teachers, and supervisors over many years and in several different locations, particularly Singapore, Hong Kong, Canada, South Korea, and the United States. We are grateful to colleagues who read earlier versions of the manuscript and gave valuable feedback: Melchor Tatlonghari and Linda Hanington (Regional Language Centre, Singapore), Willy Renandya and Anthony Seow (National Institute of Education, Singapore), Caroline Bentley and Josie Gawron (Indonesia Australia Language Foundation, Bali, Indonesia), Neil England (University of Sydney), Marlene Brenes Carvajal and Verónica Sánchez Hernández (Benemérita Universidad Autónoma de Puebla, Mexico), Tim Steward (Kyoto University, Japan), Alan Hirvela (Ohio State University), Gloria Park (Indiana University of Pennsylvania), Margo DelliCarpini (The City University of New York), and Rob Dickey (Gyeongju University, Korea). Caroline, Josie, Marlene, and Veronica allowed us to cite comments from their student teachers in places throughout the text. Rose Senior (University of Western Australia) kindly gave permission for us to cite teacher comments from her book *The Experience of Language Teaching*. Student teachers with whom we have worked piloted earlier versions of the manuscript and we would particularly like to thank Mona Irwin, Nancy Harding, Sadia Asif, and Vidya for their suggestions.

CHAPTER I

Learning to Teach Through Practice Teaching

INTRODUCTION

Practice teaching is a part of most teacher education programs in language teaching and is intended to provide a link between the academic courses you studied in your university or other institutional TESOL program and the "real" world of teachers and students in a language-learning classroom (Brenes-Carvajal 2009; Farrell 2007). Many teachers find their practice-teaching experience to be one of the most useful courses they took during their teacher preparation, as these teachers confirm:

Teaching practice gave me a taste of teaching proper. It presented to me the tip of what to expect and thus allowed me to prepare myself better mentally for real teaching.

Mariana, Brazil

Practice teaching gave me the chance to observe my cooperating teacher, and this allowed me to make different mental notes about how to deal with problems that sometimes come up in a lesson.

Yono, Japan

I learned a lot from teaching practice. It allowed me to put some ideas and thoughts from my teacher education courses into actual practice. It provided a kind of testing ground for me to try out different approaches to teaching.

Mee-Ho, Korea

Practice teaching serves a number of goals (Baird 2008). Perhaps the most obvious one is for you to have an opportunity to apply some of the things you have studied in your academic and teacher-training courses. Your coursework will have included not only the theoretical knowledge expected of today's language teachers – often derived from courses in areas such as second language acquisition, linguistics, and discourse analysis – but also the practical knowledge derived from coursework in areas such as methodology, materials design, and language assessment. The content of such coursework is usually selected on the assumption that as a teacher, you will be able to access it and use it in your teaching.

However, academic courses cannot replicate the actual experience of teaching and many things happen in teaching that coursework does not usually prepare teachers for. Coursework cannot prepare you for such things as adjusting a lesson to respond to learners' difficulty with a planned activity, redesigning a teacher-led grammar practice activity during a teaching moment to turn it into a group task, or dealing with a disruptive student so that he or she does not distract the class from learning (Farrell 2007; Senior 2006). Likewise, reading about peer tutoring or scaffolded learning is no substitute for arranging them to happen in your own classroom. And reading about philosophies of teaching is one thing, but developing your own philosophy of teaching through the experience of teaching is another.

Two Kinds of Practice Teaching: Microteaching and Teaching an ESOL Class

Two different kinds of teaching experience are often provided during practice teaching – the first is *microteaching*, and the second is *teaching an ESOL class*. Most of the activities in this book focus on teaching an ESOL class but some of them can also apply to microteaching. We will first explain what each approach consists of and then describe it in more detail.

Microteaching generally involves planning and teaching a short lesson or part of a lesson to a group of fellow student teachers (or sometimes to ESOL students who have volunteered to serve as students in a microteaching class). The microteaching session is followed by feedback on your teaching by your supervisor and your fellow student teachers. It is often conducted as part of a group activity on teacher-training courses, where students are put into groups and asked to plan and teach certain parts of a lesson. They then observe each other and provide peer feedback. In some programs, such as the CELTA (Certificate in English Language Teaching to Adults), toward the end of the course, candidates teach *whole* lessons, usually of 60 minutes. The lesson you teach or coteach (if several student teachers teach a lesson segment) is normally a language lesson, although sometimes it could be a lesson segment you prepare on other content of your choice, such as a demonstration of how to make or prepare something or a short talk. The purpose for planning and teaching a short lesson (known as a microlesson) rather than a full lesson is generally so that you can focus on a specific teaching skill or strategy (such as, how to open a lesson, how to introduce vocabulary, how to carry out group work) and get immediate feedback on how well you managed to do so, something that may be difficult to do when you teach a full lesson (Wallace 1991). Microteaching can thus be regarded as "teaching in miniature" and is intended to provide a safe and stress-free environment in which to develop and practice basic teaching skills (Roberts 1998).

The second type of teaching experience in practice teaching is teaching an ESOL class. This will normally make up the major part of your practice-teaching experience and may constitute the entire teaching experience if you are not taking part in microteaching (Senior 2006). Your practice teaching will normally involve working with an experienced teacher in his or her ESOL class (your cooperating teacher) and teaching part of lessons or entire lessons for an extended period of time. You will work closely with your cooperating teacher, sharing your lesson plans with him or her (or collaborating on planning lessons). Your cooperating teacher will also observe your lessons and give you feedback on your teaching. In some situations student teachers are actually teaching their own classes, either in the language institute on campus or because they already have teaching jobs. In such cases the supervisor generally takes the role of the cooperating teacher and assists through regular observation, consultation, and review.

PROCEDURES USED IN MICROTEACHING

Microteaching has a long history as a teacher-training strategy. An approach that is sometimes used is based on a sequence of *plan*, *teach*, and *critique* and has three essential features:

1. The student teacher teaches a microlesson of 5 to 10 minutes.
2. The lesson has a very specific and narrow focus.
3. It is immediately followed by a critique of the student teacher's performance.

This may be followed by a new cycle of *re-plan*, *re-teach*, and *re-critique*. As Wallace (1991) and others have pointed out, this view regards effective teaching as involving the mastery of specific skills and competencies that can be taught and practiced individually. It focuses on the behavioral and managerial aspects of teaching and as a consequence tends to approach teaching prescriptively, an approach often considered suitable for trainees with no teaching experience. The stages that are normally involved can be summarized as follows (Wallace 1991: 99–102):

- *The briefing*: The supervisor presents the skill to be practiced and explains how this can be accomplished (e.g., such as conducting a group activity). The presentation may be through an oral discussion by the supervisor, it may be based on readings or checklists, or it might involve "modeling." Modeling might be through the use of a video demonstration, with or without transcripts of the lesson, or the supervisor might demonstrate how the skill or technique is used.
- *The planning*: The student teachers plan their microlesson, incorporating the skills they have been assigned to practice. They should also prepare a description of the objectives for their lesson, to provide a context for the lesson for the observers.
- *The teaching*: The student teacher now teaches his or her microlesson, either to peers or to actual ESOL students. The lesson is often videotaped. The observers take notes.
- *The critique*: The lesson is discussed, analyzed, and evaluated. The student teacher generally starts by explaining what he or she was trying to do and whether the lesson went according to the way it was planned. If the microlesson was videotaped, the group can review the video and discuss different aspects of what they observed. The supervisor will comment on the strengths and weaknesses of the microlesson and suggest ways in which it could be improved.
- *The re-teach*: The microlesson is taught again. During this phase the student teacher tries to incorporate the feedback that was given during the first teaching.

Table 1.1 on page 6 outlines some of the advantages and disadvantages of microteaching.

Advantages	Disadvantages
• Short, so less stress compared to teaching a whole lesson • Very focused on one aspect of teaching • Opportunities to try out new ideas • Safe environment • Opportunities to "try again" based on feedback	• Short time may stress some people • "Teacher" may not be able to establish a rapport with the class • Student / teacher expectations of what can be achieved may be too high • "Decontextualized" lesson, so it may be difficult to get students involved

Table 1.1   Advantages and disadvantages of microteaching

ADVANTAGES OF MICROTEACHING

The standard approach to microteaching as described above seeks to develop mastery of a number of specific teaching skills that are considered core competencies of a novice teacher. Skills that could be the focus of this approach include questioning techniques, error correction techniques, or explaining lesson procedures (see Appendix A). In addition, student teachers can develop confidence through microteaching and an awareness of some aspects of their teaching style because they are teaching in a safe environment. For example, they can try a particular technique and know that they do not have to get it right the first time because they will obtain feedback that will enable them to try it again based on the comments they receive. The usefulness of these experiences is confirmed by these teachers:

Microteaching allowed me to observe my fellow trainee teachers. This allowed me to spot the good points and sometimes the not so good points of different student teachers.

Sarah, Canada

It provided a kind of testing ground for me to try out new teaching techniques.

Mark, United States

One of the advantages I felt was that the different lesson plans that were shared by all peers throughout the two weeks were all very useful. Also, the supervisor's feedback after microteaching was most helpful at this stage in my teacher development.

Oswaldo, Spain

DISADVANTAGES OF MICROTEACHING

By its nature, the approach to microteaching discussed in the section on procedures focuses on a specific but restricted set of skills and competencies that constitute part of a teacher's repertoire of teaching skills. The assumption is that once "learned," these skills can be transferred to real teaching contexts, an assumption that would be difficult to verify. However, these are generally based on a prescriptive "top-down" view of teaching that does not reflect the broader understanding of teacher knowledge that is described throughout this book. Aspects of teaching that cannot adequately be acquired through microteaching include things that can only be experienced in the context of a real classroom and through interacting with real students – for example, ways of responding to students' difficulties; ways of motivating reluctant learners; an awareness of learners' learning style preferences, motivations, and needs; the development of a personal teaching philosophy; and the theorizing of practice. In addition, a five- to ten-minute lesson imposes an artificial time constraint, and student teachers sometimes say they feel pressured to rush their lessons because the time was so short, as the following comments suggest:

In microteaching, classroom management is not accurately simulated. This is because when we do microteaching, we are teaching our peers and they will not be able to give an accurate representation of a class of 30 real students.

Pamela, Singapore

Because of the unrealistic environment of teaching my peers, I felt that even if my lesson was successful in a microteaching environment, it might not necessarily prove that the lesson would work in the real environment.

Stephanie, United States

A MORE REFLECTIVE APPROACH TO MICROTEACHING

Due to the limitations implicit in the traditional approach to microteaching described in the section on disadvantages, a more reflective approach has been suggested (e.g., by Roberts 1998). In this approach the microteaching experience is intended not simply to provide an opportunity to master specific teaching behaviors and skills, but rather to provide experiences that can trigger a deeper understanding of teaching through processes of critical reflection. The personal understandings of student teachers become the focus. Rather than feedback on microlessons being viewed as corrective in nature, it is seen as a way of uncovering the thinking and perceptions that provide the source of the teacher's planning decisions as well as those decisions and understandings that occurred during teaching. In contrast to the skills view of learning to teach then, reflective microteaching sessions involve thinking about the total teaching act in all its dimensions. As Komblueth and Schoenberg (1990) explain: "The task given to the students is accordingly more holistic and the expectations from the feedback sessions are both broader and less precise" (p. 17). A reflective approach to microteaching is hence one in which the ability to understand and reflect on the cognitive and affective aspects of teaching becomes a central focus of microteaching. The kind of feedback given by the supervisor will mirror this approach (see Chapter 4). Rather than being primarily prescriptive it will be reflective in nature, seeking to deepen the student teacher's understanding of teaching through a process of dialogue and reflection (Miller 2009).

STAGES IN REFLECTIVE MICROTEACHING

PLANNING THE MICROLESSON

A microlesson usually lasts from 5 to 10 minutes, as with the skills approach described in the previous section. However, whereas the focus of a microlesson could be a teaching skill, microlessons can include other types of goals related to other dimensions of teaching. For example:

- Making learning stimulating and enjoyable
- Relating a lesson to the learners' experience
- Developing awareness of learning strategies
- Using a reading text creatively
- Developing risk-taking in learners
- Developing motivation
- Managing feedback
- Utilizing student input
- Encouraging student participation
- Becoming aware of one's teaching style

The supervisor might provide a lesson-plan format as a guide for student teachers to follow, including such items as the lesson objectives, teaching procedures, and resources, or the student teacher may decide on the lesson-plan format. Planning might be done individually or in pairs or groups. An advantage of group planning is that it provides an opportunity to share and compare thinking about teaching and learning and to jointly negotiate a lesson plan. During the planning stage, features of the lesson that observers can focus on during the teaching phase of the lesson are identified. These should include aspects of the lesson related to the teacher, the students, the use of materials, and so on.

TEACHING AND OBSERVING

The student teacher teaches his or her microlesson and the observers complete their observation tasks.

REFLECTING ON THE LESSON

The observers meet to compare their observations of what was achieved. Following this, the student teacher gives his or her account of the experience, commenting on any aspect of the experience he or she would like the group to think about.

Finally the supervisor offers his or her understanding of the lesson. This should include the reflective strategies for giving feedback described in Chapter 4.

A friend of mine recorded me today for the midterm paper and even though I knew the camera was there, I did not feel the pressure I usually feel when being observed. I think I could manage the situation without the teacher's presence because there is enough confidence between me and the students by now.

Hada, Mexico

MONITORING TEACHER LEARNING THROUGHOUT MICROTEACHING

If microteaching is used on a regular basis as part of teaching practice, opportunities need to be provided for each student teacher to teach a range of microlessons and to take part in ongoing reflection on what he or she is learning about teaching and about himself or herself as a teacher throughout this process (Farrell 2008a). This may take different forms, such as keeping a teaching journal, lesson reports (see Chapter 11), or through group discussions.

In order to facilitate a reflective focus in microteaching, one strategy is for student teachers to work in small groups of four to six. One student teacher in each group is given an identical lesson to teach to his or her group. The content need not be related to language skills but could be taken from something the students are studying in their academic courses (e.g., a problem-solving task). Following the 10-minute microlesson, the student teachers are asked to recall the microlesson, reflect on it, and then discuss it in relation to broader, more general teaching issues.

To provide a link between microteaching and teaching in a real ESOL class, it is sometimes possible for the student teachers to gradually expand their microlessons into half lessons and then full lessons, while still teaching their peers in a "safe" environment. In this way, some of the disadvantages concerning the unrealistic nature of microteaching can be addressed: The student teachers now practice teaching for a whole class period, better preparing them to face a real ESOL class.

PROCEDURES USED IN TEACHING AN ESOL CLASS

Whereas practice teaching in a real second language class is regarded as a core component of many graduate and undergraduate TESOL programs (and a required component of many of them), procedures for organizing teaching practice vary from institution to institution. Sometimes well-organized procedures are in place and both the supervisor and the cooperating teacher are involved in managing the practice-teaching experience. Sometimes, however, arrangements may not have been well developed and formalized and the student teacher may be affected by the lack of adequate administrative procedures. The following issues are normally involved in setting up teaching practice in an ESOL class.

FINDING A SITE TO CARRY OUT PRACTICE TEACHING

Ideally, the institution where you are studying has identified practice-teaching sites and cooperating teachers who are used every year. Some programs may be campus-based (such as intensive English programs or language centers offering courses to the public) where liaison and communication are relatively straightforward. Although such arrangements are convenient, programs of this kind may not offer an experience that reflects the kind of teaching you will do when you graduate. Other programs may take place in schools or institutions in the community that have been selected by the supervisor. Sometimes student teachers are required to make their own arrangements, contacting schools and cooperating teachers. Student teachers who have recently completed their teaching practice are often a source for recommendations in such cases.

Accepting student teachers on a regular basis, however, is a considerable responsibility for the host institution since, if the institution accepts fee-paying students, they may not feel they are getting adequate instruction if part of their course is taught by a student teacher. Optional free classes are sometimes established to address this issue enabling the student teacher to have a "risk-free" class to teach. Often, however, you will be teaching in a class that is part of the school's regular course offerings. In this case the cooperating teacher will have the responsibility to ensure that the students in the class are receiving competent instruction from the student teacher.

WORKING WITH A COOPERATING TEACHER

Your cooperating teacher may be chosen for you by your supervisor through his or her connections with the host institutions, or you may have to make your own contacts with a school to locate a teacher who is willing to serve as your cooperating teacher. Many schools have a roster of experienced and senior teachers who are able to take on this role. Working with a student teacher is a considerable responsibility for the cooperating teacher since it will involve a lot of extra work for him or her (e.g., when reviewing your lesson plans or when giving feedback on your teaching). Furthermore, working in a supervisory role with a student teacher is often an unpaid addition to the teacher's role, and one for which he or she may have had no special training or preparation.

Cooperating teachers differ in the way they work with student teachers. The best cooperating teachers are expert teachers with a wide range of experience, who enjoy supervising student teachers and can provide supportive guidance and direction to novice teachers. They may not necessarily share your own views about teaching and learning but are willing to listen and to consider different approaches. They are able to find the time needed to meet with you outside of class time and offer constructive criticism as well as encouragement and support (Baird 2008). The following comments describe the approach used by one cooperating teacher:

My feeling is that as a cooperating teacher, supervision should not be just about evaluating student teachers, although this is still part of the process because of ultimate certification, because if this is the case, then the student teachers will just follow what they see in the evaluation forms rather than teach the students to learn English. I do not think that the checklists are really helpful and I tend not to put too much faith in them although I have to fill them out. What I look for is a student teacher who is trying to create lesson plans that have an overall connection to the curriculum and lessons that are delivered with enthusiasm and creativity. I do not care if the student teacher follows a particular method that I subscribe to but I do care that he or she follows a method that he or she subscribes to and can articulate. So during the feedback sessions I first ask the student teacher what he or she thinks about the lesson and what the students learned and then why he or she thinks this way.

John, cooperating teacher, Germany

COORDINATING THE PRACTICE-TEACHING EXPERIENCE

Arrangements for carrying out the teaching in an ESOL class vary from institution to institution, and the campus-based supervisor may have an active role in planning and coordinating your teaching experiences. Sometimes, however, it may be left entirely to the discretion of the cooperating teacher. In the former case you may be required to teach an assigned number of classes and to perform specific teaching tasks. In the latter case the cooperating teacher may assign teaching tasks to you.

LEARNING FROM PRACTICE TEACHING IN AN ESOL CLASS

In your college program the focus was on learning through academic study, with a focus on learning current findings and assumptions based on theory and research. In practice teaching the focus is not on what you know but on what you can do. And many of the skills you need to master to be an effective language teacher will not have been the focus of your academic studies. So your practice-teaching experience is above all an opportunity to learn more about the *process* of language teaching. If you have a particular interest or area of specialization in language teaching (such as teaching young children or teaching ESP) you may want to complete your practice teaching in a school where you can teach classes of this kind. On the other hand you may wish to teach in a context that is unfamiliar to you, to give you useful experience that can support your career plans (Senior 2006).

At the beginning of the first practice, I was a little nervous but the students made me feel comfortable; they were very kind with me . . . I was very nervous . . . I forgot to ask them their names and most of the time I said, "Excuse me, can you repeat your name please?" I realized that theory is different from practice; it is not the same being a student and being a teacher; your way of thinking changes drastically.

Reina, Mexico

In teaching an ESOL class your practice-teaching experience will typically involve observing your cooperating teacher's classes as well as teaching part or all of the class on a regular basis. Conversations with your cooperating teacher and observation and reflection on your own teaching experiences are important parts of the learning process in practice teaching. In order to gain maximum benefit from your practice-teaching experience you also need to become actively involved in monitoring and directing your own learning (see Chapter 11). Whereas your supervisor and your cooperating teacher will provide ongoing feedback and guidance on your teaching, you can also be responsible for your own teacher learning during practice teaching, and ways of doing so are discussed throughout this book. Table 1.2 on page 11 summarizes learning to teach through practice teaching.

1. Engage in microteaching.	• Plan and teach short lessons to groups of fellow student teachers or sometimes to ESOL students.
2. Teach ESOL classes.	• Work with an experienced teacher in his or her ESOL class (your *cooperating teacher*) and teach part of lessons or entire lessons for an extended period of time.
3. Find a site to carry out the practice teaching.	• Check out campus-based programs or schools or institutions in the community.
4. Work with a cooperating teacher.	• Note that he or she may not necessarily share your views about teaching and learning but is willing to listen and to consider different approaches.
5. Learn from practice teaching in ESOL class.	• Observe the cooperating teacher's classes and teach part or all of the class to learn more about the *process* of language teaching.

Table 1.2   Learning to teach through practice teaching

SUMMARY AND CONCLUSIONS

Your practice-teaching course may involve both microteaching as well as teaching an ESOL class, and both kinds of experience will provide useful opportunities for teacher learning. However, classroom experience in itself is an insufficient basis for teacher development. Linking experience to critical reflection and review is essential to learning to teach (Senior 2006). Through reviewing your own teaching experiences and through discussing your teaching with fellow student teachers, with your cooperating teacher, and with your supervisor, you will be able to monitor the effectiveness of your lessons and of your teaching and develop your confidence and skills as a teacher. Dialogue will play a central role in this process, so establishing good channels of communication between yourself and your cooperating teacher is essential.

Your teaching-practice experience is something you can look forward to. And although some aspects of it might prove challenging, it will provide you with invaluable opportunities for learning and professional growth and will be an essential first step in your career development as a language teacher. Although the teaching-practice course does not always accrue the same status and prestige as academic and theory-based courses you may have taken in your academic study, it is ultimately a testing ground for the relevance of those courses in the classroom and in your understanding of language teaching and learning. And in considering a teacher for employment, a typical director of studies in a private language school would generally be more interested in your results for teaching practice than your other course grades. Teaching practice may not be assessed in the same way as your academic coursework, yet in many ways it will prove to be the most important learning experience that you have gained so far. We hope that the information and activities that are provided in this book will help make it both a constructive and memorable one.

Further reading

Crookes, G. (2003). *The practicum in TESOL: Professional development through teaching practice*. New York: Cambridge University Press.

Senior, R. (2006). *The experience of language teaching*. Cambridge: Cambridge University Press.

Ur, P. (1996). *A course in language teaching*. Cambridge: Cambridge University Press.

Discussion questions

1. What do you expect to learn during practice teaching?

2. What concerns do you have about your practice-teaching assignment?

3. How can you best prepare for teaching practice?

4. One cooperating teacher had the following expectations for student teachers on teaching practice:

    a) A high level of proficiency in the language and the skills needed to access relevant information and resources as needed;

    b) An awareness of a variety of teaching and learning approaches, methods and techniques, and the flexibility to employ them according to the context they are working with;

    c) Organizational and functional skills required for the daily routines of teaching;

    d) A rapport with their students which may be uniquely their own, but generally positive;

    e) An open mind to explore their teaching with me as a supervisor in order to improve;

    f) A sense of their own professionalism as teachers and all that comes with that as they join an educational institution and the profession.

To what extent do these reflect your own expectations for practice teaching? Would you add others to the list?

5. In what ways do you think the theory you learned during your academic courses will be useful to you during the practicum?

6. What aspects of teaching do you hope to master during your practicum experience?

Follow-up activities

1. Prepare a set of questions you can use to interview two or more student teachers who have completed practice teaching. Carry out the interviews and share your findings.

2. Individually or in a small group, prepare a set of questions you can use for discussion with your cooperating teacher. These should focus on the class content and goals of your practice-teaching class, the students, the teacher's expectations of you, and the mechanics of interaction and communication between the two of you. Review your responses to Questions No. 1 and No. 2 and make notes as a basis for sharing your ideas with your cooperating teacher if time allows. Carry out these discussions as soon as possible.

3. Review the list of skills in Appendix A. Can you suggest other skills that could be the focus of microteaching?

4. Review the vignettes on teaching practice presented throughout the chapter and in Appendix B. What did these student teachers find most helpful from their microteaching and practice teaching experiences?

Appendix A: Examples of teaching skills and behaviors that could be the focus of microteaching lessons

- Extent to which a lesson realized its objectives
- Number of questions the student teacher asks
- Types of questions that occurred during the lesson
- How questions are responded to
- Responses to student performance
- Ways used to check students' understanding
- How students were chosen to respond to questions
- Explanations of lesson procedures
- Use of visual aids
- Use of technology
- Organization of pairs / groups
- Use of gestures and eye contact
- Use of voice and voice projection
- Evidence of organization and planning
- Lesson opening and closure
- Selection of appropriate materials for the planned lesson
- Transitions between activities
- Sequencing of activities
- How vocabulary is presented
- How grammar is presented
- How skills are presented
- Amount of teacher talk in the lesson
- Amount of student participation in the lesson

Appendix B: Vignettes from teaching practice

Microteaching gives students a chance to take an initial stab at preparing a lesson and to actually get up in class and teach, all in comparatively nonthreatening surroundings (by which I mean not nearly as stressful as on the day you get up in front of your first real class).

Mona, Canada

Microteaching gave me the opportunity to hear feedback from both my tutor and fellow trainees while the event was very fresh in my mind. We weren't using video, but since it had only been a few minutes earlier I could recall very clearly what they described. And opinions from my peers were often easier to accept than critique from the almighty tutor.

Robert, Korea

My teaching practice gave me the opportunity to try out different materials that I hadn't tried before. I also learned how to use an overhead projector, cue a tape player, and make my own overhead transparencies. These all seem like quite minor things to a seasoned teacher, but they were quite challenging for me initially.

Michelle, Indonesia

I feel that the biggest disadvantage of peer teaching is that it takes place in a very artificial environment. I know from experience that real teaching is a very dynamic process and certain real-life circumstances can never be imitated in a peer-teaching class. Moreover, I find that peer teaching reflects a rather Eurocentric concept and as such its universality is rather doubtful.

Vidya, Canada

I feel we have the foundations, which are those subjects that have given us the foundations, have given us the theory, and now comes the practice and through the experience and everything we acquire in our practicum and in our professional lives we will be able to be good teachers, well, with time.

Anita, Mexico

My biggest problem when I started the teaching practice was underestimating how long activities would take to complete. The main reason for this was that I wasn't allowing time in my lesson plan for correction and incidental issues, which invariably arise. Now I am more conscious of allowing time in the planning phase for error correction stages in my lessons.

Mark, Indonesia

I'd prepare and prepare and prepare and probably learn by rote how it was going to be. I didn't want to allow the students to interrupt, because it was like, "This is what I have to do. How can I fit the students in around it?"

Teacher (cited by Senior 2006: 46)

I like the idea of "ongoing reflection" as a good way of looking at microteaching. I think each student should reflect on their lesson (perhaps in pairs or a small group) and consider if any changes may need to be considered for future lessons.

Nancy, Canada

CHAPTER 2

The Nature of Teacher Learning

INTRODUCTION

Your teaching-practice course aims to provide an opportunity for you to develop or improve your teaching skills through experiences provided by microteaching, by teaching in a second language classroom, and through reflecting on your teaching experience in discussions with your supervisor, fellow student teachers, and your cooperating teacher. The most crucial experiences will be those provided when you do your practice teaching in a real classroom (Richards and Crookes 1988). The words "practice teaching," however, may give a misleading impression of what we understand by "learning to teach," or as we shall refer to it throughout this book, "teacher learning." "Practice teaching" suggests that development as a language teacher primarily involves acquiring a set of specific teaching skills, and that these gradually develop and improve through practice. Whereas aspects of teaching can certainly be regarded as skilled performance as we saw in Chapter 1, this book is predicated around a broader and, we hope, more meaningful understanding of what competence and expertise in teaching consist of, and consequently what the goals of teacher learning are. In this chapter we will consider the nature of competence and expertise in language teaching and examine eight different dimensions of teacher learning that are involved. The account we present here will provide the rationale for the approach to practice teaching we present throughout this book.

DEVELOPING THE DISCOURSE SKILLS OF A LANGUAGE TEACHER

English is both the target of learning as well as the medium of teaching in ESOL classrooms. Your proficiency in English and your use of English in the classroom will therefore make an important contribution to how well you are able to teach English (Richards and Farrell 2005). It will influence many crucial aspects of your teaching, such as your ability to provide good language models, to maintain use of English in the classroom, to give explanations and instructions in English, and to give correct feedback on learner language. Learning how to carry out these aspects of a lesson fluently in English may be an important dimension of teacher learning for those whose mother tongue is not English. For these teachers as well as those who *are* native speakers of English, other discourse skills will also need to be acquired – skills that enable you to manage classroom discourse so that it provides opportunities for language learning. These discourse skills relate to the following dimensions of teaching:

- Understanding and using the *metalanguage* (i.e., the technical terms used within the profession) of classroom language teaching when discussing your teaching with your cooperating teacher and supervisor (see below)
- Providing language input at an appropriate level for your learners (see Chapter 10)
- Using appropriate "teacher talk," i.e., speech that is comprehensible to students but which is not oversimplified or unnatural
- Providing opportunities for students to develop and extend their linguistic resources (both grammatical and discoursal)
- Providing opportunities for interactive and collaborative uses of language among learners (see Chapter 8)

Becoming a language teacher also involves learning to "talk the talk," that is, acquiring the specialized discourse that we use among ourselves and that helps define the subject matter of our profession. This means becoming familiar with several hundred specialized terms, such as *learner-centeredness, discourse markers, clause, finite verb, progressive aspect, learner autonomy, self-access, alternative assessment, blended learning, task-based instruction, phoneme*, and *Common European Framework,* that we use on a daily basis in talking about our teaching. Being able to use the appropriate discourse (and of course, understand what they mean) is one of the criteria for membership of the language-teaching profession. This is emphasized in the following observation from a student teacher:

My cooperating teacher often uses different terms for talking about teaching from the ones we use in my college course. For example, to practice grammar she recommended "back-chaining" and "concept checking" and until I saw her using these techniques in her teaching I was not sure what exactly they referred to.

Anna, Canada

DEVELOPING THE IDENTITY OF A LANGUAGE TEACHER

One of the things that has to be learned in becoming a language teacher is what it means to be a language teacher – that is, to have a sense of the *identity* of a language teacher. Identity refers to the differing social and cultural roles you will enact through your interactions with learners and your cooperating teacher during the process of teacher learning. These roles are not static but emerge through the social processes of the classroom. Your sense of identity (i.e., who you feel you are and who others take you to be) may be shaped by many factors, including your personal biography, culture, working conditions, age, gender, and the school and classroom culture (Burns and Richards 2009). The concept of identity reflects how we see ourselves as individuals and how we enact our roles within different settings. In a training course or campus-based teacher education program your identity as a student teacher emerges through the acquisition of new modes of discourse, that is, new ways of talking about teaching and learning, as well as new roles in your campus classroom.

And through practice teaching, your identity will now be further reshaped as you gradually assume the role of teacher. At times during your practice teaching you may experience a sense of unease because of the tension between your role as student and your role as teacher (Thornbury 1991).

This transition is not always easy and can create stress and anxiety. For many ESL teachers their identity may partly reflect their wish to empower immigrants, refugees, and others for whom English is a way out of their current circumstances (Cooke and Simpson 2008), as these comments suggest:

When I went into the class first to observe my cooperating teacher I was so shocked at the reality of the differences in ethnic backgrounds of all the students and wondered how I would manage this and what my role was as a teacher of English. When I started to teach the class and got to know them better I realized my role would not only be to teach them how to speak English but also how to navigate the culture outside the classroom because now they were in a new country (USA). I realized that I would take on another role as that of cultural ambassador as I explained more and more about the US to them during and even after class. Eventually, I had them all over to my house.

Eva, United States

Since I have been in teaching practice and inside teaching a real class with real ESL students I no longer feel an outsider in this profession even though I am a nonnative speaker of English. Now that I have had a chance to prove myself as a teacher in front of these students and show them that I know many different techniques as well as my skills using English (yes, and even if I still have a bit of an accent), they have begun to accept me as their teacher and I am beginning to feel more like a teacher of English.

Momoko, Japan

Teacher learning thus involves not only discovering more about the skills and knowledge of language teaching but also what it means to be a language teacher, and it may affect native speaker and nonnative-speaker teacher learners differently. If you are a native speaker of English for example, you may find your students credit you with an identity you are not really entitled to (the "native-speaker-as-expert-syndrome"), whereas a nonnative-speaking English teacher may feel she or he has to establish a sense of credibility as an English teacher, as this teacher observes:

As a nonnative English speaker I was worried about my language skills at first when I started to teach English in a campus-based language institute because I was placed with a cooperating teacher who was teaching a high-level writing class. The scheme of work that the class was using in this writing class came from a genre approach to writing. Thankfully we had covered this in my teacher education course so I did not have any difficulties understanding the concepts associated with this approach. For example, I remembered that within each genre, students are required to perform reading, comprehension, and writing tasks, with little emphasis on the grammatical aspect of the genre although the cooperating teacher told me that her students would be required to attempt grammar-based questions in their midyear examinations. When I was given the class to teach by myself and because I had a very open-minded cooperating teacher I found myself experimenting with different ways to bring the genre and its characteristics across to the students. At first this was somewhat difficult for me because it was difficult to relate to the materials because when I learned writing we only focused on various aspects of the language at a generic level, whereas now I was required to plan specific activities to cover particular aspects of the genre. As the lessons progressed I became more confident in my teaching and I actually forgot that I was a nonnative speaker of English while I was teaching because I became so engrossed (and interested) in delivering my lessons.

Raul, Canada

DEVELOPING A REPERTOIRE OF TEACHING SKILLS

A priority in teacher learning is to develop confidence and fluency in the basic classroom skills needed to present and navigate language lessons. Microteaching aims to provide a safe environment in which to practice some of these skills. Teaching from this perspective involves developing a repertoire of routines and procedures for such things as opening the lesson, introducing and explaining tasks, setting up learning arrangements (group work, pair work, whole-class learning), checking students' understanding, guiding student practice, monitoring students' language use, making transitions from one task to another, and ending the lesson (see Appendix A).

Such skills are acquired through teaching in a variety of different situations with different kinds of learners and with different kinds of content. Over time, experience will enable you to perform these skills fluently and with less conscious thought and attention, so you can focus on other dimensions of the lesson. Research on teaching suggests that as teachers accumulate experience and knowledge, there is a move toward a degree of flexibility in teaching and the development of improvisational teaching. Senior comments:

> Just as they deviate in major ways from what they intended to do in their lessons, so language teachers routinely digress in a variety of minor ways during the course of their daily teaching. Teachers talk about "sidestepping," "bringing in little extra bits and pieces," or "dealing with things as they pop up." They behave in these ways as a matter of course – perhaps 10 or 20 times in any one lesson. (Senior 2006: 157)

Experienced teachers are hence more willing to depart from established procedures and use their own solutions, and to improvise, than novice teachers (Borg 2006). They are able to anticipate problems and have procedures available to deal with them, and they deal with routines and procedures more efficiently, spending less time on them. Your practice-teaching experience will be a chance to develop fluency in the use of different aspects of teaching and also to experience improvisational teaching. Here a student teacher describes an important transition in her teaching:

I was required to teach English grammar to Level 2 students in the elementary school where I was placed for my teaching practice. In the class I was assigned to work with the cooperating teacher usually followed a deductive "production practice method" of teaching grammar that has the teacher explain the rules of grammar and then has the students complete fill-in-the-blank-type grammar exercises after as a way of evaluating that learning. As I was educated in such a similar manner when I was learning English, I had no problem following this approach and did as I was told. Then about five weeks into my teaching practice, as I was used to the class and they were used to me, I asked the cooperating teacher one day if she would allow me to change the approach to teaching grammar to the class and try a more inductive way to teach grammar where I would give them activities that would encourage them to discover the rules for themselves. Although somewhat skeptical she nevertheless allowed me to try as she could see that I was gaining in my levels of confidence and so I started to teach basic tenses using this approach. To my delight the class was generally able to discover the grammar rules by themselves. My CT was so impressed with what I pulled off that she said she will incorporate such an approach along with her usual production practice exercises; at first she said she will continue with her usual way because students are more familiar with production practice and may be a bit unsure if she changes totally to the inductive approach. But now she sees that the inductive approach can really help in their learning of English language.

Diana, Canada

Teaching practice enlightened me with the fact that one skill (reading, writing, grammar) can be taught in so many varied ways. I think I feel a little more secure knowing that I will have some ideas to refer to or modify when the need arises when I become a full-time teacher.

David, Hong Kong

LEARNING HOW TO APPLY PROFESSIONAL KNOWLEDGE

Practice teaching is generally thought of as an opportunity to apply some of the knowledge that you have studied or are studying in your teacher-training or academic courses (Brenes-Carvajal 2009). The academic courses provide the theory, and teaching practice provides an opportunity to make the connections between theory and practice. However, the courses you will have studied in your TESOL programs are generally of two different kinds. Some belong to the domain of *disciplinary knowledge* whereas others are in the domain of *pedagogical content knowledge*. Disciplinary knowledge refers to a body of knowledge that is considered by the language-teaching profession to be essential to gaining membership of the profession. Possessing such knowledge leads to professional recognition and status and is part of professional education but does not translate into practical skills. For example, courses in the history of language-teaching methods, contemporary linguistic theories, psycholinguistics, critical pedagogy, and sociolinguistics belong to the domain of disciplinary knowledge and are not intended to have practical application in the classroom.

Pedagogical content knowledge (Shulman 1987), on the other hand, refers to knowledge that provides a basis for language teaching. It is knowledge which is drawn from the study of language teaching and language learning itself and which can be applied in different ways to the resolution of practical issues in language teaching. It could include coursework in areas such as curriculum planning, assessment, reflective teaching, teaching children, teaching the four skills, and so on. So we would expect teachers with a sound grounding in relevant pedagogical content knowledge to be better prepared than teachers without such knowledge to understand learners' needs, to diagnose learners' learning problems, to plan suitable instructional goals for lessons, and to select and design learning tasks. Practice teaching, therefore, provides opportunities for you to make use of pedagogical content knowledge acquired through your academic courses, as the following commentary illustrates:

When I did factual writing with my class during teaching practice, I remembered the way my instructor taught us during my B.ED. course because she had small story charts to help students generate ideas for the topic, such as on teenage crime. I modified her idea a bit by adding several boxes on a worksheet; each box asked a question about the topic (in this case, Bus Drivers), which the students were to write on. By answering the questions, students unwittingly generate points for their factual writing, and at the same time, the boxes are sequenced in such a way that the points would flow in a correct paragraphing order.

I also thought my instructor's use of visual organizers was very helpful for me during teaching practice when it came to assisting students in getting down their ideas in an orderly and systematic manner, which would aid their understanding and increase the speed of internalization. Thus, when I conducted a lesson on descriptive writing during teaching practice, I had the students draw a Venn diagram to illustrate the three types of descriptive writing – on people, places and events, and occasions. The chart also helped the students to understand that these three types of descriptive writing topics would overlap (when the three circles in the Venn diagram overlap) and when that happens, students must be able to write descriptively on a combination of people and place, people and occasions, or a mix of all three.

I even transferred this idea to my reading course and had students do a plot sequencing on the board using the labels again. This time, the labels were for the major sections of the novel, and the class was split into groups and told to do a summary for each major part and then to stick their summary under the respective labels. The groups then took turns to go up to the board to read the summary of the entire novel.

Emily, Singapore

A further important component of professional knowledge in today's classrooms has been termed "technological pedagogical content knowledge," or TPCK (Mishra and Koehler 2006) – that is, the ability to incorporate and integrate technology into teaching. Reinders (2009: 231) points out that depending on the teacher's level of technological expertise, this could involve "being able to first, *use* a certain technology; second, being able to *create* materials and activities using that technology; and third, being able to *teach* with technology." The use of technology in teaching becomes more important in present times because teachers also have to be able to keep up with the technological knowledge of their students. Young learners today have more access to information and more tools available to them to manage their own learning. Reinders (2009: 236) suggests that "the challenge for teachers will be more one of helping learners develop the skills to deal successfully with the increased control and independence that technology demands."

DEVELOPING AN UNDERSTANDING OF HOW LEARNING IS SHAPED BY CONTEXT

Practice teaching takes place in many different contexts. You may have a chance to teach young learners or adults, to work in a public school or a private institute, to work in mixed-level classes or in a homogeneous class, or to teach general English or ESP. Each teaching context reflects different rules, facilities, values, expectations, and dynamics that can substantially shape teaching and learning. One group of learners may have very different characteristics from another. This constitutes what is meant by "situated learning." Hence you may find that what works well in one teaching context, does not work so well or in the same way in a different context.

Teacher learning thus involves discovering the "hidden curriculum" that needs to be understood in order to function effectively in the school context. And in order to function in a specific context you will need to acquire the appropriate contextual knowledge that will enable, for example, an Australian teacher to learn how to be an effective teacher in China or vice versa, or a Singaporean teacher to learn how to be an effective EFL teacher in Japan. Different contexts for teaching create different potentials for learning that the teacher must come to understand. This means trying to understand the nature of the school and the school culture, the students' expectations and learning styles, and their cultural and linguistic background (see Chapter 3).

Senior (2006) points out that norms for classroom interaction vary from culture to culture and that teachers with a Western educational background typically seek to establish an informal atmosphere in their classroom, which may not be typical of teachers from a different cultural background. Teachers from a Western background try to establish a relaxed classroom atmosphere in a number of ways:

> They encourage adult students to remain seated as they enter the room, to address them by their first names, and to call out answers without raising their hands. They may call the class roll as they sit perched on the corner of their desk, perhaps making light-hearted remarks to the class as they do so. . . . [They] regularly say things in a joking manner to lighten the mood of their classes – and reinforce the notion that their classes are informal rather than formal learning environments. (Senior 2006: 82)

Teacher learning thus involves understanding the specific values, norms of practice, and patterns of social participation of your host school. In teaching practice your cooperating teacher will play a crucial role in orienting you to the context in which you will be teaching.

Going through teaching practice helped me realize how every ESL class is unique and different with its own identity, I guess. So I realized some things we learned during the teacher education courses (such as the course on collaborative learning) were not really applicable for me when I went to teach in a school that had a majority of students from a particular religious background. I was not able to conduct much group work and indeed they never allowed me to use a mix of girls and boys in any pair or group work. So this aspect of teaching practice was a real challenge to me.

Andrew, Canada

When I walked into my class for teaching practice I thought I was in Korea because eighteen of the twenty students were all from Korea and the other two were from Japan. On the first day at one point I sat on the teacher's desk and I saw the look of horror on the students' faces because they were not used to seeing a teacher sit on the desk in their country and because they had just arrived in Canada, they were still not used to Canadian culture which allowed this to happen. I moved back from the desk quickly and stood beside the board and remembered not to sit on the teacher's desk again unless I wanted to make a cultural point.

John, Canada

DEVELOPING THE COGNITIVE SKILLS OF A LANGUAGE TEACHER

An important dimension of teaching is the specialized thinking skills it involves. Teaching involves many different kinds of thinking and decision making, and teachers draw on complex cognitive processes before, during, and after a teaching experience or episode. One important dimension of teacher thinking involves the processes that are employed in planning lessons. These call upon what has been termed a teacher's "pedagogical reasoning skills," that is, the ability to:

- Analyze potential lesson content (e.g., a piece of realia, a text, an advertisement, a poem, a photo, etc.) and identify ways in which it could be used as a teaching resource.
- Identify specific linguistic goals (e.g., in the area of speaking, vocabulary, reading, writing, etc.) that could be developed from the chosen content.
- Anticipate any problems that might occur and ways of resolving them.
- Make appropriate decisions about time, sequencing, and grouping arrangements.

(adapted from Shulman 1987)

Shulman (1987) described this ability as a process of transformation in which the teacher turns the subject matter of instruction into forms that are pedagogically powerful and that are appropriate to the level and ability of the students. Experienced teachers use these skills every day when they plan their lessons, when they decide how to adapt lessons from their coursebook, and when they search the Internet and other sources for materials and content that they can use in their classes. It is one of the most fundamental dimensions of teaching, one that is acquired through experience, through accessing content knowledge, and through knowing what learners need to know and how to help them acquire it.

Teachers also employ other cognitive skills when they monitor their teaching and make on-the-spot decisions about the lesson based on their assessment of how effective the lesson is and whether adjustments in the lesson plan, lesson activities, timing, and other factors need to be made based on their understanding of how well the lesson is achieving its goals. Senior observes:

> Sometimes teachers abandon what they intended to do mid-way through lessons, sensing that something dynamic is happening in the form of high levels of student interest and engagement. One teacher described this experience as "having a sudden insight into what the students are actually experiencing." When moments such as these occur, teachers are often prepared to surrender temporary control over the direction of their lessons and be guided by their students – sensing that such opportunities are too valuable to let slip. (Senior 2006: 155–56)

Practice teaching is therefore an important way in which you can develop your pedagogical reasoning skills and develop the ability to reflect on and revise your teaching during actual teaching moments as this student teacher describes:

When I started teaching classes on my own during teaching practice the cooperating teacher asked me to plan the lessons to give me practice. For this I had to write the specific objectives of the lesson so that she could look at them before and then she would ask me if I could anticipate any problems or issues that may occur in that lesson. If I pointed out anything that I was worried about concerning the lesson, she asked me to try to solve the problem myself. I found this process very useful too because it helped me to have a clearer picture of how the lesson is going to be delivered and what is going to be achieved at the end of the lesson. After all this sometimes my cooperating teacher would also show me her own lesson plan for that particular lesson that she would have taught if I had not been assigned to her. I found the whole process demanding because I realized that I was not only planning what was to be covered but how it would be covered and of course how I would evaluate its eventual success. I wonder how experienced teachers do all this in their heads but I prefer to write my plans on paper and keep them with me in class but as my cooperating teacher has recommended, I am not afraid to adjust these as I go along in class.

Gloria, Canada

DEVELOPING LEARNER-FOCUSED TEACHING

Although in some ways teaching can be viewed as a type of teacher performance, the goal of teaching, of course, is to facilitate learning. Novice teachers are often initially more concerned about their own performance as teachers than on the impact of their teaching on their learners. With more experience, however, teachers come to think about teaching less in terms of teacher performance and more in terms of learner engagement. Learner-focused teaching is reflected in such things as the degree of engagement learners have with the lesson, the quantity of student participation and interaction that occurs, the ability of the teacher to present subject matter from a learner's perspective and to address learners' needs, how well the teacher is able to reshape the lesson based on learner feedback, and how he or she responds to learners' difficulties (see Chapter 9).

We see these different perspectives on lessons in how two student teachers responded to the question, "What constitutes an effective language lesson from your perspective?"

It's important to me that I achieve the goals I set for the lesson and don't skip things I planned to cover. I need to feel I did a good job on covering the different stages of the lesson – the presentation phase, the practice stage, and the free production stage, for example.

Teacher A

To me the most important thing is that the students enjoyed themselves and had useful practice. And that the lesson was at the right level for them – not too easy or too difficult so that they felt it was really worthwhile coming to class today.

Teacher B

It is natural when you first start teaching to be preoccupied with your own performance as a teacher, to try to communicate a sense of confidence, competence, and skill, and to try to create lessons that reflect purpose, order, and planning. It is a period when things are being tried out and tested, when your role and identity is being developed, and when many new challenges have to be overcome. Hence studies of teachers in their first year of teaching have revealed a transition from a survival and mastery stage where the teacher's performance is a central concern, to a later stage where teachers become more focused on their students' learning and the impact of their teaching on learning (Fuller and Brown 1975). The challenge in practice teaching is to ensure that such a transition occurs and that your initial teaching experiences do not lead to a style of teaching that sticks, one that provides a comfort zone for you but that fails to provide learners with the opportunity to achieve their full potential as learners. Strategies for addressing this are discussed in Chapter 9.

When I started on teaching practice I was determined to plan every aspect of my lesson so I would leave nothing to chance. To me the lesson plan is just like a script in a play where every minor detail is spelled out on paper and the teacher is just like the "actor" who will "act" according to the "script," thus placing great importance on the "script." Also, I believed that a good lesson is a well-thought-out lesson with proper planning, which explains why lesson planning is so instrumental in producing a good lesson, especially for beginning teachers like me – with little teaching experience. So when I started teaching the class by myself I was so focused on the lesson plan and I was determined to follow that plan that I forgot about monitoring if my students were learning anything from the lesson. I remember one day I had planned a grammar activity that called for me to prepare some students for the activity in advance in the front of the class for about five minutes and I totally forgot about the other students and when the 'prepared' students finally got what I wanted them to do (which took fifteen minutes rather than the five I had planned) the other students did not seem interested in the lesson at all but I forced them to participate. Lucky for me the cooperating teacher was observing because she pointed all this out to me and asked me to think more about how students react during the class rather than following the lesson plan. From that moment on I began to ask myself what my students were actually learning during each class because, as the cooperating teacher reminded me, this is the reason we teach.

Carrie, United States

Senior (2006) suggests that a central aspect of learner-focused teaching is creating a classroom that functions as a community of learners.

> It is sometimes forgotten that language classes operate as communities, each with its own collection of shared understandings that have been built up over time. The overall character of each language class is created, developed, and maintained by everyone in the room. (Senior 2006: 200)

Effective teachers use different strategies to develop a sense of community among their learners, including using group-based activities, addressing common student interests and concerns, regularly changing seating arrangements so that students experience working with different classmates, using humor and other ways of creating a warm and friendly classroom atmosphere, and recognizing that students have both social as well as learning needs in the classroom.

LEARNING HOW TO THEORIZE FROM PRACTICE

Mastery of teaching skills and the specialized thinking skills expert teachers make use of are essential aspects of teacher development (Borg 2006). But teacher learning also involves developing a deeper understanding of what teaching is, of developing ideas, concepts, theories, and principles based on your experience of teaching. The development of a personal system of knowledge, beliefs, and understanding drawn from practical experience of teaching is known as the *theorizing of practice*. This involves making connections between one's practical and experience-based understanding of teaching and the theoretical understandings of teaching developed within the language-teaching profession. The belief system and understanding teachers build up in this way helps them make sense of their experience and also serves as the source of the practical actions they take in the classroom. To better understand the concept of theorizing of practice it will be useful to contrast two ways of thinking about the relationship between theory and practice. The first is the *application of theory*. This involves making connections between the concepts, information, and theories from your teacher education courses and your classroom practices, of putting theories into practice. So after studying the principles of task-based instruction or collaborative learning, for example, you might try to find ways of applying these principles in your teaching.

The *theorizing of practice*, on the other hand, involves reflecting on your practice and developing an understanding of its underlying meaning in order to better understand the nature of language teaching and learning. The information you make use of is the experience of teaching, observations of how your learners learn or fail to learn, and your reflections on things that happen during your lessons. The theorizing that results from these reflections may take several different forms. It may lead to explanations as to why things happen in the way they do, to generalizations about the nature of things, to principles that can form the basis of subsequent actions, and to the teacher's personal teaching philosophy.

The following examples taken from student teachers' narratives and journals illustrate teachers beginning to theorize from practice.

ARRIVING AT EXPLANATIONS AND GENERALIZATIONS

Children are much better language learners than adults because they are not worried about making mistakes and are much more prepared to take risks.

When we begin learning a language it's better to follow the natural way, using imitation. But when you are more advanced then you need to know more about the grammar.

The essential thing in language learning is knowing how to say what you want to say but not why you have to say it in a particular way.

Learners learn more when they work in groups because they can learn from each other and they get more opportunities to talk than when the teacher is conducting the class.

Error correction works best when you ask students to monitor their own language, rather than having them depend on the teacher all the time.

DEVELOPING PRINCIPLES AND A TEACHING PHILOSOPHY

A further stage in theorizing from practice is when teachers formulate principles that they refer to when planning and evaluating their teaching and a personal philosophy which guides their decision making. Here is an example of a teacher describing some of the beliefs and principles she brings to her teaching:

I think it's important to be positive as a personality. I think the teacher has to be a positive person. I think you have to show a tremendous amount of patience. And I think if you have a good attitude you can project this to the students and hopefully establish a relaxed atmosphere in your classroom so that the students won't dread to come to class but have a good class. I feel that it's important to have a lesson plan of some sort because you need to know what you want to teach and how you are going to go from the beginning to the end. And also taking into consideration the students, what there ability is, what their background is, and so on. I have been in situations where I did not understand what was being taught or what was being said, and how frustrating it is, and so when I approach it I say: How can I make it the easiest way for them to understand what they need to learn?

Pauline, Hong Kong

This teacher's philosophy emphasizes the teacher's attitude and the need to create a supportive environment for learning in the classroom. She stresses the need for lesson planning, but her justification for lesson planning is based on helping the students rather than helping the teacher.

Other examples of theorizing from practice are the principles that teachers often refer to when reflecting on the assumptions and beliefs that guide their practice and decision making. For example:

- Follow the learners' interest to maintain students' involvement.
- Always teach to the whole class – not just to the best students.
- Seek ways to encourage independent student learning.
- Make learning fun.
- Build takeaway value in every lesson.
- Address learners' mental processing capacities.
- Facilitate learner responsibility or autonomy.

Practice teaching provides the basis on which you can begin to articulate and test your theories, beliefs, and principles, and the theorizing that results from these procedures will often provide the basis for interpreting and evaluating your own teaching as well as the teaching of others. Table 2.1 summarizes the eight dimensions of teacher learning in practice teaching.

1. Develop the discourse skills of a language teacher.	• Develop proficiency in and use of English in the classroom.
2. Develop the identity of a language teacher.	• Negotiate social and cultural roles through interactions with learners and cooperating teacher.
3. Develop a repertoire of teaching skills.	• Develop confidence and fluency in basic classroom skills needed to present and navigate language lessons.
4. Learn how to apply professional knowledge.	• Apply knowledge gained in teacher-training / academic courses.
5. Develop an understanding of how learning is shaped by context.	• Reflect on different rules, facilities, values, expectations, and dynamics that shape teaching and learning.
6. Develop the cognitive skills of a language teacher.	• Develop different kinds of thinking and decision making teachers draw on before, during, and after teaching.
7. Develop learner-focused teaching.	• Develop thinking about teaching in terms of learner engagement.
8. Learn how to theorize from practice.	• Develop ideas, concepts, theories, and principles based on the experience of teaching.

Table 2.1   Eight dimensions of teacher learning in practice teaching

SUMMARY AND CONCLUSIONS

There are many different dimensions of effective teaching, and in this chapter eight of these have been the focus of discussion. The teacher's use of language is a key part of professional competence in language teaching and involves acquiring both the discourse of TESOL as well as the ability to use effective classroom language. It is also part of the process by which the teacher constructs a sense of the identity of a language teacher. Knowing how to teach involves becoming familiar with a range of different teaching skills, but also knowing how to use these skills flexibly. Good teachers also have a solid knowledge base derived from their academic studies as well as the ability to apply this knowledge in teaching. In drawing on this knowledge they make use of sophisticated processes of analysis and reasoning, known as pedagogic reasoning skills. In addition they need to be sensitive to the norms that operate in the contexts in which they work. Effective lessons reflect the teacher's ability to create learner-centered classrooms. Reflecting on their practice enables teachers to develop theories and concepts that can support and further develop their teacher development.

Teaching practice seeks to develop many different dimensions of teacher knowledge, skill, and awareness. The activities provided through teaching practice, which typically include planning lessons, adapting published materials, teaching different parts of a lesson, observing your cooperating teacher's teaching, reviewing your teaching sessions with your cooperating teacher, and reflecting on your own teaching through activities such as lesson reports, narratives, or journal writing, will provide you with the opportunity to develop your skill, confidence, and understanding of teaching and of yourself as a teacher.

Further reading

Borg, S. (2006). *Teacher cognition and language education: Research and practice.* London: Continuum.

Freeman, D., & Richards, J. C. (Eds.). (1996). *Teacher learning in language teaching.* Cambridge: Cambridge University Press.

Richards, J. C., & Schmidt, R. (2010). *Longman dictionary of applied linguistics and language teaching* (4th ed.) Harlow: Pearson.

Thornbury, S. (2006). *An A–Z of ELT.* Oxford: Macmillan.

Discussion questions

1. How can the way the teacher uses language, i.e., his or her "discourse skills," support classroom language learning? Can you give examples from your experience?

2. It is sometimes said that student teachers teach the way they were taught and find it difficult to adopt new teaching approaches. Do you think the ways you have been taught languages might have influenced your understanding and approach to teaching?

3. What are some ways in which you feel your sense of your identity as a language teacher has been influenced by your teacher education course? What other factors do you think influence your sense of identity as a teacher?

4. Review the list in Appendix A from the CELTA program. Which of these is of particular importance to you in your current teaching practice situation and at this present point in your teacher development?

5. Give two or three specific examples of how the pedagogic content knowledge you have acquired so far has prepared you for teaching.

6. Discuss ways in which learner-centeredness can become a feature of your lessons.

7. Read the vignette in Appendix B. Why do you think the writer felt that learning from classroom experience was more powerful and effective than learning from lectures in the course room? Why did he feel that "structuring" was an important skill to master?

Follow-up activities

1. Think about the last two classes you taught or observed. Try to identify one principle that was evident in these lessons. Relate this principle to what happened in the classroom, particularly in terms of how it clarifies what was taught and / or how it was taught.

2. Write a short description on one of your personal principles and how it influences your approach to teaching. Then share your description with other student teachers and compare.

3. Compare two different contexts for ESL programs and discuss ways in which contextual factors contribute to the uniqueness of each context.

Appendix A: Knowledge and skills required in the Certificate in English Language Teaching to Adults (CELTA) (summary of the test from https://www.teachers.cambridgeesol.org/ts/digitalAssets/ 104480_celta8_251103.pdf)

Learners and teachers and the teaching and learning context

- Cultural, linguistic, and educational backgrounds
- Motivations for learning English as an adult
- Learning and teaching styles
- Context for learning and teaching English
- Varieties of English
- Multilingualism and the role of first languages

Language analysis and awareness

- Basic concepts and terminology used in ELT for describing form and meaning in language and language use
- Grammar – grammatical frameworks: Rules and conventions relating to words, sentences, paragraphs, and texts
- Lexis: What it means to "know" a word; semantic relationships between words
- Phonology: The formation and description of English phonemes; features of connected speech
- The practical significance of similarities and differences between languages
- Reference materials for language awareness
- Key strategies and approaches for developing learners' language knowledge

Language skills: Reading, listening, speaking, and writing

- Reading
  - Basic concepts and terminology used for describing reading skills
  - Purposes of reading
  - Decoding meaning
  - Potential barriers to reading
- Listening
  - Basic concepts and terminology used for describing listening skills
  - Purposes of listening
  - Features of listening texts
  - Potential barriers to listening

- Speaking
  - ○ Basic concepts and terminology used for describing speaking skills
  - ○ Features of spoken English
  - ○ Language functions
  - ○ Paralinguistic features
  - ○ Phonemic systems
- Writing
  - ○ Basic concepts and terminology used for describing writing skills
  - ○ Subskills and features of written texts
  - ○ Stages of teaching writing
  - ○ Beginner literacy
  - ○ English spelling and punctuation
  - ○ Key strategies and approaches for developing learners' receptive and productive skills

Planning and resources for different teaching contexts

- Principles of planning for effective teaching of adult learners of English
- Lesson planning for effective teaching of adult learners of English
- Evaluation of lesson planning
- The selection, adaptation, and evaluation of materials and resources in planning (including computer- and other technology-based resources)
- Knowledge of commercially produced resources and nonpublished materials and classroom resources for teaching English to adults

Appendix B: Learning from teaching practice

While I was completing my practicum I realized that I learned a lot over the course of 12 weeks of practice teaching. In fact, I might have learned more practical skills for ESL teaching during those 12 weeks than I did during the four years of my undergraduate degree from coursework. One of the main skills that I learned was establishing classroom routines and procedures. Of course when I practice taught my first class, I really didn't have much of a clue of how to order and structure a "proper" ESL class. That, however, changed rather quickly as I observed from my first experience that for a class to be successful and function properly, ordered routines and procedures are very necessary. I learned to always start off my class with a greeting and a question, such as "How was your weekend?" or "What do you guys think about this crazy Canadian weather?" By doing so, I discovered that I could easily grasp the attention of the entire class as well as try and create some humor, which always works well as a crowd-calming technique.

After gaining control of the class, the next step in a routine is to review and recap from the previous lesson or day. By doing this, I learned that students will start to get into the "work mode" and start to get serious. After some review and some preactivity comes introducing and explaining tasks. I found out the hard way that an ESL teacher needs to explain and describe a new task more than once as many students do not always seem to understand everything the first time you explain it. I found that it is helpful (if I didn't create a worksheet of some kind) to write steps on the boards so that students have a visual outline of what to do.

The next step in setting up a classroom is to put students into groups. It is always easy to put students into pairs, but I learned over time that the best way to group students is in groups of three as the most meaningful discussion and learning opportunities seem to come in groups of three. However, I learned from experience that it is necessary for the instructor to think out the groups so that certain students are / aren't together in a group. Of course, this reminds me of the Vygotskian theory of Zone of Proximal Development . . . something that was touched on numerous times in my undergraduate classes. After the students completed their task in groups or pairs, I found that it is very useful to take up the activity as a whole class. The way I learned to structure whole-class activities is to first ask students to volunteer answers, and then to pick on specific students for answers as some of the best answers to questions never seem to be volunteered! After finishing a task, it is either time to wrap up the class or transition to another task.

Ruben, Canada

CHAPTER 3

Understanding the Teaching Context

INTRODUCTION

Teaching practice may take place in one or several very different contexts. For example, you might be teaching in a campus-based ESL program, in a local public school, in a community college, or a private language institute. Depending on the context, the learners you teach may be children, teenagers, or adults and may represent a variety of different social, economic, cultural, and educational backgrounds. Different teaching contexts present different notions of the process of learning to teach (Zeichner and Grant 1981). Campus-based teaching experiences (e.g., in a language center) may be quite different to those occurring in schools off campus. The students may be undergraduate international students rather than immigrants. The program may be supported with well-trained staff and superior support systems that do not always reflect conditions found in off-campus programs (Richards and Crookes 1988). Whatever the context in which you will be teaching, you will need to develop not only the skills of teaching but also the norms of practice expected of teachers in your school, both inside and outside the classroom. This will include understanding such things as the role of the prescribed curricula, the school culture, the routines of the classroom, and the school's procedures for lesson planning, as well as learning how to interact with students, school authorities, and colleagues.

In order to prepare for a successful practice-teaching experience, before you start your teaching practice you should therefore try to find out as much as possible about the school or institution where your teaching will take place, the kinds of language programs offered there, the kinds of teachers and students that you will work with, and what facilities and learning resources will be available. In this chapter we will examine how the context in which you complete your teaching influences the nature of your teaching practice.

CONTEXTUAL FACTORS IN TEACHING

Every teaching context is different and learning to teach involves understanding what the characteristics of the teaching context are and how they shape the nature of teaching and learning, as the following comments by student teachers reveal:

I love the school where I am working. The teachers I have met seem real friendly and helpful and my cooperating teacher goes out of her way to make me feel comfortable in her class.

Judy, United States

The teachers in the school where I am teaching seem to have little contact with each other. There are a lot of part-time teachers who just teach their classes and disappear. I get a sense that there is not a strong feeling of collegiality among the teachers in the school.

Robert, Korea

The teacher I am working with is very strict about everything. Seems like the school has lots of procedures teachers have to follow and I have to do things exactly the way they like to do them.

Andrew, Canada

My first few weeks went really well, then I had to work in a different class and I found the students very difficult to work with. They didn't seem to be interested in learning.

Anna, Japan

Teaching involves understanding the dynamics and relationships within the classroom and the rules and behaviors specific to a particular setting. For this reason teaching is sometimes described as a "situated" activity. Schools have their own ways of doing things. In some schools, textbooks are the core of the curriculum and teachers follow a prescribed curriculum. In others, teachers work from course guidelines and implement them as they see fit. In some institutions there is a strong sense of professional commitment and teachers are encouraged to cooperate with each other. This is reflected in many different aspects of the way the school functions.

The notion of "context" here is a very broad one, since it includes issues such as a school's goals and mission, its management style and "school culture," its physical resources including classroom facilities, media, and other technological resources, the curriculum and course offerings, the role of textbooks and tests, as well as the characteristics of teachers and learners in the school. Some of these factors have to do with "structural influences" (i.e., those to do with life in the classroom and the school in general), whereas others belong to the domain of "personal influences" (i.e., they come from other persons you will interact with while at the school, including the learners you will be teaching, your cooperating teacher and other teachers in the school, and in some cases your learners' parents). Learning to teach within a specific teaching context can thus be thought of as a process of socialization. As Calderhead (1992) remarks, learning to teach involves becoming "socialized into a professional culture with certain goals, shared values, and standards of conduct" (p. 6). There are a number of practical ways in which you can prepare yourself for this process.

I have worked in two different institutions in the past. The work cultures in the two places were almost opposite to one another. The personality of the head of the institutions had a lot to do in shaping the working environment in both. In the first place, there was hardly any discipline in the campus and most of the senior members of the staff dominated the juniors. The next institution was headed by a strict principal, who nevertheless, was a great teacher. So the whole working atmosphere was student centered.

Vidya, Canada

A Preliminary Visit to the School

A preliminary visit to the school or institution where you will be working is an invaluable opportunity to learn more about the nature of the school and its programs and practices. The school may also have a website that provides useful information about the school. There may be protocols to observe in setting up a school visit concerning who you should contact first (e.g., the principal or an administrative assistant), how to do this (e.g., in person or by letter), and whether a letter of introduction is needed. Usually half a day should be sufficient for a visit of this kind and can involve:

- a short meeting with the school principal
- a meeting with the cooperating teacher (and other teachers if possible)
- observation of some of the classes in the school
- familiarization with the layout of the school and its resources
- conversations with some of the learners you as a student teacher will be working with

Such visits can be very informative, as these student teachers attest:

The first thing that struck me when I entered the school was how organized everything was. There was a map of the school right beside the main entrance and so I could see where I was going immediately and there were notices everywhere for staff and students about upcoming events and all placed on notice boards rather than put up on walls all over the place. I was able to find the teachers' room easily and this was well maintained with small cubicles for each teacher. One cubicle was allotted to me for the period of my teaching practice, which was nice.

Zubeda, Turkey

Students were mulling about everywhere and seemed to be in a constant struggle but not with wanting to get to their next classes; rather they seemed to be in conflict with each other so I feared for the worst even before teaching practice. Even the principal seemed stressed when I met her a few minutes later.

Clarence, Singapore

It is important to prepare carefully for the preliminary visit, both in order to make a good impression at the school and to make the best use of the limited time available for the visit. It is a good idea to prepare a set of questions in advance that will help you learn more about your host institution, the courses it offers, the learners, and any other important issues you think you will face during your teaching practice. Some of these questions can include:

- How is the school organized in terms of the administration?
- Does each department in the school have a head teacher and are there any level coordinators or skill coordinators?
- For level coordinators, are they based on each skills area, such as a reading coordinator, a writing coordinator, etc., or are they based on levels, such as Level I coordinator, Level II coordinator, etc.?

(ctd.)

(ctd.)
- What is the role of the coordinator?
- Will I attend all staff meetings?
- Will I have any recess and / or lunch duties?
- Will I have to go on field trips with the students?
- What resources would be available to me in terms of photocopiers and computers? Is there a computer room where I can go to use the computers? Are there any other resources I could use?
- Who should I go to for photocopying during my teaching practice?
- Where will I be based during my teaching practice? Will I be in the main teachers' room or is there a separate location for student teachers?
- How many other student teachers will be placed in the same school with me and will they be located near me during teaching practice?
- What are the main school rules that I should know about and which ones should I be sure to monitor when I interact with students?
- Are there any rules specific to speaking English in class that I should be aware of?

However, it is important to remember that teachers and principals are extremely busy people and may have only a few minutes time to spare for your questions. Make sure your visit does not turn into an interrogation session!

THE SCHOOL OR INSTITUTION

Becoming familiar with the physical layout of the school, its resources and resource centers, and rules for their use, is an important first step in preparing for a teaching practice assignment. It is also necessary to find out as much as possible about the school's human resources, that is, the administrators, the teachers, and the students in the school. Williams et al. (2001) suggest that the culture of a school exists on a continuum from a highly individualistic school culture, where teachers see themselves as working individually to achieve their goals, to a collaborative culture, where teachers work more as a team and are willing to help one another. Morris similarly observes:

> Schools are organizations and they develop a culture, ethos, or environment which might be favorable or unfavorable to encourage change and the implementation of innovations. A school with a relatively open climate, where the teachers collaborate with each other and where the principal and senior teachers are supportive of teachers, is more likely to try to implement a change. In contrast, a school where the principal focuses on administrative matters, the teachers work in isolation or in narrow subject-based groups, and where there is no mechanism to discuss and try to solve problems is less likely to change. (Morris 1994: 109)

This is obviously a sensitive issue and one that cannot be easily determined from a first visit, although from observation of teachers and students in and outside of classrooms and from conversations with them, you may be able to get a sense of the professional and personal qualities of the teachers in the school. Both they and the school director or principal will help you understand the rules, protocols, procedures, and routines of the school. Some of these may be stated on the school's website or in printed information about the school. Other information may initially be more difficult to obtain since it is part of the "hidden curriculum" of the school, that is, the often unstated values, rules, expectations, and norms of practice that operate in the school (see Appendix for student teachers' accounts of the schools they worked in).

Depending on the nature and duration of your practice-teaching experience, you should try to get information about the following kinds of issues in order to understand the school's practices and other aspects of the school culture:

- What are the school's expectations of student teachers?
- Is there a dress code for teachers?
- Is there a dress code for students?
- How have learners in the school in the past reacted to being taught by a student teacher?
- When will my practice teaching take place and how often?
- Will I be dealing with anyone other than my cooperating teacher?
- What sort of problems might I encounter during my teaching practice?
- If I have any problems, who should I go to for advice?
- If I am sick, what are the school procedures I should follow?
- What discipline procedures should I follow when dealing with students?
- Do I have to do any extracurricular activities such as sports and field trips?
- Do I have any involvement with parents?
- Who will be giving me overall feedback about my teaching practice performance?

One of the concerns of a student teacher is described in this comment:

I'd want to know how strict the rules are (assuming there are any). I know one of my observation teachers used to remind her students, "English in the classroom, please!" but she wasn't excessively heavy-handed about it.

Mona, Canada

THE ENGLISH COURSE YOU WILL BE TEACHING OR ASSISTING WITH

The circumstances in which you will be teaching may vary considerably from one school to another. In one setting, the school policy may be to follow a textbook linked to a prescribed curriculum, while in another school, teachers may have the freedom to construct their own curriculum and design their own teaching materials. English courses take many different forms depending on the goals and content of the course, the teacher's teaching style and approach, the learners, and the resources used. Hence two student teachers both carrying out their practice teaching in a college writing program may have very different experiences. And since you will generally be teaching a course or part of a course designed by the regular class teacher it is important to study the course outline or syllabus and the course materials or textbook and to understand the teacher's approach to teaching the course. Issues which can be the focus of your initial familiarization visit include:

- What kind of course will you be teaching on?
- Is there a course outline and syllabus for the course?
- What teaching materials and resources will you be using?
- Where does the teaching take place (e.g., classroom, media lab, seminar rooms)?

(ctd.)

(ctd.)
- Does the course make use of technology (e.g., computers, video, media lab)?
- Will you be teaching part of lessons or whole lessons from Day 1?
- What is the role of tests and assessment in the course?
- What is the role of assignments and homework?
- Will you be using the school's materials or be expected to prepare your own materials?

Here is what student teachers said about the courses they were assigned to teach:

I had to teach on an introductory course for engineers. I had never taught an ESP course before and the materials were very unfamiliar to me. My cooperating teacher provided me with the course materials, which were very detailed and included lesson plans, homework assignments, and midterm and final examinations. I also had to factor in that most of the students in the class were from the Middle East and I was not familiar with the culture there as I had never been there, nor had I had any interaction with people from that part of the world. So I had to learn quickly on two fronts: the new materials and become familiar with the cultural background of my students. I was lucky that I had such a good cooperating teacher to guide me because I felt overwhelmed most of the time.

Oliver, United Kingdom

I was given a writing course on teaching practice that followed a genre-based approach because the school as a whole had decided to follow this system of teaching writing. Luckily I had covered this in my teacher education courses and so while I was teaching the class, I directed my students' attention to the choice of words by the writer, such as the concentration of "action" and "emotive" words in different parts of the model. Even though I tried as much as possible not to use technical terms, my cooperating teacher noticed that I often did, so that was one thing I picked up quickly – I think this is a direct result of hearing my teacher education instructors explaining it in class. Anyway I followed my cooperating teacher's advice and I tried only to highlight the text structure such as orientation, complication, and resolution to assist the students' understanding.

Mark, Singapore

I was asked to take over my cooperating teacher's reading class for a few lessons during teaching practice and I was given complete freedom to teach as I wanted provided I had reading comprehension lessons. So, even though the lessons were to be on comprehension, as I was given freedom I decided to incorporate a reading activity (skimming and scanning) to keep students on-task and focused. So instead of having the students read the passage from the text directly as the cooperating teacher usually did, I decided to divide the text into five parts. Students were assigned into groups of five and each of them had to read a part of the passage. Students were tasked to answer two simple questions based on their section of the passage. The first question required them to read and pick out specific details from the passage (scanning) and the other required them to pick out the main idea from the passage. This was to be done individually and after that, students were to share with their respective groups about their part of the passage (i.e., provide a summary of their part). The groups were then tasked to piece the different parts of the passage together. The main objective of the activity was to provide an alternative avenue for the students to comprehend the passage instead of having them read the whole passage monotonously. My cooperating teacher seemed to like this a lot and she continued to encourage me to experiment during teaching practice.

Walter, Canada

In some cases you may find that the teaching methods and strategies you focused on in your academic or training courses are not necessarily those that are used or recommended by your cooperating teacher. This does not mean that you need to abandon everything that you have been taught. As an experienced teacher educator comments:

So long as the student teacher understands how to mediate between theory and practice, any method (or strategy) that works is a good method. The host school is likely to welcome student teachers who are innovative and who have more effective ways of teaching to ensure that real learning takes place in the classroom.

Anthony, teacher educator, Singapore

THE LEARNERS YOU WILL BE TEACHING

A primary concern for you will be to find out as much as possible about the kind of learners you will be teaching. Are they immigrants, college students, teenagers, or working adults? Why are they taking the course and what kinds of learners are they? ESL classrooms are typically characterized by the diversity of their students, often containing people with very different life experiences, needs, and expectations. The following are not untypical of the kinds of students you might be working with in your teaching practice:

Mee Gyung is an 18-year-old student from South Korea. She came to the United States because her parents wanted her to learn English so that she could get into a university in the United States and thus eventually get a good job back in Korea. So she went to attend language school in the United States for one year and then transfer into the private university that the language school was affiliated with.

Abdullah is an oil executive from Saudi Arabia and has signed up for language classes in the language school attached to the nearest university in Saudi Arabia so that he can update his English language skills in order to be able to travel abroad for business.

Georgio is an immigrant from Colombia who came to Canada one month ago. As the Canadian government has English language programs that are free for all landed immigrants, Georgio decided to enroll in the government-run programs (called LINC) so that he can better fit into his new homeland and ultimately get a good job.

Whei Neng is from China and has conditional acceptance into a U.S. university undergraduate program already but she has to go through all the levels of the language institute successfully and get an acceptable TOEFL score also. So she arrived and started at Level 1 and attends most classes but does not really finish her homework and occasionally feels less motivated to study English.

Establishing a classroom culture in which students with very different needs and expectations such as the ones above can work together cooperatively and form a cohesive learning community – one in which they feel comfortable interacting among themselves and with their teacher – takes time to achieve (Senior 2006). Your cooperating teacher will generally have tried to create this culture in the classroom and you will need to build on it and become a part of it (see Chapter 8).

In addition it will be important to understand what the learners' expectations are for their English course, and whether their understanding is the same as yours. Brindley states:

> When learners and teachers meet for the first time, they may bring with them different expectations concerning not only the learning process in general, but also concerning what will be learned in a particular course and how it will be learned. The possibility exists, therefore, for misunderstanding to arise. It is accordingly, of vital importance that, from the beginning of the course, mechanisms for consultation are set up, in order to ensure that the parties involved in the teaching-learning process are aware of each other's expectations. (Brindley 1984: 95)

Procedures for identifying learners' needs and goals are discussed in Chapter 9. Another issue that you will encounter in relation to the students you will be working with concerns your identity as a student teacher. How will the class perceive you? Will they judge you to be an "expert-in-training" and accord you the same level of respect that they accord their regular teacher? Meeting a new class of learners can therefore be a somewhat challenging experience for novice teachers. Finding out as much as possible about the learners in advance is essential preparation for teaching practice, and in conversations with the people you meet at the school you should try to clarify questions such as these:

- What kind of learners attend a typical ESL class in the school?
- What kind of learners will I be teaching?
- Why are they taking the course?
- How do learners like these typically perform in the course?
- Are they usually highly motivated?
- Is this the first time they will have been taught by a student teacher?
- Do they have any particular preference for teaching methods and materials?
- Do I assign homework and what do I do if they do not complete their homework?
- Is there an assigned textbook and do I decide what to cover?
- What do the students think about the textbook – do they expect it to be followed in detail?
- Are they generally very active and participatory in class?
- What seating arrangements should I follow and can I change their seating arrangements?
- How do I form pairs and groups or are these combinations already formed?

A common concern is expressed by this student teacher:

I was very nervous because it is not the same to do microteaching in my classroom and with my classmates as to teach in a real context where someone is observing and evaluating you.

Anita, Mexico

YOUR COOPERATING TEACHER

Your cooperating teacher plays a crucial role in facilitating your practice-teaching experience (Farrell 2008b). The cooperating teacher may be in this role through volunteering to do so, but in other circumstances it may be a normal expectation of experienced teachers in a school. Working with a cooperating teacher should therefore always be regarded as a privilege, since it involves extra work for the teacher. The first meeting with the cooperating teacher is therefore an important one and an opportunity to find out what his or her expectations are and how he or she plans to arrange and manage the practice-teaching experience. In initial conversations with your cooperating teacher, discussions will usually focus on the teaching you will be doing and the arrangements the cooperating teacher will set in place for working with you during your teaching practice.

Issues for discussion with the cooperating teacher will normally include the following:

- What are his or her expectations for teaching practice?
- What kind of working relationship does he or she like to have with student teachers?
- How does he or she think you should prepare for your practice teaching?
- What are some things you should anticipate?
- Have there been any problems in the past in relation to practice teaching in his or her class?
- Will you have contacts with any other teachers or classes in the school?

The following comments were made by student teachers about their cooperating teachers:

From the moment I met her, my cooperating teacher was really great. She had all arranged for me and even had folders ready for me that I heard she paid for herself. She took complete charge of my time at the school from the very first day and brought me everywhere with her: to meetings, to classes, to lunch, to sports, and even to her home. She was great.

Mee Soo, Korea

My cooperating teacher made his expectations for me clear from the very beginning. He had a system in his class that he wanted me to follow and he told me he would provide me with all the necessary information to do this. And he did. He gave me the course details, the lesson plans, and evaluation rubrics that I would need. All he asked of me was not to deviate much from the plan while I was teaching, as he wanted to follow his system that he had worked out in 20 years of teaching. I followed it as closely as possible and we got on very well during teaching practice.

Lynn, Australia

CONTACTS WITH OTHER TEACHERS IN THE SCHOOL

Apart from the cooperating teacher, you may also have the chance to interact with other teachers in the school or institution. Although some of the regular teaching staff may feel that you and other student teachers are only in the school for a short period of time and hence they may not feel particularly responsible for you, others may be willing to spend time with student teachers, offering advice and support or even inviting the student teacher to observe their class from time to time. If you meet other teachers in the school you may like to discuss issues such as these:

- What is their experience with student teachers?
- What was their student-teaching experience like?
- What advice would they give student teachers?
- Would it be possible to observe them teach?
- What do they think about the atmosphere / culture of that particular school?
- How do they think you can best use your time on teaching practice?

(ctd.)

(ctd.)
- What do they think you can expect to learn from teaching practice?
- Where should you go to look for a job after teaching practice?

Table 3.1 summarizes the contextual factors teacher learners can consider during their practice teaching.

1. A preliminary visit to the school	• Learn about the nature of the school and programs and practices.
2. The school or institution	• Discover information about the school's physical resources (layout, rules) and human resources (administrators, teachers, students).
3. The English course you will be teaching or assisting with	• Find out about the course curriculum, goals, policy, use of textbook, and teacher's teaching style.
4. The learners you will be teaching	• Find out about the learners' learning styles, needs, goals, and expectations.
5. Your cooperating teacher	• Find out about the cooperating teacher's expectations and plans for managing your practicum experience.
6. Contacts with other teachers in the school	• Find out about interacting with other teachers in the school.

Table 3.1   Contextual factors to consider in practice teaching

SUMMARY AND CONCLUSIONS

Different contexts for carrying out teaching practice create different opportunities for teacher learning and pose different kinds of challenges. Teaching contexts vary greatly and your campus course will not have been able to predict exactly the kinds of conditions you will encounter in your host school. So the more you can find out about it the better prepared you will be to teach there. Schools have different traditions of practice and different expectations for teaching and learning, and becoming familiar with these is an important preparation for teaching practice. You might experience approaches to teaching that differ from those you are familiar with from your academic or teacher-training course. It is important to keep in mind that teaching practice is both an opportunity to apply what you know and to learn things you can only learn in a real language classroom. You can learn a lot from a preliminary visit to a school, through conversations with teachers in the school, and through observation of their classes. Adequate preparation for practice teaching means finding out as much as you can about the kind of class you will be teaching, who the learners are, and what curriculum and materials you will be expected to follow or use. Understanding your cooperating teacher's expectations is also crucial. Whereas there will inevitably be a period of adjustment and perhaps rapid learning, your cooperating teacher will have had experience working with other student teachers and will doubtless be able to help you make a smooth transition into teaching practice.

Further reading

Gebhard, J. G. (2006). *Teaching English as a foreign or second language: A teacher self-development and methodology guide* (2nd ed.). Ann Arbor: University of Michigan Press.

Randal, M., & Thornton, B. (2001). *Advising and supporting teachers*. Cambridge: Cambridge University Press.

Richards, J. C. (1998). *Beyond training*. New York: Cambridge University Press.

Discussion questions

1. Can you give an example of how schools differ from one culture to another?

2. Discuss a school context you are familiar with. How do assessment practices in the school affect teaching and learning?

3. What aspects of school life in the community where you live might strike visitors from a different culture as unusual or surprising?

4. What different expectations as to how language classes should be conducted might you expect among the following learner groups: young children, teenagers, and adult working professionals?

5. What roles do textbooks play in a school context you are familiar with? How do they influence teaching and learning?

6. In the vignettes on page 36, Oliver, Mark, and Walter all had different experiences with the courses they were asked to take over. Discuss each one and explain what you would have done in each case.

7. Read the student teachers' accounts in the Appendix of the schools they worked in during their teaching practice. In the first account, Vic encountered a situation where he perceived that he was not getting any support from other teachers in the school and he was tolerated rather than welcomed. Now contrast Vic's story with Ting's who had a very positive experience during her teaching practice because the school welcomed her as a student teacher.

- Do you think Vic should have shared his worries with his cooperating teacher?
- What would you have done if you had found yourself in a similar situation?
- Do you think Vic could have done anything more to help himself?
- What steps can student teachers adopt to make their time at the school as meaningful as possible given that some schools may be more welcoming than others?

Follow-up activities

1. Draw up your own list of questions to ask the school principal and your cooperating teacher on your preliminary visit to your school placement.

2. When you commence your teaching practice, survey your students about their expectations for their study of English and their expectations of you as a student teacher. Compare your findings with those of other student teachers.

Appendix: Student teachers' accounts of their teaching contexts

After about two to three weeks of teaching practice I realized that I was probably in a school that exhibited a culture of individualism among the full-time teachers. This culture of individualism really started when I entered the school on the first day and was put in an isolated room with another student teacher, both of us beside the photocopiers. Then I was told that I would not be allowed to observe any teachers teaching even though I was under the impression that this would be part of my training. Throughout the period of teaching practice there were limited opportunities of sharing because full-time colleagues were not easily visible or accessible since they were not all sharing the same staff room. So I didn't really talk much with the other teachers beyond my cooperating teacher because they were always busy and into cliques of teachers who have been there a long time, newer teachers, and student teachers like me. Anyway, the cooperating teacher did her duty and evaluated me on regular intervals but she then "gave" me her class and I had to teach it by myself with nobody in the room observing. I really had to learn-on-the-job in order to survive, but survive I did and I am actually still in touch with some of the students to this day. But this is in spite of the school, as I got the impression that we were to be tolerated as student teachers by all but not really welcomed by any. I was glad to get out of that school in the end because I felt I was really self-educated during my teaching practice.

Vic, Singapore

I remember the first day I entered the school for my teaching practice. Because I had made a preliminary visit to the building I knew where to go and who I was going to meet and at what time. I arrived on time and went into the Assistant Director of the Institute's office and she was ready for me with all kinds of school pamphlets and folders with school maps, rules, and regulations. She also had my school special I.D. to wear at all times while I was on teaching practice and then we set off for a walking tour of the school. Yes, I had already been given an informal tour of the school during my preliminary visit but this time the Assistant Director was giving me an official welcome as she brought me to the staff room and introduced me formally to everyone there who seemed genuinely eager to welcome me and offered me help whenever I would need it. We also visited some classes while they were in session and the teachers did not seem to mind the interruption and stopped to shake my hand. Then we returned to her office where my cooperating teacher was waiting for me so that he could take over the formal first-day introduction and give me more details. I was so impressed with this first day and I felt very welcome not only into the school but also the profession. I wondered how long this would last but it was great throughout my teaching practice because not only did my cooperating teacher go out of his way to help me but also the other teachers all remembered my name and stopped to chat each time we met in the corridor or in the staff room. The atmosphere in that staff room was great and each of the teachers seemed to be taking a continuous interest in each other and I never really heard anyone complaining about anything except when a student was difficult to deal with. I was hoping I could get a job in a similar institution when I graduated because I really enjoyed my teaching practice experience in that school with those teachers.

Ting, Vietnam

CHAPTER 4

Working With Your Cooperating Teacher

INTRODUCTION

Your cooperating teacher is one of the people who will greatly influence the nature and impact of your practice-teaching experience (Guyton and McIntyre 1990). He or she will support you in a number of ways during your teaching practice – as guide and mentor, as critical friend, as expert, as model teacher, as evaluator, as counselor, and as resource person – so developing a positive working relationship with your cooperating teacher will make your practice-teaching experience both fruitful and positive. When you start your practice teaching many of the crucial decisions involved in planning and teaching your lessons may be made principally by your cooperating teacher, but as you gain experience and confidence you will gradually assume greater responsibility for all aspects of your teaching. Often your practice-teaching experience will begin with observation of the cooperating teacher's class, and later you will take over different areas of responsibility for teaching. During practice teaching you are likely to be involved in a different kind of experience from those you had during your campus program. The latter will most likely have focused on an academic or theoretical understanding of teaching and language learning, drawing on academic research and theories. But your practice teaching will focus more on the practical experience of teaching and your cooperating teacher may feel that this is more crucial to your professional development than your academic studies. This may pose a dilemma for you at times since you may receive different kinds of messages from what you were taught during your campus or training center program and from your teaching practice experience. The important role of the cooperating teacher is emphasized in these comments from a student teacher:

I feel that the cooperating teacher is one of the most important components of practice teaching. In fact, he / she can make it an enriching experience or otherwise. I see my cooperating teacher as a link between me and the students. The students who are used to her way of teaching can find it difficult to get used to someone else teaching them. So her advice on conducting the class is crucial, especially in the initial stage.

Vidya, Canada

THE FUNCTIONS OF THE COOPERATING TEACHER

There are many different ways in which your cooperating teacher can help you improve your understanding and practice of language teaching.

HELPING YOU PREPARE FOR TEACHING

- by orienting you to the class and its goals
- by inducting you into the school culture
- by familiarizing you with the curriculum and the materials
- by helping you plan your teaching
- by reviewing your lesson plans

You cooperating teacher will be able to introduce you to the kind of course you will be teaching on and the materials you will be expected to teach, and suggest how these can be used in class. If he or she has copies of previously used lesson plans, it is important for you to ask to see these to get a sense of how the cooperating teacher likes to plan lessons and what aspects of lessons he or she feels need greater attention or focus, as the following student teacher describes:

On teaching practice I have been assigned to teach the best class (highest level). So I must work very closely with my cooperating teacher in order to coordinate the lessons. Indeed, she explained her goals for the class and she showed me the scheme of work that she has to follow which was very illuminating for me because the scheme of work for this high-level class dictated that I should alternate a composition and a comprehension exercise every week. For lesson planning for the high-level class my cooperating teacher said she would focus on oral and structured writing while I was to focus on narrative writing, comprehension, grammar, and perhaps listening comprehension. She reviewed all my lesson plans before I went into class and made some suggestions, and she also showed me how she usually teaches narrative writing and told me to watch her model this as she took some of the first lessons. After these demonstrations, we discussed some different methods that I learned in the teacher education course and if they would be suitable for her class. Because of all this I felt I was well prepared before the lesson.

Sze Seau, Singapore

SHARING INSTRUCTIONAL STRATEGIES

- by modeling teaching strategies
- by letting you observe his or her classes
- by discussing effective practices

Your cooperating teacher may have a very different teaching style and approach from you, one that you may not feel you can use yourself. If you plan to use a different teaching approach you should discuss this with your cooperating teacher to check if he or she feels it will be effective or appropriate. There may be good reasons why your teacher prefers to do more whole-class teaching than small group work, or vice versa.

I realized that my cooperating teacher uses very deductive methods in teaching descriptive writing after observing her teach a class and so I thought they can be assigned more individual written work during the class and if they did not finish then it could be done at home after the teaching of a lesson. My cooperating teacher decided to let me try this way and I learned quickly that these students have extremely short attention spans and their behavior took a turn for the worse when they were allowed to work alone. They would only try behaving themselves after much scolding and nagging by me and my cooperating teacher but this process has to be frequently repeated as they did not do any real work by themselves and most spoke in their native language to each other. Now I know why my cooperating teacher preferred to teach the whole class together in a deductive mode.

Bruce, Korea

DEVELOPING YOUR AWARENESS OF YOUR TEACHING

- by observing your lessons
- by collecting information about your teaching
- by giving feedback on your teaching
- by supervising your teaching sessions
- by discussing your teaching philosophy

You may be a little nervous when your cooperating teacher observes you teaching, and one of his or her roles is to give you both positive and negative feedback. Student teachers sometimes feel nervous or uncomfortable when they receive negative feedback on their teaching from their cooperating teacher or supervisor. However, if you both negotiate a focus for these observations and see observations as an opportunity for sharing and reflecting on teaching experiences, observation can become a positive rather than a negative experience. Getting the cooperating teacher to understand that his or her help and advice is appreciated and valued is critical to developing a positive relationship between the cooperating teacher and the student teacher from the very start (see Chapter 7). This is described in the following student teacher's comments:

After my cooperating teacher observed my class we went back to the staff room and found a quiet corner where we reviewed my teaching. I was so scared about this process because I had felt that I had just encountered some class management problems for this lesson. I felt the students were fidgety because they could not stay still and study the text closely although they knew they were going to be tested on it the following lesson. I wondered if they were really getting what I was trying to cover in the text. But to my surprise and delight after the lesson my cooperating teacher mentioned that she had always had some trouble covering the same part of the textbook because there were so many grammar rules for the students to remember and worse, they knew they were having a test on that material the following lesson as was mandated in the school's curriculum. During the post-observation review the cooperating teacher broke down the lesson into various parts and I came away from the discussion really energized and with the realization that what we think we do and what we really do while teaching may not be the same.

Frank, Canada

HELPING YOU RESOLVE PROBLEMS

- by discussing problems you experience
- by presenting alternatives
- by exploring teaching incidents

Doubtless some unanticipated issues will arise during your practice teaching. Your cooperating teacher will probably have encountered similar issues and will be able to suggest effective strategies for resolving them, so think of him or her as a key resource person when you encounter problems.

When I was teaching I decided to put students together in groups in order to better interact with each other and practice the language. So I decided one day to mix up the genders in each group by placing two boys and one girl together in a group. The result was not good because the girl was left out completely as the two boys only talked to each other and in their native language, which was different from that of the girl's native language. I noticed that this also occurred when the girls were in a majority and they also left the boy out of their discussion. When I reflected on this after the class my cooperating teacher said that it was important to be concerned about the issue of student gender in my classes in general and in my case the realization that some students did not like working in groups with members of the opposite sex. Until this incident and the advice I received from my cooperating teacher I must say that I had never thought about gender issues in class and I now believe that cooperation among the genders in class can and should be cultivated, given the time and opportunity.

Jasmine, Malaysia

ENCOURAGING AND MOTIVATING YOU

- by praising aspects of your teaching
- by commenting on your progress

Hopefully your cooperating teacher will find many positive things to say about your teaching and this will help you develop your confidence as a teacher, as we see from the following comments:

After my teaching practice lesson my cooperating teacher showed me what she had written while I was teaching and I was really encouraged as a result. Here is some of it: "To me planning a lesson properly is crucial as it enhances the confidence of the teacher in class and it gives the lesson direction. This lesson was really well planned by Sarah and really well delivered as she displayed sound knowledge of the topic taught. Her use of materials was also appropriately selected to match the different abilities of students. The different procedures of the lesson were always smooth and orderly in all cases." I was really delighted with this result and felt that I was making some progress in my desire to be a real teacher.

Sarah, Canada

APPROACHES TO SUPERVISION

Traditionally *supervision* has been seen as the primary function of the cooperating teacher, however, our understanding of the nature of supervision has changed as our understanding of the nature of teacher development has changed. We can compare traditional "top-down" approaches to supervision with current, more "bottom-up" approaches. By a top-down approach we mean one where the cooperating teacher adopts a prescriptive role, emphasizing the need to conform to established norms and practices and intervening directly to correct instances where the student teacher departs from these practices. Often the prescriptions reflect a particular teaching philosophy or method:

I don't think your lesson was very communicative. There was too much emphasis on controlled practice and grammar and not sufficient emphasis on free practice and real communication.

A less prescriptive approach is the "non-directive approach" (Freeman 1982, 1989), where the cooperating teacher serves as a sympathetic listener and tries to develop nonjudgmental conversations about the lesson. For example:

How did you feel about the lesson? What kind of balance were you aiming for in the activities you chose, and how successful do you think the balance of activities was?

Another style has been termed "the alternative approach," where the supervisor seeks to help the teacher discover alternative ways of approaching teaching. For example:

I noticed you took a fairly direct role in modeling the language you wanted the students to use during the activity. What do you think are some other ways of focusing on the accuracy of student language? Shall we look at one or two other strategies that would work and see what their advantages and disadvantages are?

This can be compared with a "collaborative approach," where the student teacher and the cooperating teacher work in a team relationship and share the processes of reflecting on teaching and reviewing different teaching strategies. For example:

So if you want to make use of more cooperative learning in your classroom, let's see if we can find some ways to set that up. What do you think would be a good place to start?

Unlike the prescriptive approach, the other three approaches discussed in this chapter represent a more reflective approach to supervision in which the cooperating teacher's role is to facilitate the student teacher's understanding of teaching through a process of collaborative observation and reflection. These different approaches to supervision reflect different perceptions of status, power, authority, and identity. In considering alternative styles of interaction between the student teacher and the cooperating teacher, however, we need to recognize that the role of the supervisor may differ from one context to another. In some cultures a more direct form of supervision may be favored, whereas in others more of a consultative style is preferred. We also need to recognize that some aspects of the cooperating teacher's role by their nature can arouse negative feelings, since he or she may be the bearer of both good and bad news about your teaching. Offering criticism on your teaching may not be something a cooperating teacher enjoys but he or she may feel it is part of his or her responsibility.

You were not allowed to do things differently – and that was very difficult for me. I kept wanting to take the language from the textbook and teach it in my own way. I mean, I wanted to do the same thing – but in a different way that might be more appealing or more captivating for the students.

Teacher cited by Senior 2006: 49

Bailey (2006: 284–285) describes a study that investigated teachers' views of what constitutes a productive relationship between teachers and supervisors, the results of which are summarized by Bailey in terms of three macro categories and ten subthemes as follows:

    i. *The supervisor's task-oriented approach toward the teacher*

        a) The supervisors gave immediate, nonpunitive feedback about the teaching.

        b) The supervisors took a collaborative approach to problem solving.

        c) The supervisors made the teachers feel they were experts on teaching.

        d) The supervisors were genuine in their relationship with teachers.

        e) The supervisors made the teachers feel they were intelligent.

    ii. *The supervisor's interpersonal set toward the teacher*

        a) The supervisors made the teachers feel that they were always available to them.

        b) The supervisors made the teachers feel they were being listened to.

        c) The supervisors were open about what they knew or didn't know.

        d) The supervisors made them feel they were interested in them as people.

        e) The supervisors made the teachers' interests their interests.

    iii. *The supervisor's own competence as an educator*

        (Bailey 2006: 284–285)

You may have discussed your cooperating teacher's approach to supervision in your first meeting with him or her. If not, before you start your practice teaching you should establish a clear understanding of how the cooperating teacher understands his or her role and the kind of interaction and feedback you can expect during your practice teaching. Cooperating teachers work in different ways based on their own experience and beliefs about their role, as these comments from a teaching-practice supervisor illustrate:

Personally and professionally, I view student teaching supervision to be a highly prioritized work in our field. It is high priority work due to the fact that the nature of what we do in our field IS ABOUT teaching and doing teacher supervision / education work. Unfortunately, many believe, mostly the traditionalists in our field, that teaching English language can be compartmentalized into a "one size fits all" approach. Because of this false belief, many teacher education programs often perceive the transition from taking courses to doing student teaching can be transitioned smoothly. On the contrary, teaching English is highly politicized due to the ways in which the English language is situated in these worldwide contexts.

    With an increase in the number of culturally and linguistically diverse (CLD) learners (students as well as student teachers) in both K-12 and teacher education programs, it is important to (re)structure teacher supervision components of TESOL programs as to include the critical voices in our field. These critical voices can deepen our exploration and our teacher supervision work within and beyond the teacher education programs to include the wide array of knowledge domains in teacher education: knowledge of learners, knowledge of social, political and cultural contexts, knowledge of pedagogies, knowledge of subject matter, knowledge of assessment, and educational goals. To this end, my feedback to student teachers would be examining how they tailor their teaching materials and practice within the aforementioned domains.

Gloria, United States

YOUR OBLIGATIONS AS A STUDENT TEACHER

As a student teacher you now have a different role and responsibilities from those you have as a student on campus. These include:

PRESENTING A PROFESSIONAL IMAGE AND CONDUCT

You may find that codes of dress and behavior that are considered appropriate on the college campus are not necessarily acceptable in your host institution. You will need to find out what your host school considers appropriate norms for dress and conduct. For example, in your college classroom your instructor may occasionally sit on the edge of the classroom desk as he or she teaches. This may not be considered a suitable way to conduct your teaching in your host institution. While you were a student, individuality of behavior and expression was often valued. But as a student teacher in a school you will be expected to follow standards of behavior and expression that schools expect, including such details as punctuality, care and attention to the preparation and use of teaching materials and resources, relations and contacts with the students you teach, as well as other aspects of behavior that reflect the professional image of a language teacher. Here, a student teacher comments on building rapport with her students:

During the first few lessons I discovered that most of the students were the same age as me, or even older. As a result, I tried very hard to build a rapport with them as equals and use similar interest as the basis for my teaching.

Bryony, Indonesia

BEING A GOOD LISTENER

You may feel that in your university program or training course you have worked with famous professors and learned all the latest ideas and theories about language teaching. You may feel you want to try out everything you have learned as quickly as possible, without considering the body of knowledge and experience possessed by your cooperating teacher and others in the school. They have worked with many similar student teachers to you and may be a little skeptical of your enthusiasm and confidence. Likewise they know that your attachment will be temporary so they may not want to depart significantly from their established procedures. So in order to develop a good working relationship with your cooperating teacher you need to be a good listener and to carefully consider the advice your cooperating teacher gives you before offering your own opinions, as this student teacher observes:

The detailed feedback I have received has sometimes matched my own evaluation of my teaching, but in other cases I have been alerted to shortcomings I was not aware of and possibly would never have become aware of if it had not been for the teaching practice component. I now feel more confident that I can translate theory into practice more effectively so that each hour my students spend in class will be productive.

Cheryl, Indonesia

BEING A LEARNER OF TEACHING

You need to remember that you are still a student and that teaching practice is a chance to deepen your learning and not an occasion to constantly try to demonstrate your expertise. This means that you should always be willing to ask questions of your cooperating teacher or other teachers in the school. That is what they are there for and they will not judge you to be foolish because you let it be known that there are many things that you want to learn. These may sometimes be things that seem relatively trivial (e.g., whether students should call you by your first name), or at other times things that are more complex (e.g., how best to deal with reluctant learners). Being an inexperienced teacher also offers you certain advantages because it gives you a chance to try out things you have never done before and to learn from your successes or failures. Remember that in order to develop your teaching skills you need to be extending the boundaries of what you know and feel comfortable with, rather than simply becoming more relaxed and fluent in doing the things you are already familiar with. Table 4.1 summarizes the functions of your cooperating teacher and your obligations as a student teacher.

• The functions of the cooperating teacher	• Helping you prepare for teaching • Sharing instructional strategies • Developing your awareness of your teaching • Helping you resolve problems • Encouraging and motivating you
• Your obligations as a student teacher	• Presenting a professional image and conduct • Being a good listener • Being a learner of teaching

Table 4.1   Working with cooperating teachers

THE NATURE OF YOUR TEACHING PRACTICE EXPERIENCES

Your teaching practice will normally consist of observations of your cooperating teacher's class, observations by the cooperating teacher of your own classes, preparation of teaching materials, and a series of practice-teaching experiences that may range from teaching part of a lesson to taking full responsibility for lessons. You will also normally take part in conversations or meetings with the cooperating teacher prior to and after teaching a lesson.

The cooperating teacher's expectations of you

Cooperating teachers vary in how much dependence or autonomy they expect of student teachers. Some want to be closely involved with many aspects of your teaching. Others may leave you to largely work things out for yourself. It is good to have a clear understanding of what each other's expectations are. It is also important to remember that in order for you to complete your teaching practice, the cooperating teacher has probably given up one of his or her classes temporarily, freeing the teacher to perform mentoring responsibilities to one or more student teachers. The cooperating teacher will naturally be concerned about what happens to the class when it is being taught by a student teacher.

Your goals for teaching practice and those of your cooperating teacher

You need to determine exactly what you hope to gain from your teaching practice experience and compare your goals with those of your cooperating teacher. Your cooperating teacher may consider you as little more than a teaching assistant and not want to become too closely involved in helping you develop your teaching skills. On the other hand you may have little teaching experience and feel that much more guidance would be beneficial. You might want to focus on general skills, such as classroom management skills, lesson planning skills, awareness of teaching styles, and ability to interact with students. However, your cooperating teacher might be more concerned that you give adequate coverage of material from the class textbook and give students sufficient preparation for the end-of-term assessment.

The nature of the course you will be teaching and its goals

During your practice teaching you will be teaching on a course that has been planned by your cooperating teacher. The teacher may have very specific goals for the course and for its learning outcomes. You will need to understand what these are and share your own goals with the teacher so that you do not lead the students in a different direction when you teach the course.

The kind of observations you will be involved with

It will be useful to agree on a schedule of observations, both those involving your cooperating teacher's class, and those when you are being observed. The goals of these observations should also be clarified (see Chapter 7).

The nature of conferences with the cooperating teacher

Before you teach a lesson you will normally have an opportunity to discuss your lesson with your cooperating teacher, and to review it after the lesson. These sessions are referred to as pre- and postlesson conferences.

The prelesson conference may serve to:

- Review your lesson plan
- Discuss anticipated difficulties
- Decide on a focus for the teacher's observation, if he or she will observe the lesson
- Decide on criteria to use in evaluating the lesson
- Decide on how feedback will be delivered after the lesson – immediate or delayed

The postlesson conference may serve to:

- Review how well the lesson went
- Provide encouragement and support for the student teacher
- Discuss difficulties and problems
- Decide on areas for improvement
- Decide on the next steps for teaching

However, the nature of the postlesson conference will depend on the cooperating teacher's approach to supervision. Practice teaching may also be viewed as a type of coaching. When this happens, the student teacher and the cooperating teacher agree on a teaching strategy that the student teacher wants to practice. The "coach" suggests how best to carry this out and the lesson is a chance to practice it. During the postlesson conference the student teacher and the coach assess how well the strategy was implemented.

The process-writing approach is a requirement of the school's scheme of work where I was placed for my teaching practice. My cooperating teacher wanted me to try one approach that she found successful over the years and that was using the mnemonic POWERS (prepare, organize, write, edit, rewrite, and share) to represent the process-writing approach. So with the cooperating teacher acting as "coach" as she gave me the basis in this method before I entered the class, I prepared to teach this two-period class. To make POWERS come alive, I decided to use an analogy from the cartoon "Captain Planet" where, when all the powers combine, Captain Planet will appear to save the earth with the idea that when students use the POWERS writing process, they will be able to produce a good story.

I selected some students who have watched the cartoon to role-play the part where all the powers combine to make Captain Planet appear. I used POWERS as I thought that the students would find it easier to remember as compared to prewriting, editing, and revising. It was also to make the lesson more interesting. I had the students mindmap the POWERS approach after explaining it. I then introduced the students to their "P – Prepare" task where they had to brainstorm ideas on a narrative related to the story of King Arthur. The students were to share their stories about King Arthur (which my cooperating teacher had asked them to research beforehand), then brainstorm and share their ideas.

Thereafter, they had to "O – Organize" their ideas with the story web provided and so on until I reached the end of "R – Rewrite" when I ran out of time. So, I could not finish the lesson because I had prepared too much for one lesson but I got valuable feedback from my cooperating teacher on how I carried out the lesson and, as she said, even though I could not finish it, I mastered the main aspects of using this mnemonic.

Monica, Portugal

SUMMARY AND CONCLUSIONS

Your cooperating teacher will play a crucial role in your practice-teaching experience. The cooperating teacher will help you prepare for your teaching, share teaching suggestions and strategies with you, provide feedback on your teaching, help you deal with problems that may occur during your teaching, and encourage and motivate you during your teacher learning. Cooperating teachers and supervisors may adopt different approaches to the supervision process. Some may try to orient you toward a particular way of teaching, one that does not necessarily reflect your own understanding of teaching. Others may work in a more collaborative relationship with you, working with you to explore your strengths and limitations as a teacher and suggesting ways to improve your teaching. It is important to establish good channels of communication with your cooperating teacher to ensure that the relationship is positive and constructive. Pre- and postlesson conferences, even very brief ones, are a good opportunity to clarify your intentions in a lesson and to reflect on how well the lesson went.

Cooperating teachers interpret their responsibilities in different ways, and the nature of their interactions with you will vary according to how they see your role as student teacher and how they view their own role as your mentor and supervisor. Establishing a clear understanding of how your practice teaching will be conducted, what your responsibilities will be, what procedures will be followed, and how your teaching will be supported and reviewed is essential for a satisfactory working relationship between you and your cooperating teacher. Reaching an awareness of each other's expectations at the beginning of your practicum will help you avoid any misunderstandings throughout your teaching practice.

Further reading

Bailey, K. M. (2006). *Language teacher supervision: A case-based approach.* New York: Cambridge University Press.

Johnson, K. E. (1996). The vision versus the reality: The tensions of the TESOL practicum. In D. Freeman and J. C. Richards (Eds.), *Teacher learning in language teaching* (pp. 30–49). New York: Cambridge University Press.

Nunan, D. (1999). *Second language teaching and learning.* Boston, MA: Heinle and Heinle Publishers.

Discussion questions

1. One cooperating teacher had the following expectations for student teachers on teaching practice. Compare these with your own expectations for teaching practice:

   a) some proficiency in the language and the skills to access the information as needed
   b) an awareness of a variety of teaching and learning approaches, methods, and techniques, and the flexibility to employ them according to the context they are working with
   c) organizational and functional skills required for the daily routines of teaching
   d) a rapport with their students which may be uniquely their own, but generally positive
   e) an open mind to explore their teaching with me as a supervisor in order to improve
   f) a sense of their own professionalism as teachers and all that comes with that as they join an educational institution and the profession

2. What aspects of your teaching do you feel your cooperating teacher can most usefully help you develop or improve?

3. How would you prefer your cooperating teacher to give you feedback on your teaching? Check your preferences below:

   ○ To give me written comments on my lessons
   ○ To discuss each lesson I teach
   ○ To let me observe his / her class only
   ○ To let me teach his / her class with him / her always present
   ○ To make only occasional visits to my class
   ○ To review my lesson plans before I teach them
   ○ To let me take full responsibility for all aspects of the classes I teach including lesson planning, teaching, and evaluating

4. What do you think you can learn from observing your cooperating teacher's lessons?

5. How do you think you should respond when you disagree with the feedback your cooperating teacher gives you?

6. Do you think it is sometimes appropriate for the cooperating teacher to adopt a prescriptive approach to supervision?

Follow-up activities

1. Read the vignette in the Appendix and consider George's discussion of class discipline. In groups discuss what you consider to be the principles of maintaining class discipline, then compare with others.

2. George (see Appendix) writes about the tension that sometimes occurs when a student teacher wants to try out creative and novel teaching strategies but is constrained by the fact that the class does not belong to him or her. Discuss how you would deal with a situation in which you felt you had a much better teaching strategy for dealing with a particular teaching problem than the one suggested by the cooperating teacher.

Appendix: A student teacher's account of working with his cooperating teacher

I did my teaching practice in an elementary school where many of the students were second language speakers of English and so I teamed up with a teacher of ESL in that school. One of the first major issues I had to get used to was to plan for the week, or even two weeks in advance, instead of simply planning for the next lesson as happened in my microteaching classes. Initially I found this quite difficult to do but gradually got used to it. Another issue that needed to be tackled was that of class discipline. I felt that it was quite an important aspect of teaching that I had to get a hold of.

Teaching practice brought me face to face with 40 young energetic students, all eager to impress either their friends or the teacher. I had to admit that the issue of class discipline was on my mind very much during the duration of my teaching practice. This was because I felt that class discipline was very important to the class actually learning. If the class did not have good discipline, students would not learn. In this area, I felt that although the cooperating teacher provided me with great assistance throughout the practicum, with this issue she would simply tell me to "be more firm with the class," but did not give me any other form of help or advice regarding class management. Perhaps she felt that I needed to learn classroom management myself, or find my own individual style, which I did.

So, teaching practice really brought me into the real world of teaching and quickly. Indeed, there were times where lessons had to be changed at the last minute, there were also times where lessons had to be changed because of the lack of time. There was a time where I had to change my lesson at the last minute because my cooperating teacher insisted that a reading comprehension exercise had to be covered. This incident made me realize that during teaching practice, the class we were teaching ultimately does not belong to me. So at times I felt that I did not have the freedom of trying out different ideas even if I wanted to because of the different policies of the school, the department, and finally the cooperating teacher that was guiding me. That said, the cooperating teacher always encouraged me where she could and she seemed concerned that I would get good practical experience to become a well-qualified teacher.

George, Singapore

CHAPTER 5

Planning Your Teaching

INTRODUCTION

Planning a lesson before teaching is generally considered essential in order to teach an effective lesson and often receives considerable emphasis in teacher-training programs, although teachers vary in the nature of the planning they do and the kinds of information they include in lesson plans. Experienced teachers generally make use of less detailed lesson plans than novice teachers and often teach from a mental plan rather than a detailed written lesson plan (Richards 1998). And lesson plans often differ from the lessons teachers using them actually teach, since there are sometimes good reasons for departing from a lesson plan, depending on the way a lesson proceeds and develops (see Chapter 6). However, lesson planning is an administrative requirement of many schools, and teachers are often required to prepare yearly, term, unit, weekly, and daily lesson plans. As a student teacher you may find that the general framework and content of the course you are teaching has already been planned in some detail by the cooperating teacher. Nevertheless you will generally be required to plan for the lessons that you are going to teach or coteach so it is important to become familiar with the procedures used in lesson planning. The following comments describe student teachers' views on lesson planning:

As a student teacher, I find a detailed lesson plan to be very helpful. My cooperating teacher e-mails me a broad lesson plan every week. But it is up to me to work on the details. I remember when I first started teaching practice, I was more focused on "what" to teach than "how" to teach. This was probably due to my past experience of teaching in a grammar-translation method to huge classes. The expectations from a teacher in my old setting were radically different from how it is here in Canada. There a teacher was expected to know everything and she was expected to teach every bit of the textbook. The role of a student was a passive one. Moreover, huge classes did not permit any pair or group activities. Under such a circumstance, lesson planning did not play a very important role. However, after starting to practice-teach here in Canada, I have realized the importance of a well-structured lesson plan. I find that a lesson plan helps me in many ways. First, it helps me remain focused to the overall curriculum objective. Second, I feel more confident when I go to a class with a lesson plan. Third, I have noticed in the past that I find it difficult to move on from one activity to another – so now I pay a greater attention to transitions while planning my lessons. This has helped me manage my time much better than before. The only disadvantage of a detailed lesson plan is that it creates an amount of stress in me when things don't go as planned. Sometimes, I find it very difficult to anticipate the students' reaction in a class. Recently, I found that I took about 20 minutes to complete an activity I had anticipated to take just about 5. I discovered that the students did not know some of the vocabulary that I had believed to be very simple. My lesson plan was not very helpful that day! Minor problems apart, I feel the benefits of a lesson plan to be a lot more than the disadvantages. Maybe as I gain more experience, I would need a less detailed lesson plan. However, till then, I guess I will stick to a very detailed and elaborate lesson plan.

Vidya, Canada

The teaching practice has made me realize how careful and thorough a lesson plan must be to reach my aims. There are so many things to consider: the class profile; variety of topics; materials; interaction patterns; language awareness – to name but a few.

Joyce, Indonesia

PLANNING IN TEACHING PRACTICE

As a student teacher working in the classroom of a cooperating teacher you may have a limited say over what you will teach, since the English program in the school or institution and the choice of teaching materials, resources, and textbooks will typically have been planned by the senior teachers and other teachers based on such factors as the kind of program it is (e.g., a general English program, a vocationally oriented program, a program designed to mainstream students, or a program to prepare students for college or university studies), the students' proficiency level, or the intensity of the program. So, although long-term planning will not necessarily be part of your responsibility, if you are attached to a school for an extended teaching block (say, a full term of ten weeks), involvement in term planning may be required. However it is still important for you to become familiar with the long-term curriculum plans and the range of English courses offered in the school, which can be a focus of a preliminary visit to the school (see Chapter 3). More typically, as a student teacher you will be involved in short-term, week-by-week, day-by-day planning, and it may be difficult to prepare for this before arriving on site to teach and being given specific teaching assignments.

My cooperating teacher liked me to give her plans for my week's lesson, however she didn't want a detailed plan, mainly what I was planning to cover and the main things the students would be working on. She needed this for record keeping. However for my own purposes I felt I needed a much more detailed lesson plan for every lesson since I wasn't confident I could teach a good lesson without a well-developed plan.

Rosi, Colombia

I was teaching from a commercial ESL series and the teacher's manual provided fairly detailed lesson plans for every unit. However, after a while I found that they didn't always work for me so I modified them and eventually found I was using my own very different plans for the units.

David, Korea

Senior comments on the fact that although teacher preparation courses usually emphasize the importance of preparing detailed lesson plans, student teachers find that experienced teachers often make different use of planning in their teaching:

> They notice that few teachers around them spend time writing detailed lesson plans – and certainly not ones containing formal aims and objectives. They notice that it is far more common for teachers to be making lists of items in the order to teach them, or jotting down rough notes or reminders to themselves about what they intend to cover. (Senior 2006: 142)

Senior (2006) suggests that the reason for this is because experienced teachers have a substantial knowledge and experiential base to draw upon in their teaching and are generally familiar with the specific needs and interests of the students in their class. Conversely, novice teachers without such an experiential base will make greater use of lesson plans and use more detailed lesson plans during their initial teaching experiences (Richards 1998).

TEXTBOOKS AS LESSON PLANS

Schools make different uses of commercial textbooks in language teaching. In some contexts the textbooks *are* the curriculum and the lessons teachers teach closely follow the content of the textbook. Particularly in situations where the English teachers are not native speakers of English and may not have an advanced level of proficiency in English (perhaps the majority of the world's English teachers in EFL contexts), textbooks often provide the major source of input to language lessons. Teachers may have had limited opportunities for teacher training and the textbook and the teacher's manual are their primary teaching resources. For both teachers and learners, the textbook provides a map that lays out the general content of lessons and a sense of structure that gives coherence to individual lessons as well as to an entire course. This can give learners a sense of autonomy, which dependence on daily or weekly teacher-prepared lesson handouts does not provide. Crawford notes:

> It may well be this sense of control which explains the popularity of textbooks with students. Consequently a teacher's decision not to use a textbook may actually be 'a touch of imperialism' . . . because it retains control in the hands of the teacher rather than the learner. (Crawford 1995: 28)

However, experienced teachers make much less use of textbooks, particularly if they are trained teachers and fluent users of English, instead making greater use of teacher-made or authentic materials (Senior 2006). These have the advantage of more closely addressing students' needs and interests and allowing the teacher to teach in a more creative and flexible manner rather than following the sequence of exercises found in a textbook. If they do use a textbook, they tend to use it selectively, adapting it to meet their needs. These adaptations may involve:

- *Modifying content:* Content may need to be changed because it does not suit the target learners, perhaps because of factors related to the learners' age, gender, occupation, religion, or cultural background.

(ctd.)

(ctd.)

- *Adding or deleting content:* The book may contain too much or too little for the program. Whole units may have to be dropped, or perhaps sections of the book omitted. For example, the English course may focus primarily on listening and speaking skills and hence writing activities in the book will be omitted.
- *Reorganizing content:* The teacher may decide to reorganize the syllabus of the book, and arrange the units in what he or she considers a more suitable order. Or within a unit the teacher may decide not to follow the sequence of activities in the unit but to reorder them for a particular reason.
- *Addressing omissions:* The coursebook may omit items that the teacher feels are important. For example, the teacher may add vocabulary activities or grammar activities to a unit.
- *Modifying tasks:* Exercises and activities may need to be changed to give them an additional focus. For example, a listening activity may focus only on listening for information. It is adapted so that students listen a second time for a different purpose. Or an activity may be extended to provide opportunities for more personalized practice.
- *Extending tasks:* Exercises may contain insufficient practice and additional practice tasks may be needed.

(Richards 2001: 260)

In preparing for your practice teaching it will be important to clarify the role of textbooks in the course you are teaching by discussing questions such as the following:

1. To what extent does the course make use of (a) a commercial textbook; (b) teacher-prepared materials; (c) authentic materials?
2. Will I be expected to prepare my own materials for my lessons or will I mainly use materials that have been prepared by the cooperating teacher?
3. Should I show any materials I prepare to my cooperating teacher before I use them?
4. If a textbook is used, is it used (a) regularly as the main teaching text or (b) as one source among other materials for the course?
5. If a textbook is used, what does the cooperating teacher feel are the strengths or limitations of the book?
6. How does the cooperating teacher feel the textbook should be used?
7. If supplementary materials are used, what are some good sources for these?
8. If I am teaching from a textbook, how far can my lesson plans deviate from the contents of the book?
9. Will the students be tested on the contents of the textbook?
10. Will I be expected to write a test on the supplementary materials I use in class?

Although we point out the advantages of using a textbook during your teaching practice, some novice teachers feel constrained if they are having to follow a textbook on teaching practice and become frustrated when told they are deviating too much from the text. Senior gives one such example of a trainee teacher on a CELTA course who was told that she suffered from "text avoidance syndrome," as the trainee teacher explained:

Their argument was, "The people who wrote the textbook are the experts. Why are you recreating the wheel? They've done the hard work for you, they're the brilliant ones who have been in the industry forever. Just use their knowledge." Which is true – I mean, I'm a new teacher, so what do I know about it.

Trainee teacher cited by Senior 2006: 49

UNIT PLANNING

As we saw above, planning can involve both long-term and shorter-term planning, although you will generally be involved with the latter. This may not be limited to planning and teaching individual lessons. Sometimes teaching may be grouped into a series of lessons, which are known as *units*. A unit is a group of lessons planned around a particular theme or instructional focus and linked to a defined learning outcome. For example, *teenage smoking, persuasive writing*, and *a sales presentation*, could all be the focus of a unit. A unit is hence a series of integrated lessons that takes place over a period of time (e.g., two weeks) and which leads toward a culminating task or activity. MacDonald (1991: 76) outlines some useful steps for planning units:

i. *Identify the main purposes of the unit.* This involves determining the overall focus and goals for the unit. For example, a unit could be a plan for a sequence of lessons linking listening, speaking, writing, and reading, and focusing on a specific theme, such as *adventure sports.*

ii. *Prepare a content outline for the unit.* This involves selecting the topics, skills, genres, language focus, etc., of the unit.

iii. *Determine the types of learning outcomes to be addressed.* Specific learner outcomes are now determined for the different components of the unit (e.g., for the listening, speaking, reading, writing, and other strands).

iv. *Select teaching strategies and activities.* The unit is now organized in terms of lessons and teaching techniques and strategies are chosen.

(MacDonald 1991: 76)

See Appendix D for an example of a unit plan.

INDIVIDUAL LESSON PLANS

Lesson planning serves a variety of purposes in teaching practice. One important purpose is to help you develop your pedagogic reasoning skills – those specialized skills that enable teachers to transform potential lesson content into effective means of learning (see Chapter 2). But in addition to the conceptual and cognitive processes activated through lesson planning, it also serves a number of other functions. These include:

- to provide a framework or a "road map" for the lesson you will teach
- to help think through and rehearse the teaching process
- to provide security
- to determine the sequence and timing of activities
- to help realize your principles and beliefs
- to provide a record of what has been taught

Here are some comments by teachers on why they make use of lesson plans:

The lesson plan is essential for me in creating a cohesive lesson. It reminds me of the different elements I need to pay attention to in bringing the whole lesson together.

I find unless I have a lesson plan I tend to forget things, and never get half the things done I planned to do.

It helps me clearly organize how I'm going to present the language to the students.

It provides a framework for me to follow during the lesson.

It helps me clarify my aims and gives the lesson structure.

Teachers cited in Richards: 1998

Even if you are teaching from a textbook (which contains lessons that have already been planned), further planning is usually necessary to adapt the textbook to the teaching context and to supplement it based on the learners' backgrounds, interests, learning styles, and abilities. For example, you will want to consider the specific instructional objectives for the lesson and choose tasks and activities that address the language skills the lesson addresses. You will need to think about the resources you will use in the lesson as well as how much time you will spend on different activities. Your plan may also include thoughts on how you will monitor your students' understanding and learning.

The lesson planning, in the beginning, seemed like the biggest mountain a person could climb and I really struggled trying to develop the "perfect" lesson plan. I knew I would be able to write a plan that fulfilled the tutor's expectations, but it wasn't happening fast enough for me. I felt even more determined to deliver because I wanted to show the course tutors that I actually care about it and I care about doing it in the best way possible.

Lyndsay, Indonesia

From the start I loved the idea of a lesson plan. I don't think that this was necessarily a universal experience but I loved having the structure and from my first lesson I saw the benefits in being as thorough as possible. When I completed the form in the recommended order, the lesson itself flowed more smoothly. Yes, it takes a lot of time but building the stage detail after I have identified my aims is much easier.

Elizabeth, Indonesia

DEVELOPING THE PLAN

There are no simple formulae for lesson plans, because what constitutes an effective lesson will depend on many factors, including the content of the lesson, the teacher's teaching style, the students' learning preferences, the class size, and the learners' proficiency level. Fujiwara describes the process an experienced teacher uses in lesson planning:

> Though now I do try to articulate objectives, my method of planning still begins with activities and visions of the class. It's only when I look at the visions that I can begin to analyze why I'm doing what I'm doing. I also need to be in dialogue with my students, so it's hard for me to design a year's course in the abstract. Just as my language learning process is no longer in awareness, so my planning process is based on layers and layers of assumptions, experiences, and knowledge. I have to dig down deep to find out why I make the decisions I do. (Fujiwara 1996: 151)

A lesson plan will reflect your assumptions about the nature of teaching and learning, your understanding of the content of the lesson (e.g., what you have learned from your coursework about paragraph organization, the present perfect tense, reading for main ideas, or whatever the focus is for the lesson), your role in the lesson and that of your learners, and the methodology you plan to implement (e.g., cooperative learning, process writing, communicative approach).

I feel that I create a relaxed classroom environment in which the students will participate and learn. I feel that if a teacher has a positive and enthusiastic attitude toward the class, the students will feel the same. I try to prepare lessons that take their previous knowledge and expand on it. In their regular classroom, they have had exposure, but have had little or no actual speaking practice. By using simple instructions, encouraging group participation and spontaneity is difficult to achieve because of "losing face," therefore praise is essential to encourage the student to try. At the same time, the teacher must tactfully correct, and also have students correct each other in group activities.

Anna, United States

I see my role in the classroom as an instructor or a resource person. I'm able to present a language point and, being culturally sensitive, show how they can use it effectively when necessary. I would and do encourage them to ask questions to better understand. In each class, I strive to help the students to use what they know and expand that knowledge, overcoming the obstacle of "peer pressure" or acceptance – losing face among their classmates. By encouragement and praise, I help them to verbalize what they already know or are learning.

José, Puerto Rico

Generally however, a lesson plan will reflect decisions that you have made about the following aspects of a lesson:

- *Goals*: What the general goals of the lesson are
- *Activities*: What kinds of things students will do during the lesson, such as dialogue work, free writing, and brainstorming
- *Sequencing*: The order in which activities will be used, including opening and closing activities
- *Timing*: How much time will be spent on different activities
- *Grouping*: When the class will be taught as a whole and when they will work in pairs or groups (see Chapter 8)
- *Resources*: What materials will be used, such as the textbook, worksheets, and DVDs

Richard-Amato (2009) suggests that language lessons can be generally divided into five different phases:

Opening: Links are made to previous learning or the lesson is previewed.

Simulation: A lead into the main activity is provided to create interest in the lesson.

Instruction: The main activity of the lesson is taught.

Closure: The lesson may be reviewed and future learning previewed.

Follow-up: Independent work or homework is assigned.

See Appendix C for examples of lesson plans.

THE ROLE OF THE LESSON PLAN IN TEACHING

Teaching is much more than enacting a lesson plan, however, since during the process of teaching many individual decisions have to be made that shape the nature and progress of the lesson and not all of these decisions can be planned for in advance. These unplanned decisions are known as "interactive decisions." They include decisions relating to the following issues:

- *Task effectiveness*: Are tasks and activities working effectively?
- *Language focus*: Is there a sufficient language focus to an activity?
- *Language support*: Do students need more language support for an activity (e.g., additional vocabulary, grammar)?
- *Grouping*: Should the grouping arrangement be changed?
- *Interest*: Are the students interested or should something be done to maintain motivation?
- *Sequencing*: Should the planned sequence be changed in any way?
- *Transitions*: Is a better transition needed between activities?
- *Pacing*: Should the planned timing be modified?
- *Difficulty*: Is the lesson proving to be at the right difficulty level?
- *Student understanding*: Is clarification needed?
- *Student behavior*: Is intervention needed to control noise levels or disruptive behavior?

A lesson plan can therefore be regarded as a blueprint for action. In teaching your lessons you will still have to "play by ear" and teach according to the changing circumstances of the actual teaching situation. So your lesson plan will sometimes have to be renegotiated according to the things that occur during the lesson itself. Nunan describes the lesson planning processes employed by teachers with different levels of experience, and observes that the teachers' plans had a significant impact on their lessons, although their lessons were substantially modified during the process of teaching:

> While it is naïve to assume that what gets planned will equate with what gets taught, and that what gets taught will equate with what gets learned, this does not mean that planning, including the formulating of objectives, should be removed from the equation. While the plans that teachers lay will be transformed, if not metamorphosed, in the act of teaching, such plans provide a framework and structure for those interactive decisions which the teacher must make. They also provide a set of criteria against which such interactive decisions must be evaluated. (Nunan 1992: 161)

The following examples show some of the decisions student teachers had to make during a lesson:

The students finished quicker than I thought they would, so I kind of filled in a little at the end. That's why I went back and had them do some sentences at the end. Because I originally planned that they had done the game on the board and then copied it on paper and that would be the end of it. So it all went in sequence and I just had to add some extra at the end. I think sometimes you can prepare a lesson plan but you don't know often how fast or slow it will go in the classroom.

Karen, United Kingdom

I had planned for most of the lesson with my low-level learners to be spent on a writing activity. I started with some free writing to get their ideas for the topic (a report of a school trip) and did an activity on paragraph organization based on sequence makers. However, when it came to the writing part I noticed that their sentence grammar was really poor so I abandoned my plan for the last part of the lesson and did some grammar work. I will pick up the report writing later in the course.

Marcia, Colombia

Bailey (1966) studied the departures six experienced ESL teachers made from their lessons during teaching. She describes the reasons for these departures in terms of the principles they hold about good teaching (see Chapter 5). The teachers gave the following justifications for departing from their lesson plans:

1. *Serve the common good* (e.g., an issue raised by an individual student was thought to be worth pursuing because it would benefit the whole class).

2. *Teach to the moment* (e.g., the teacher drops the lesson plan and pursues an issue likely to be of particular interest to students at that moment).

3. *Accommodate students' learning styles* (e.g., the teacher decides to incorporate some explicit grammar instruction since the learners have a preference for this mode of grammar learning).

4. *Promote students' involvement (*e.g., the teacher drops a planned activity to give students more time to work on an activity that they have shown a high degree of interest in).

5. *Distribute the wealth (*e.g., the teacher keeps one student from dominating the class time to enable the whole class to benefit from a learning opportunity).

(Bailey 1996: 24–35)

EVALUATING THE LESSON PLAN

After teaching a lesson it is important to take time to review how well the lesson went. This involves asking questions such as the following:

1. Did my students enjoy the lesson?

2. Were there sufficient activities to engage the students throughout the lesson?

3. Which aspects of the lesson were the most successful?

4. Which were the least successful?

5. Did I manage to achieve what I set out to teach? What evidence do I have for this?

6. What difficulties did the lesson pose?

7. Will I teach it in the same way next time?

Since every lesson you teach has a life of its own, you will often find that even if a lesson worked perfectly on one occasion, teaching it in the same way the next time may not have the same results. Teaching always involves adjusting your lesson plans according to the way the lesson evolves. In other words, it requires you to build a lesson around your plan based on the students' reactions to the lesson, rather than enacting your lesson plan based on your prior intentions for the lesson. Table 5.1 summarizes how you can plan your teaching.

1. Check with cooperating teacher.	• Teacher checks how much planning he / she is allowed do.
2. Check role of textbook.	• Teacher checks if textbook (and teacher's manual) is primary or secondary teaching resource; also if teacher can modify, add / delete, or reorganize content; address omissions; modify or extend tasks.
3. Prepare unit plan.	• Teacher identifies main purposes of unit; prepares content outline for unit; determines types of learning outcomes to be addressed; selects teaching strategies and activities.
4. Prepare lesson plan.	• Teacher prepares plan depending on content of lesson, teacher's teaching style, students' learning preferences, class size, and learners' proficiency level.
5. Evaluate lesson plan.	• Teacher reviews how well the lesson went.

Table 5.1   Planning your teaching

Summary and Conclusions

Lesson planning is an important component of teacher-training programs, although experienced teachers tend not to use detailed lesson plans, drawing instead on their profound knowledge of students' interests and needs. Novice teachers, however, are generally required to use lesson plans when they begin their teaching. Student teachers are mostly responsible for planning individual lessons or groups of lessons, rather than a whole course, which is the responsibility of the regular class teacher. In some situations, your practice teaching may make extensive use of a commercial textbook, in which case considering how to adapt it to your students' needs may be important. Planning a lesson not only provides support for teaching but also serves to clarify your thinking about the principles of effective teaching. However, your lesson plan should not control the lesson. You should be prepared to teach "from" the lesson plan rather than to teach "to" it, that is, to use it flexibly and creatively based on how students respond to the lesson.

Lessons are complex and dynamic events and in a successful lesson the teacher is engaged in many different kinds of monitoring, attending to learners' responses to the lesson to ensure that issues such as pacing, development, task difficulty, motivation, learner understanding, and language focus are addressed and adjustments made where necessary to ensure a successful outcome. For that reason a lesson plan is just that, and the fact that a lesson realizes its lesson plan is no guarantee that it was a good lesson. The success of a lesson is based on the extent to which it contains worthwhile and appropriate learning experiences and engages the learners in meaningful learning. This may sometimes mean departing from the lesson plan to ensure the principles of good teaching are realized.

Further reading

Bailey, K. M., & Nunan, D. (1996). *Voices from the language classroom.* New York: Cambridge University Press.

Farrell, T. S. C. (2002). Lesson planning. In J. C. Richards & W. A. Renandya (Eds.), *Methodology in language teaching: An anthology of current practice* (pp. 30–39). New York: Cambridge University Press.

Richards, J. C. (1998). *Beyond training.* New York: Cambridge University Press.

Richards, J. C., & Renandya, W. A. (2002). *Methodology in language teaching: An anthology of current practice.* New York: Cambridge University Press.

Woodward, T. (2001). *Planning lessons and courses.* Cambridge: Cambridge University Press.

Discussion questions

1. What do you think are the features of an effective lesson plan?

2. What are the advantages and disadvantages of using a detailed lesson plan?

3. Do you think a good lesson is one that follows its lesson plan? What are some of the things that might happen during a lesson that could prompt a teacher to depart from his or her lesson plan?

4. How useful do you think commercial textbooks are in teaching?

5. If you could create the ideal textbook for the class you are teaching, what would some of its main characteristics be?

6. Look at the list of questions under "Evaluating the lesson plan" on page 63. Are these questions appropriate for your teaching situation? Are there others you would use?

7. Suggest some ways in which links can be made to previous lessons as part of a lesson opening, and ways in which interest can be created in the lesson during the opening phase, as described by Richard-Amato (2009).

Follow-up activities

1. Choose a unit from a textbook and suggest how you might adapt it for a specific teaching situation.

2. Choose some authentic materials relevant to a specific teaching situation and, in groups, prepare a lesson plan showing how the materials could be used.

3. Read the comments in Appendix A from five students on their teaching practice course. What roles do lesson plans play for these teachers?

4. Read the vignette in Appendix B and describe the student teacher's lesson plan. Suggest a different lesson plan that might address the difficulties the teacher experienced.

5. Appendix C outlines two different reading lesson plans: Lesson Plan I is more detailed than Lesson Plan II. Discuss the advantages and disadvantages of each plan.

6. Appendix D outlines a five-week plan for a unit on writing skills. It is designed for three to four 45-minute periods of instruction per week. The unit combines a functional approach to language with the emphasis on content-centered instruction. How has the teacher built a focus on student involvement into her lesson plan?

Appendix A: Student teachers' comments on lesson planning in teaching practice

1. *Lesson plans at the standard expected were a totally new thing for me. At first it was very difficult for me to process all the new information that I had to put into my lesson plans. Still now I have difficulty getting as much detail in the plans as I should, but I know now that I must allow enough time to plan a lesson thoroughly as it will be beneficial to myself and to the students in the end.*

Hannah, Korea

2. *I had never thought how time consuming planning a lesson could be. Before each lesson I spent whole afternoons and evenings planning, and often becoming upset that it had to take so much time. But when I saw that my students enjoyed my lessons and when I achieved my aims because I followed the plan and procedures closely, then I felt better.*

Joyce, United States

3. *I've learned that it is really important to make detailed lesson plans, and how a seemingly easy topic can turn into a disaster if the lesson isn't well prepared.*

Sari, United Arab Emirates

4. *My biggest problem when I started the teaching practice was underestimating how long activities would take to complete. The main reason for this was that I wasn't allowing time in my lesson plan for correction and incidental issues which invariably arise. Now I am more conscious of allowing time in the planning phase for error correction stages in my lessons.*

Mark, Singapore

5. *I often had difficulties achieving my lesson aims as I would tend to plan quite broadly with little consideration to the stages of the lesson. This would often lead to divergence and the lesson would lose its shape. The pace would then become erratic as I tried either to frantically catch up or slow down to fill the time when I hadn't planned enough activities. The aspect of lesson planning involving the articulation of stage aims with respect to their support of the main lesson aims is the area I have made the most progress in.*

Deborah, Canada

Appendix B: A student teacher's account of an unsuccessful lesson

I learned a lot from one of my early practice-teaching classes. I was teaching a speaking class and I was asked to teach a fluency class, using materials of my choice. I thought it would be useful to plan a role-play activity around the situation of renting a car, since I was teaching summer school students from Japan and I assumed that some of them wanted to rent cars and do some sightseeing. So I put together plans for what I thought would be a good lesson.

It started with looking at some ads for car rental companies and a discussion activity on what type of car would be good to rent. Then I had prepared a dialogue to practice the sort of interaction I wanted them to practice. I also made some role-play cards for the students to use in pairs – one student was the person who wanted to rent the car and the other was the person from the rental company. So far so good. And then came my lesson.

I introduced the topic for the lesson and the idea of the role play and asked some questions to get them talking about renting cars. Total silence. No one had a word to say. I realized that none of them had ever rented a car. So I moved on to the rest of the lesson plan. Practicing the dialogue was OK but took about two minutes and then the students looked bored. So I moved on to the actual role play. I asked a couple of students to try it out in front of the class as a model but as they fumbled their way through it, I realized that they didn't have the language resources to do so. The task was beyond them. So I had to take over the class and spent most of the lesson drilling vocabulary and doing question and answer drills to fill out the lesson. I felt really disappointed with the way the lesson went. Luckily my cooperating teacher was not there to observe it!

Ricardo, Spain

Appendix C: Lesson plans

Lesson Plan I: Main idea (from Farrell 2002)

Time: 12 P.M. to 12:35 P.M.   *Class:* English

Language Focus: Reading   *Topic*: Sport

Objectives: To teach the students to skim to find the main idea of the passage

Prior knowledge: Students know how to locate information by reading and finding the main sentence of each paragraph. This lesson is to increase reading speed by scanning and skimming for information.

Materials:

1. Reading materials – article from a book on sport
2. Overhead projector / OHT's
3. Whiteboard

Step	Time	Tasks (Teacher)	Tasks (Pupils)	Interaction	Purpose
1	5–10 mins.	Opening: Introduction to the topic sport. T activates schema for sport.	Listen	T ⟷ Ss	Arouse interest. Activate schema for sport.
		T asks students to help him / her write down as many different kinds of sport as they can think of on the whiteboard within three minutes.	Ss shout out the answer to the question as the T writes the answers on the board.		
		T asks students to rank their favorite sports in order of importance.	T writes the answers.		
2	5–7 mins.	Teacher distributes handout on sports schedule from the newspaper.	Ss read the handout and answer the questions.	T ⟷ Ss	Focus attention of Ss on the concept of skimming for general gist with authentic materials.
		T asks Ss to read it quickly and answer the true–false questions that follow it within three minutes.	Ss call out their answers to the T.		
		T goes over the answers.	Ss check their answers.		

(ctd.)

(ctd.)

Step	Time	Tasks (Teacher)	Tasks (Pupils)	Interaction	Purpose
3	15 mins.	T tells students that they just practiced skimming to get the general meaning or gist of a passage. T gives another handout on sport from the textbook (*New Clue*).	Ss read the handout and answer the questions.	Ss ⟷ T T ⟷ Ss Ss ⟷ T (S ⟷ S possible)	Getting Ss to read passage quickly to get the overall meaning.
		T asks the Ss to read and answer the true–false questions written on the paper within 5–7 mins.			
		T asks Ss for answers and writes them on the board.			
4	5 mins.	T summarizes the importance of reading a passage quickly first in order to get the gist.	Ss call out their answers to the T.	T ⟷ Ss	To remind students what they have just done and why – to develop pupil metacognitive awareness.
		T gives homework of reading the next day's newspaper front page story and writing down in four sentences the gist of the story.	Ss check their answers.	T ⟷ Ss	
		Follow-up: Next lesson: To teach the students to skim to find the main idea of the passage.			

(T = teacher; Ss = students)

Table 5.2   Lesson plan

Lesson Plan II: DRTA Lesson

Directed reading teaching activity (DRTA; Stauffer 1969) is intended to develop students' ability to read critically and reflectively. Here is a DRTA lesson outline based on the story "What Goes Around, Comes Around!" below (from Farrell 2008c):

What Goes Around, Comes Around!

John had been watching the two prison guards for two days now. He both hated and feared them. There were many reasons for both. While he was a prisoner these two guards were the most brutal when disciplining prisoners and many had died from their beatings. He had not had much to do with these two particular guards but before he escaped, he had heard enough from the other prisoners not to cross them in any way. Now both were on his trail and so he purposely led them into an area of quicksand, an area he had grown up in and thus knew all too well.

Lesson Plan

Phase I: Ask the students what they think the words in the title, "What Goes Around, Comes Around!" mean.

Phase II: Distribute a copy of "What Goes Around, Comes Around!" to each student and do prediction activation exercises with this first paragraph. Show them questions (either on the OHT or written on the board) as follows:

- Title: What Goes Around, Comes Around!
    - ○ *What do you think this story is about? Why?*

- John had been watching the two prison guards for two days now.
    - ○ *Who is John?*
    - ○ *How do you know this?*

- He both hated and feared them. There were many reasons for both.
    - ○ *Why do you think he hated them?*
    - ○ *Why do you think he feared them?*

- While he was a prisoner these two guards were the most brutal when disciplining prisoners and many had died from their beatings. He had not had much to do with these two particular guards but before he escaped, he had heard enough from the other prisoners not to cross them in any way.
    - ○ *Which country do you think John is from? Why? What clues tell you that?*
    - ○ *Why do you think John did not have experiences with these two prison guards before? How did he avoid them?*
    - ○ *So far, do you think your prediction of the title is correct?*

- Now both were on his trail and so he purposely led them into an area of quicksand, an area he had grown up in and thus knew all too well.
    - ○ *What does this tell you what may possibly happen? Why?*

Distribute each of the remaining paragraphs in sequence and do similar activities with each paragraph.

Phase III: Ask the students to either continue the story or to draw a sketch of the sequence of events in the story and to continue the sketch with what they think may happen.

Appendix D: Example of a unit plan
(reprinted with permission from Reppen 2002: 321–327)

Unit Outline

The outline that follows presents an overview of the four genres that were highlighted in the five-week unit on "Explorers" through a variety of talks, reading, and other media.

I. *Genre: Narrative (1 week)*
    A. Explorers
        1. Ponce de León
        2. Christopher Columbus
        3. Vikings
            a. Eric the Red
            b. Leif Ericson
            c. Bjarni Herjólfsson
    B. Activities
        1. Students read a one-page story about Ponce de León. After reading the text, students are asked to
            a. Underline the first time the main character appears

        b. Put a box around the location of the story
        c. Underline what the explorers were in search of
        d. Put a line in the margin by the exciting portion of the story
    2. Students discuss the location and purpose of these narrative features in story text.
    3. Students write a story and locate Features a to d, listed above in Activities No. 1, in their stories. Then students compare the location of these various features in the text they wrote with the text they read.
  C. Map work: Locating countries of explorers and exploration

II. *Genre: Descriptive (1 ½ weeks)*

  A. Explorers
    1. Vikings
    2. Hérnan Cortés
    3. Marco Polo
    4. John Wesley Powell
  B. Activities
    1. Joint text construction on the overhead projector of a description of a cactus. Teacher and students brainstorm features prior to writing the text. The need for a general topic sentence is discussed.
    2. The cactus text is compared and contrasted to the Ponce de León text. Verb types are discussed. Students become aware of the action verbs associated with the narrative in contrast to the static verbs (e.g., *be, have*) of the descriptive text. Students also become aware that both texts – narrative and descriptive – need an introduction or some type of initial framing to orient the reader.
    3. Students construct group texts at four poster centers depicting sights from four areas explored by the featured explorers. The posters show scenes from China, Mexico (Aztec), the Grand Canyon, and Greenland and Iceland. In addition to scenes from the area, each poster has a map of the world with that region highlighted. Students work in groups to construct a descriptive text at each of the four poster centers. For each poster, students also complete a sheet that identifies the country of exploration, the explorer, and the explorer's country of origin.
    4. Students then select one center that they develop into an individual's descriptive text.
  C. Map work: Locating countries of explorers and exploration

III. *Genre: Persuasive (1 ½ weeks)*

  A. Explorers
    1. Marco Polo
    2. John Wesley Powell
    3. Christopher Columbus
  B. Activities
    1. Oral discussion of persuasive strategies. Different types of reasons used in persuasion are discussed and related to the influence of the audience on the reasons selected. Students become aware of the need to see things from someone else's perspective in order to construct a strong argument.
    2. Group work: Working in pairs and taking turns, one student assumes the role of an explorer and tries to persuade their partner of their point of view (e.g., go on an expedition, found an expedition, explore an area).

3. Joint text construction: On an overhead projector, students write a persuasive text representing an explorer's attempt to persuade royalty to fund an expedition.

4. Individual text construction: Students choose either to persuade a crewmember to join them on an expedition or to persuade someone to fund their expedition.

IV. *Genre: Expository (1 week)*

  A. Explorers

    1. Vikings

    2. Ponce de León

    3. Marco Polo

    4. Hérnan Cortés

    5. Christopher Columbus

    6. John Wesley Powell

  B. Activities

    1. Various ways of organizing expository texts are discussed. Information about various explorers is brainstormed and recorded on the board according to the following types of report formats:

      a. compare and contrast

      b. problem and solution

      c. pros and cons

      d. cause and effect

    2. Joint text construction on the overhead projector provides students with an opportunity to practice cause and effect expository writing.

  C. Map work: Reviewing all countries related to explorers

CHAPTER 6

Teaching an Effective Language Lesson

INTRODUCTION

Once you begin your practice teaching, an expectation that you will share with your supervisor, your cooperating teacher, and your students is that you will teach (or soon learn to teach) an effective and successful language lesson, or to put it a different way, to master the skills of good language teaching. But what does success and effectiveness in a language lesson consist of? The notion of effective teaching is a difficult one to pin down precisely because two teachers may both teach the same lesson from a textbook or teach from an identical lesson plan and teach it very differently, yet both lessons may be regarded as very effective. And are success and effectiveness the same thing? Learners may enjoy a lesson a great deal even though it fails to achieve its goals. On the other hand, a teacher may feel that he or she covered the lesson plan very effectively, yet the students did not appear to learn very much from it. And a student teacher may feel that she did a great job in teaching a difficult lesson, although the cooperating teacher felt that the lesson was not successful. As Medgyes states, "all outstanding teachers are ideal in their own ways, and as such, are different from each other" (2001: 440). And as we saw in Chapter 3, teaching is very much shaped by the context in which the teacher is working and by his or her understanding and beliefs about teaching.

At the same time we recognize that there is always a degree of ambiguity and tension in teaching practice because it generally serves two different purposes. On the one hand, it is an opportunity to develop your teaching skills and to apply what you have learned through classroom teaching. However, it is also an examinable component of many teacher-training courses. Once you have completed your teacher-training course or program you are now expected to demonstrate your ability to put what you have learned into practice and to teach effectively. Initially your cooperating teacher will provide transitional guidance and support but once this phase has passed, he or she will expect to see you show initiative on teaching and to make less use of the cooperating teacher's support.

In this chapter we will attempt to throw some light on what we understand by effective and successful teaching, since your ability to teach well will be the principal criterion by which your practice teaching is assessed. We will examine a number of core principles that are central to the concept of good teaching.

1. THE LESSON AND YOUR CONDUCT IN IT REFLECT THE PROFESSIONAL STANDARDS EXPECTED OF ENGLISH LANGUAGE TEACHERS

Language teachers, like teachers of any subject area, belong to a profession that is defined by standards, that is, by norms of knowledge and behavior expected of teachers. For example, the ministry of education in one country has described 18 standards for English teachers, and the following examples are from the domain called *Planning and Management of Learning*:

- The English teacher uses a variety of instructional strategies and resources appropriately.
- The English teacher plans instruction according to the Ministry's educational goals, English curriculum, and assessment framework.
- The English teacher adapts instruction to take into account differences in students' learning styles, capabilities, and needs.
- The English teacher plans activities that will assist students in developing language skills and strategies.

(Katz and Snow 2009: 66)

The professional standards expected of you will be reflected in many aspects of your teaching, such as by the degree of knowledge and skill that is displayed in your teaching, by the extent to which your lessons reflect careful planning, by the extent of your emotional competence (e.g., how well you control emotions such as frustration and anger in the classroom and do not treat students arrogantly, insensitively, or patronizingly), by your behavior in and out of the classroom including your use of language, your dress code, your sensitivity to cultural diversity in the classroom, your relations with your cooperating teacher, and by the respect you show for your students – interacting with them appropriately in terms of their age, gender, culture, or religion. In your initial school visit you will have found out what the school's norms are for the way teachers dress and behave in the school and the standards the school expects for things that might strike you as trivial and unimportant – such as the way handouts are prepared and the condition that the classroom is in when you finish your lesson.

Here are some comments from a school principal and a student teacher:

As school principal I expect all student teachers on teaching practice to have a sensitive and positive attitude from the very first day in the school. You should get to know your school, your new colleagues, the students, and the administration as quickly as possible, as everyone in the school expects you to blend in as soon as possible. Get to know and respect your cooperating teacher and make sure to carefully prepare your lessons so that you consider the learning needs of your students. Learn from your cooperating teacher how to be successful with classroom management as she has reached master teacher status because of her successes as a teacher. Dress well and remember that at all times while you are on the school campus you are, in all definitions of the word, considered a teacher and therefore a professional.

Laura, United States

When I entered the class for the first time, all the students stood and said in halting English, "Good morning, teacher." At that moment I felt like I was a teacher and that I had to live up to their expectations and act like a teacher. I also realized that I had students who looked up to me as a teacher. When I was teaching I could hear teachers in other rooms talking and teaching and I felt as if I was part of a profession and so when I finished teaching that class I made sure that I had cleaned the board and moved the desks back to their original rows after my group activity. Just before the end of the lesson, one student (the class representative) reminded me that at the end of the class, they would also stand and say, "Thank you, teacher."

Paul, Japan

2. THE LESSON REFLECTS A THEORETICALLY GROUNDED AND PRINCIPLED UNDERSTANDING OF LANGUAGE TEACHING

A good language lesson is much more than a series of activities and exercises that the teacher has strung together to occupy the available amount of classroom time. Whereas this might indeed reflect the kinds of lessons that "amateur teachers" sometimes provide (for example, the untrained native speakers of English who sometimes find temporary employment in language schools around the world to finance their sightseeing and back-packing world travels), as you will have realized from your academic studies, language teaching is a career in a field of educational specialization, it requires a specialized knowledge base obtained through both academic study and practical experience, and for which membership is based on entry requirements and standards. A good language lesson therefore reflects the specialized thinking and knowledge of an educated language teaching professional, and in planning for your teaching you should think carefully about how you understand the nature of the teaching and learning you will be participating in (Nunan and Lamb 1996).

In the following extract from a student teacher's journal the writer describes a connection he is making between his teaching and his academic coursework:

Journal Entry: When I was teaching a listening lesson during my teaching practice to elementary-level adult learners it really confirmed what I had studied about the importance of communication strategies in language learning. For example, I remember learning that communication strategies, which Tarone defines as "a mutual attempt of two interlocutors to agree on a meaning in situations where requisite meaning structures do not seem to be shared," can be divided into production and reception strategies and it is the latter that are really difficult for my students. Indeed, I realized what a very demanding task listening is for all my students because it involves not only interpreting incoming speech correctly, but also and in many circumstances, responding appropriately to the speaker. Because listening is interactive especially in conversations, listeners must be able to contribute verbally to the discourse, and this often means switching roles with speakers in their effort to reach mutual understanding. In such cases, the success of communication relies heavily on the listener's use of strategies to give feedback to the speaker, to signal understanding. During my teacher education course this was really all theory for me but now it was a reality and I am still searching for ways of better teaching my students these reception strategies.

Chris, France

The nature of this specialized knowledge, however, will vary, based on the kind of academic courses that you studied in your teacher education courses. Although there is a commonality of subject matter contained in these courses (such as required courses in language theory, second language learning, curriculum issues, and methodology), the specific content you studied will depend on where you are studying. Some programs may seek to induct students into a particular method or approach (such as communicative language teaching, genre-based teaching, or task-based instruction; cf. Richards and Rodgers 2001), whereas others may operate on the basis of principled eclecticism, where student teachers are introduced to a variety of teaching approaches and encouraged to blend or adapt them based on the contexts in which they will teach. Bell (2007: 137) comments, "Most teachers think of methods in terms of techniques which realize a set of principles or goals and they are open to any method that offers practical solutions to problems in their particular teaching context."

Kumaravadivelu proposes ten general principles that he suggests can be used as guidelines, to be adapted or applied based on the needs of a specific situation. The principles are:

1. Maximize learning opportunities.
2. Facilitate negotiated interaction.
3. Minimize perceptual mismatches between teacher intention and learner interpretation.
4. Activate intuitive heuristics (for example, by providing enough textual data for learners to infer underlying grammatical rules).
5. Foster language awareness.
6. Contextualize linguistic input.
7. Integrate language skills.
8. Promote learner autonomy.
9. Raise cultural consciousness.
10. Ensure social relevance.

(Kumaravadivelu 1994: 32)

Whatever approach you are familiar with, if you are to escape the charge of drawing on an "unprincipled bag of tricks," your cooperating teacher will expect you to be familiar with instructional methods and their underlying principles as well as effective classroom techniques, materials, and assessment strategies appropriate to the kind of course and the kind of students you will be teaching. These might be young learners or adults, a reading or writing course, literate or nonliterate adults, a survival English or a vocationally oriented course, and so on.

In your initial conversations with your cooperating teacher, an important issue to discuss will be to share your understanding of the teaching approach you plan to use and to negotiate an understanding of whether the teacher finds this appropriate or in need of modification. Your cooperating teacher might have a different understanding of what will or will not work, and although you have enthusiastically adopted a methodology advocated in your academic or training program, your cooperating teacher might feel that this is not suitable for the kind of class you are teaching and might not provide an adequate preparation for the end-of-course assessment the students will be required to take. Your practice-teaching experience will therefore be an opportunity to reflect on your assumptions and principles and either confirm and deepen them, or, perhaps, revise or adapt them based on your teaching experience.

When I was in the teacher education course the instructor who led the grammar course told us that when marking English mistakes in compositions, selective marking is most desirable, especially, she said, when the piece of work contains very unique language features. For example, the use of imperatives is essential in writing a set of instructions to someone, so teachers may want to check whether students can produce imperatives in this kind of writing and hence, mark exclusively on imperatives for the language component. She added that we would practice selective marking if we foresee that there is going to be insufficient time to mark many compositions. In such situations, she suggested we should intentionally set out writing tasks that allowed us to mark only on the prominent grammatical aspects.

So when I started teaching practice and was teaching English composition and started to mark the compositions I only marked the past tense mistakes because that was what I was focusing on the week before. When I did this, however, the students all wanted me to mark for every grammatical error in every piece of essay as far as possible. I asked the cooperating teacher what she usually does and she said that she disliked selective marking because she found it difficult to restrict her marking to only one particular type of error, not to mention the students thinking that she was not doing her job, or worse, did not know how to do her job. From this experience I decided to drop the idea of selective marking of mistakes in compositions during my teaching practice.

Grace, Canada

3. THE LESSON IS EFFECTIVELY MANAGED

An important aspect of a successful lesson is the extent to which you are able to create a positive environment for learning. Classroom management refers to ways in which both the physical and the affective dimensions of the class are arranged in order to provide an environment that promotes successful teaching and learning, and good classroom management is a prerequisite to an effective lesson. Classroom discipline is an important aspect of classroom management. Classroom management is discussed more fully in Chapter 8 and so will merely be dealt with in summary form here.

When observing classes you may notice a number of differences in the atmosphere of different classes. Sometimes you may observe a class in which you sense a very supportive and positive atmosphere. As Dörnyei puts it:

> [There is a] . . . pleasant-and-supportive-classroom atmosphere . . . you can sense it after only a few minutes' stay in the particular class. There is no tension in the air; students are at ease; there are no sharp – let alone hostile – comments made to ridicule each other. There are no put-downs or sarcasm. Instead there is mutual trust and respect. No need for anyone to feel anxious or insecure. (Dörnyei 2001: 41)

These dimensions of a lesson have to do with the classroom ethos or climate of the class, and achieving such an atmosphere depends on how both the teacher and students build up a sense of mutual trust and rapport. This often proves a challenge for novice teachers, as the following comments illustrate:

Classroom management is a real issue for me. Don't get me wrong, I love all the students but I am having a hard time motivating them because they just don't seem to want to learn anything connected to English. I guess they are all sent here and so don't feel the need to listen to this foreign teacher (me!) and so they are always misbehaving during class, either talking out of turn or just not listening to me at all. At times I think I should get more support, but I am afraid to ask as it may seem a sign of weakness so I just endure it.

Michael, United Arab Emirates

Another aspect of classroom management has to do with the procedures you make use of to organize student behavior, movement, and interaction in such a way that there are minimal disruptions to the flow of the lesson. In dealing with a new class for the first time, class routines need to be quickly established by the student teacher. Experienced teachers have a repertoire of procedures at their fingertips that enable them to arrange student groups, to handle equipment and lesson procedures, and to respond to interruptions and disruptions appropriately. An important focus of your observations of your cooperating teacher will be to see how he or she handles these aspects of the lesson. These are things that cannot be learned through reading about them in your academic course but have to be learned through the experience of teaching. Teachers deal with management issues differently, depending on the kind of class they are teaching, their relationships with their students, and their own individual teaching style:

When I was observing my cooperating teacher's lessons I paid special attention to the way she not only set up groups but also broke them up and returned to whole-class teaching and how she handled the class in general because I had no first-hand experience of this. I was amazed when I observed the way she had prearranged the groups before class and when she said, "go into your groups of four," I saw all the students move quickly and quietly into their prearranged groups and I discovered that she had assigned all her students to different groups each week at the beginning of the semester and gave the lists to her students so that she would not waste any class time doing this. She also had a similar prearrangement for pair work. Then, when the group broke up after the activity, each group had a reporter ready to report to the whole class. In fact, each group role (reporter, leader, time keeper, and scribe) was also predetermined each week. This was really efficient and great management and when I took over her class for my teaching practice, I was able to follow the same system she had set up. For sure I am going to try this system when I begin teaching my own class.

Candice, United States

4. THE LESSON PROVIDES APPROPRIATELY STRUCTURED AND SEQUENCED LEARNING EXPERIENCES

A language lesson consists of a sequence of activities that lead toward your lesson goals or objectives. Here we would like to consider two aspects of a lesson sequence that support both the shape and the impact of the lesson. Wong-Fillmore characterized these dimensions of lessons in the following way:

> How classes are organized and how instructional events are structured deter-
> mine to a large extent the nature of the language that students hear and use
> in the classroom. . . . Two sets of characteristics appear to distinguish classes
> that work for language learning from those that do not. The first set relates
> to the way the classes are organized for instruction, the second to the way
> language is used in lessons. (Wong-Fillmore 1985: 23–24)

The structure of a lesson is determined by how you deal with three essential stages of a lesson: *openings*, *sequencing*, and *closings* (Richard-Amato 2009).

OPENINGS

This phase of the lesson serves primarily to focus the students' attention on the aims of the lesson, to make links to previous learning, to arouse their interest in the lesson, to activate background knowledge, or to preview language or strategies they may need to understand in order to complete activities in the lesson. You may have studied various ways in which successful openings can be achieved, for example:

- by using questions to assess background knowledge or to activate schema
- by using brainstorming and discussion activities
- by showing a DVD or video clip related to the lesson theme
- by giving a short test
- by doing or showing something unusual to arouse their interest in the lesson

The following lesson plan extract shows a student teacher's way of conducting a lesson opening:

Lesson Plan: Opening

Language Focus: Reading

Topic: Sport

Objectives: To teach the students to skim to find the main idea of the passage

Prior Knowledge: Students have learned how to locate information by reading and finding the main sentence of each paragraph. This lesson is to practice increasing their reading speed within scanning and skimming for information.

Level: Elementary

Materials: Reading materials – article from book on sport; overhead projector / OHT; whiteboard

Opening:

- *Introduction to the topic "Sport"*
- *Ask students to help me come up with a list of as many different kinds of sport as possible on the whiteboard within three minutes.*
- *Students rank their favorite sports in order of importance.*

John, Canada

The following comment shows how another teacher usually begins her class:

Before my cooperating teacher starts class she always stops for a few minutes and asks her students if there is anything on their minds because she said that she had lots of experience trying to begin her lesson with the idea of teaching a particular skill in English only to have the students thinking about something different and not really ready to begin the lesson. One time she said that her students were so worried about previous homework that she could not start the lesson proper until she reduced their anxieties about it. So now she makes a point of asking them if they have anything on their minds like homework or a bad previous class that is upsetting them. This, she says, saves time in the long run.

Margaret, Hong Kong

The two different strategies discussed in this section suggest that one teacher uses the opening phase of the lesson to prepare students for the content of the lesson, whereas the other tries to create a positive class atmosphere before she begins the lesson. Both strategies can of course be used together.

I noticed that when a student arrives late, the teacher normally does not stop to look or even glance at the student. Instead she let's the student sit and settle in (take out the textbook etc.) and then when she has a moment of pause in whatever she is explaining (usually at this opening stage of the lesson she is giving some instruction or other), she now looks directly at the student and points to the left corner of the whiteboard to the instructions she has written <u>before</u> the class and calls out the number (she numbers each instruction she will give during the lesson) and that way each student who is late or who has to leave the classroom during the lesson for whatever reason (bathroom or the like) knows exactly where the teacher is and what she is doing. I was amazed to see this as it all happened very fast and the students seemed to be socialized into the system very well.

Mark, United States

SEQUENCING

A lesson is normally devoted to more than one type of activity and teachers often have a script that they follow when teaching a particular type of lesson, such as a speaking lesson, a reading, writing, or listening lesson (Richards and Lockhart 1994). A common lesson sequence, found in many traditional language classes for example, consists of a sequence of activities referred to as P-P-P: *Presentation, Practice*, and *Production*. Reading lessons often follow a format consisting of *Prereading, While-Reading*, and *Postreading* activities. Lessons based on a task-based approach often consist of a sequence consisting of *Pretask activities, The task cycle, The language focus*, and a *Follow-up task*. Text-based teaching (an approach in which units of work are built around different types of spoken and written texts) on the other hand often uses a five-part sequence of activities consisting of *Building the context, Modeling and deconstructing the text, Joint construction of texts, Individual construction of a text*, and *Linking the text to related texts*.

I teach my student teachers to use an alternative version of the P-P-P structure: P-P-P-P. P = Preparation, P = Presentation, P = Practice (Guided), P = Production (Independent). This works very well with my students. If the student teacher does not <u>prepare</u> well for what he or she is going to teach (i.e., preparing the teaching resources, reading up to compensate for any knowledge limitations, etc.) and to <u>negotiate</u> for what will really work in his or her teaching-learning situation (e.g., having a sense of the students' prior knowledge, the type of lesson to conduct, etc.), the student teacher may still fail at the Presentation stage of the P-P-P. A well-prepared teacher is also often a more confident teacher.

Anthony, teacher trainer, Singapore

In addition to the lesson sequence suggested by the teaching approach or language skill you are teaching, other more general considerations will also influence the stages into which you think a lesson should be divided, drawing on principles such as "simple before difficult activities," "receptive before productive skills," or "accuracy activities before fluency activities," and the suggestions you have for lesson sequencing can be discussed with your supervisor or cooperating teaching prior to each lesson. At the same time you will need to consider how you will handle the transitions between the different sequences of the lesson.

Research on how teachers tend to handle transitions (e.g., Doyle 1986; Woodward 2001) suggests that skilled teachers mark the onset of transitions clearly, orchestrate transitions actively, and minimize the loss of momentum during these activities. Less effective teachers on the other hand tend to blend activities together, fail to monitor events during transitions, and take too long to complete the movement between segments of a lesson. Effective transitions help maintain students' attention during transition times and establish a link between one activity and the next. Planning for transitions involves thinking about how the momentum of the lesson will be maintained during transitions (e.g., while moving from a whole-class activity to group work) and what students should do between transitions (e.g., if some students complete an activity before others).

CLOSINGS

The closing phase of a lesson is also an important part of a lesson sequence. Ideally it should leave the students feeling that they have successfully achieved a goal they set for themselves or that has been established for the lesson, and that the lesson was a worthwhile and meaningful lesson. Sometimes teachers and students may have very different perceptions concerning the lesson's outcomes or what they feel a successful lesson outcome is (Nunan 1999). Indeed, Richards et al. (1996) discovered that students they studied in Hong Kong had the following expectations for their language teachers, which were not necessarily those of their teachers:

- Provide useful language learning experiences.
- Provide a model of correct language use.
- Answer learners' questions.
- Correct learners' errors.
- Help students discover effective approaches to learning.
- Pass on knowledge and skills to their students.
- Adapt teaching approaches to match students' needs.

So, the teacher will normally want to summarize what the lesson has tried to achieve, to reinforce the points of the lesson, suggest follow-up work as appropriate, and prepare students for what will follow. The students may expect to be praised for their effort and performance, they may raise issues or problems that they would like to discuss or resolve, and ask for suggestions concerning how they can best learn and use what they have studied out of class. In the following comments, student teachers describe how their cooperating teachers established links between lesson activities:

I noticed my cooperating teacher always wrote the activities the students would be doing on the whiteboard at the beginning of the lesson. This gave the students a sense of how the lesson held together. It was also a good way to review the lesson at the end because she did not have to write any summary on the board as it was already there. The students could also know what was covered and what was not covered. I think it's a good idea.

Mark, Singapore

My cooperating teacher planned her activities well and was ready to move onto the next activity smoothly. For example, when she wanted her students to finish one activity because they had reached the time limit, she just flicked the lights on and off and got their attention, then she just moved onto the next activity.

Hee-Soon, Korea

It is often useful to make students aware of the structure you have planned for a lesson. For example, you might write a brief lesson outline on the board at the beginning of the lesson (or preferably, before the students come to class), listing the activities that the students will take part in during the lesson and what the purpose of each activity is. This lets the students know what will be expected of them during the lesson and gives them a sense that they are taking part in a lesson that has been planned and organized. It also orients late-coming students to what part of the lesson has been reached.

5. THE LESSON PROVIDES OPPORTUNITIES FOR LEARNERS TO PROCESS AND PRACTICE USING LANGUAGE IN A MEANINGFUL WAY

Some important questions that are at the forefront of the planning and delivery of any language class are the following:

- What kind of language-learning opportunities did the lesson provide?
- How many opportunities were there for students to practice using the language?
- Were the activities they took part in sufficiently challenging to increase their skill in using what they already know, as well as to expand their awareness of things that were new?

Some of the things that characterize a successful language lesson will depend on the kind of lesson it is. The essential components of a speaking lesson will be very different from those of a writing class for example, depending on the students' current level of proficiency and the stage they are at in their course. The initial stages of a speaking course, for example, may focus on mastering the language and conversational routines needed to carry out functions such as greetings, introductions, and small talk, whereas the contents of an intermediate speaking course might focus on expressing agreement, disagreement, sympathy, encouragement, and on performing oral texts, such as narratives and personal recounts. Whatever the kind of course you are teaching however, some core principles should be evident in your lessons and these will reflect the principles embodied in the teaching approach and the particular set of teaching skills you are using. For example, it could be argued that a successful speaking course:

- Gives all the students in the class an opportunity for extended speaking practice
- Practices talk as interaction
- Practices speech features that the students will need outside of class
- Practices appropriate features of spoken language
- Practices communication strategies
- Practices meaningful and purposeful use of spoken English
- Addresses the difficulties students experience with speaking English
- Practices forms for both expressing and managing talk
- Deals with both accuracy and fluency
- Expands the learners' speech repertoire

Statements such as these may be contained in the objectives or syllabus of the course you are teaching. If they are not, you should negotiate an understanding of the competencies or skills your course is addressing, and then refer to these in planning and reviewing your lessons.

6. THE LESSON CREATES THE MOTIVATION TO LEARN AND PROVIDES OPPORTUNITIES FOR SUCCESS

Sometimes learners look forward to coming to class. Other times learners may dread coming to class because they anticipate that they will be engaged in activities they do not enjoy doing, that appear to have little purpose, and that leave them both with a feeling of frustration as well as loss of face. As a teacher you play a crucial role in developing a classroom atmosphere that encourages and motivates students in their learning (or conversely, that fails to do so) (Senior 2006). Perhaps you can recall some of the most inspiring language teachers you have had, and what made them different and special. Among the factors that account for the qualities of exceptional language teachers is their enthusiasm for teaching, the high expectations they set for their learners, and the relationships they have with them (Dörnyei 2001). Enthusiasm can be communicated in many different ways, such as by showing interest in the students and the activities you use. If your students sense that you are positive and enthusiastic about the course book or materials that you are using, they are likely to share your enthusiasm. Expectations for student success can be achieved through praising students' performance, by giving help to weaker students when needed, and generally by demonstrating the belief which one teacher expressed as "every student in my class is a winner!" Establishing a warm and caring attitude toward students also contributes to building a positive class atmosphere. This means treating the students as people and not just as numbers, through learning their names, showing an interest in their lives, and in their interests and problems, without going further than the boundaries set by your professional relationship.

Establishing good relationships among students in the class is also important. This involves working toward a sense of cooperation rather than competition among students, using group consensus-building activities and avoiding activities that could lead to strong disagreement or tension. You can also engage the class in establishing norms of behavior and interaction for both the teacher and the class, such as rules concerning punctuality, use of mobile phones, or ways of supporting members in a group who are having difficulty with a task. And you can build in opportunities for success rather than failure in the class by ensuring that tasks are at an appropriate level of difficulty and that every lesson contains some "take away" value, that is, something that students feel they have successfully mastered when they leave the class. This could be a growing sense of confidence in how to write a paragraph, the awareness of some appropriate conversational expressions to use with friends and neighbors, or a list of 10 or more useful words or expressions. "Take away" value is achieved by reviewing your lesson plan in advance to make sure that you give sufficient time and attention to those aspects of the lesson that have greatest importance.

It is also important to work toward maintaining the motivational level of the class. You can do this by asking yourself questions such as these:

- Do I vary the way I teach my lessons?
- Do I include activities that are there simply to maintain motivation (such as songs and language games)?
- Can I find ways of making my tasks more interesting (for example, by presenting a reading text as a jigsaw reading)?
- Can I increase the personal value of my lesson to my learners (for example, by adapting an activity so that it centers on the students' lives rather than on characters in a textbook)?
- Can I build in more opportunities for success in my lessons (for example, by choosing activities that challenge but do not frustrate learners)?

In the following comments, two student teachers describe how they built motivation into their lessons:

Today's lesson was on synonyms. This was listed in the scheme of work that I was supposed to follow as closely as possible. My cooperating teacher allowed me to do what I wanted and let me come up with whatever activities I thought would motivate the students to become interested. I was so excited and I designed a crossword puzzle to help in this lesson. Before I handed out the crossword puzzle, I explained to students the meaning of a synonym.

After the students had understood the meaning, I asked for a few examples from the students before handing out the crossword puzzle. Allowing the students about 15 minutes to complete the puzzle, I used a transparency of the puzzle to give the answers. By the end of the lesson, I think the students understood the meaning of a synonym. I concluded the lesson by asking the students for examples of a synonym again, making sure that they understood what a synonym was. I think the students all enjoyed the lesson and appreciated that I had gone to the trouble of preparing the crossword for them.

James, Canada

My objectives for these two lessons were to enable my students to identify and compare the types of tenses used in narratives and infer the rule in forming the regular verb forms of the simple past tense. In the first chapter of the textbook, the students have been exposed to the use of the simple present tense in narratives and in this second chapter they will learn the use of the simple past tense. I need to teach the students the rules for forming past tenses, thus I decided to adopt the inductive approach as I strongly believe that the students will be able to better retain the rules if they discover the rules themselves.

I chose the "peanut butter sandwich" approach as it provides an opportunity for students to learn the use of simple past tense in narratives. This is in fact from a CRISP approach to grammar teaching, meaning it is Clear, Relevant, Interesting, Short, and Productive. It basically involved making a peanut butter sandwich in class and this is to help reinforce the notion of end use in meaningful situations. I printed two similar texts on the students' handouts. In the first text, they were supposed to fill in the blanks (simple present tense) while I made the sandwich and in the second text, they were supposed to reflect on the steps I had taken to make the sandwich and fill in the blanks accordingly (simple past tense). Then, to their amazement, I ate the sandwich in class. They had to extract the words used in the two texts and complete their handout. I went through the words with the students and led them to discover the patterns present in forming the singular present tenses and subsequently, the students worked in pairs to discover the patterns in forming the regular verb forms of the simple past tense.

The cooperating teacher told me that they were all very excited with this peanut butter sandwich approach and were actually able to better retain the grammar rules via this discovery approach.

Tung, Singapore

7. THE LESSON ACHIEVES MEANINGFUL LEARNING OUTCOMES

It is an obvious truism to state that every lesson sets out to teach something. A language lesson may set out to achieve a number of different kinds of outcomes however. Some may be to teach students to master or to improve their mastery of a certain type of skill. The following are outcomes of this kind for three different lessons:

- To learn how to write paragraphs containing a thesis statement and supporting ideas
- To learn how to use concessive clauses
- To learn the use of note-taking skills in academic listening

Objectives such as these refer to specific and observable skills or competencies, and at the end of a lesson or unit it should be possible to assess the students' improvements in the skill area. Many aspects of language use of course take a long time to develop, and their mastery can only be assessed after a lengthy period of instruction. In such cases lessons may provide opportunities to practice and consolidate some area of language use. For example:

- To practice self-editing skills in composition
- To practice the development of critical reading skills

Yet other objectives address processes and learning experiences rather than specific products or observable outcomes. For example:

- To help develop a positive attitude toward language learning
- To have a successful experience in language learning
- To encourage students to work productively and cooperatively
- To give students control over their own learning

When I review my student teachers' account of their aims and objectives for a lesson the adjectives I use are valid (in other words, are the aims related to language learning rather than to something the teacher is interested in, such as changing the students' views about religion?), specific (is the student teacher setting out to teach something that is not too general or ambitious?), and clear and achievable (is this something that really can be achieved in a lesson?).

Neil, teacher trainer, Australia

Language-learning goals or objectives may be both long term and short term. Whereas long-term goals may have been determined for you by your cooperating teacher or by the syllabus and teaching materials you have been assigned, you should also develop your own personal goals for your lessons, and discuss these with your cooperating teacher. Your lessons may have different kinds of goals embedded in them, but whatever their goals, they should be things you can identify, that you have thought about and, in some way, planned for. You can share your goals with your students so that they come to realize that your teaching is planned and purposeful. For example, you might write your lesson goals on the board at the beginning of each lesson to help students see the objectives the lesson is planned to achieve.

Goals are also something you can help students set for themselves. McCombs and Pope suggest the following ways in which students can think about their personal language-learning goals, and these processes are also suitable for student teachers:

1. Define your goal clearly.
2. List steps to take to reach this goal.
3. Think of problems that might come up and that would interfere.
4. Think of solutions to these problems.
5. Set a timeline for reaching the goal.
6. Evaluate your progress.
7. Reward yourself for accomplishment.

(McCombs and Pope 1994: 36)

8. THE LESSON REFLECTS YOUR PERSONAL PHILOSOPHY OF TEACHING

Whereas your academic and teacher preparation courses have introduced you to different teaching methods and approaches, once you begin your teaching you will need to learn how to teach in *your* way, based on the kind of person you are and how you see your role in the classroom. This does not mean that you can abandon everything you have learned once you start your teaching practice. Rather it means that you will now have the opportunity to interpret and understand what it means to be a language teacher and what values, beliefs, theories, and assumptions you will use to guide you in your teaching. As we saw in Chapter 2, some of these beliefs will be confirmations and elaborations of theories and principles you studied in your academic courses. Now you will have a chance to more fully understand how language learning develops in learners, the kind of feedback that facilitates language learning, and how to scaffold learning activities so that students can benefit from working together on group tasks and projects.

You will also be developing a set of your own personal theories and principles that you wish to reflect in your teaching. For example, you may arrive at two important principles that relate to how to motivate reluctant learners. For example:

- Make learning fun.
- Make learning relaxing rather than stressful.

As you plan and deliver your lessons you will then look for opportunities to build these principles into your teaching. Your cooperating teacher may not share or be aware of your personal principles so developing an appropriate set of beliefs and principles and discussing these with your supervisor and your cooperating teacher (or writing about them in a teaching journal or lesson report) is an important aspect of your teacher development. Table 6.1 summarizes the core principles that are central to the concept of good teaching.

1. The lesson and your conduct in it reflect the professional standards expected of English language teachers.	• The teacher carefully plans lessons, controls emotions and behavior in and out of classroom, and shows respect for students.
2. The lesson reflects a theoretically grounded and principled understanding of language teaching.	• The teacher is familiar with instructional methods and their underlying principles, effective classroom techniques, materials, and assessment strategies.
3. The lesson is effectively managed.	• The teacher creates a positive environment for learning, and develops and enforces clear classroom procedures.
4. The lesson provides appropriately structured, sequenced learning experiences.	• The teacher sequences activities that lead toward the successful completion of lesson goals and objectives.
5. The lesson provides opportunities for learners to process and practice using language in a meaningful way.	• The teacher negotiates an understanding of the competencies or skills the course is addressing, then refers to these in planning and reviewing lessons.

(ctd.)

(ctd.)

6. The lesson creates the motivation to learn and provides opportunities for success.	• The teacher develops a classroom atmosphere that encourages and motivates students in their learning.
7. The lesson achieves meaningful learning outcomes.	• The teacher accesses specific and observable skills or competencies at the end of lesson.
8. The lesson reflects your personal philosophy of teaching.	• The teacher teaches in his / her own way, based on personality and the way he / she views the teacher's role in the classroom.

Table 6.1   Core principles of good teaching

SUMMARY AND CONCLUSIONS

There are a number of dimensions to an effective language lesson. Your cooperating teacher will expect your lesson to reflect current ideas about language teaching that have been the focus of your professional training and to reflect the professional image and standards of professional language teachers. You should be able to justify your lessons in terms of the principles underlying them as well as the outcomes you have set for them. They should therefore both be grounded in terms of the theoretical understanding that underlies them as well as being well planned, well sequenced, and relevant to your learners' needs. At the same time, your own individuality as a teacher should be something that is evident to someone observing your classes. You will also be expected to be fully in charge of the class, able to teach with confidence, and to manage the class appropriately. And your lessons should also be meaningful and motivating for your learners.

As the review in this chapter suggests, an effective language lesson reflects both the knowledge, skills, beliefs, and values that you bring to teaching, and the decisions you make while teaching a lesson to ensure that it reflects your goals for the lesson, your awareness of learners' needs and concerns, and your ability to create a lesson that provides optimal conditions for language learning. Few teachers teach an ideal or perfect lesson every time they teach, and every lesson provides opportunities to reflect on the effectiveness of the plans you made for the lesson and the decisions that you made while teaching it. You may find that your initial teaching experience leads to lessons that are less than ideal and that developing the skills needed to achieve the goals you set for your teaching will take a considerable period of time. However, the practicum is intended for exactly that purpose, so it is always important to keep your long-term goals in mind when reviewing your practice-teaching experiences.

Further reading

Dörnyei, Z. (2001). *Motivational strategies in the language classroom.* Cambridge: Cambridge University Press.

Richard-Amato, P. A. (2009). *Making it happen: From interactive to participatory language teaching: Evolving theory and practice* (4th ed.). New York: Pearson.

Richards, J. C., & Lockhart, C. (1994). *Reflective teaching in second language classrooms.* New York: Cambridge University Press.

Richards, J. C., & Rodgers, T. (2001). *Approaches and methods in language teaching.* (2nd ed.). Cambridge: Cambridge University Press.

Discussion questions

1. Reflect on a successful language lesson that you have experienced or observed. What factors do you think accounted for its success?

2. What are some ways in which you think a student teacher can establish an expectation in the classroom that the students should take his or her class seriously and have the same expectations for him or her as for their regular class teacher?

3. Discuss an ESL class of a kind that you are familiar with (e.g., a writing class, a reading class, a listening class) and identify some of the principles that you think the activities students do in the class should reflect.

4. What are some of the causes of undisciplined and disruptive student behavior during lessons? What procedures have you seen teachers follow to successfully respond to such behavior?

5. Can you suggest some classroom management principles that you think are most likely to create a well-managed classroom?

6. Reflect on a lesson that was highly motivating, and one that was less so. What factors accounted for the differences between them?

7. How useful do you think is it to describe lesson outcomes in terms of objectives? In what other ways can you assess the learning outcomes of lessons?

Follow-up activities

1. Plan a lesson around any area of content that you choose, and describe how you will deal with the *opening, sequencing*, and the *closing* of the lesson.

2. Review the teacher trainer's view of a good lesson plan in Appendix B. Can you give examples of aims for an intermediate-level speaking class (or another lesson of your choice) that are valid, achievable, and specific?

3. How would you plan a lesson on "a class debate"? Think of how you would begin the lesson and how you would structure it. Then read Ruben's account in Appendix A of how he presented a lesson on a debate and compare.

4. Come to class prepared to discuss one effective practice or strategy that your cooperating teacher has used. This could be a technique, the use of materials or technology, dealing with a classroom management problem, or any other effective practice you observed. Explain what you observed to the class (using visuals, the board, demonstration, etc., as needed) and explain what makes this an effective practice, in your opinion.

Appendix A: A student teacher's view of lesson effectiveness

Over the course of the 12 weeks of practice teaching I did last semester, one of the many practical skills I learned and developed is how to effectively design and implement a lesson in an ESL class. From my experience, there are two crucial components to creating and completing an effective lesson. The first and most obvious is the actual lesson itself: How it is structured, what types of activities are included, how the lesson flows, how the students react to the material being taught, and what teaching strategies are being used. Second, I learned from my experiences that classroom management is also a crucial component of an effective lesson.

An example of an effective lesson from my teaching practice was a lesson I taught on debating techniques and strategies in a speaking class. In my opinion, I had a very good lesson prepared for that class. I opened the class with an example of a short debate. I then asked the class if they recognized what type of speaking structure I was using. The students guessed correctly that I was arguing or debating, and then we proceeded to pick apart the arguments and "debating vocabulary" I used. After the class discussed some ways to debate, I put them into pairs and instructed them that they were going to have a "speed debating session." Each pair would have three minutes to debate on topics I had prepared and then they would rotate and debate another topic with another peer.

After the students completed several rounds of debating, I stopped them, asked them what types of difficulties or ease they experienced, and had them reflect on their experience. Next I put the students in groups of four and explained to them that their next assignment would be to do formal debates in teams. I gave the groups their topics and their stance on the topic and told them to start thinking about pros and cons. The class ended with students working on their group debates and looking forward to completing them in the next few days.

As I reflect on this lesson, I can see that I really was capable of preparing effective lessons. I could clearly observe that my students had learned something that day and were eager to use what they learned. The manner in which I managed this lesson was also vital to its success. I had carefully planned out the timing of each activity and it worked out better than I expected. I had given the students freedom to express what they wanted in their debates while having firm control over how they were doing it and for what purpose. After this lesson, I felt really confident in my ability to deliver an effective lesson by managing the class in a way that was controlled, but not controlling. I also realized the importance of thoughtful planning and creatively getting students to use what they learned. This lesson really was a highlight of my practice-teaching experience and gave me a lot of confidence to do what I enjoy.

Ruben, Canada

Appendix B: A teacher trainer's view of a good lesson plan

When helping preservice language teachers set appropriate lesson aims and express them well in a lesson plan, I find it useful to get the teachers thinking about the following questions:

- *Are the aims valid?* Valid aims solely promote language learning and do not have an overt or covert political or even religious agenda. Valid aims are also appropriate for the level of the class and must move the learners forward in some way. For example, a lesson revising the whole of the English article system would not be valid for a beginners' class, and a lesson exclusively on the meaning and use of the Present Simple for habits or routines (e.g., *I have cereal for breakfast*) would not be valid for an upper-intermediate class.
- *Are the aims achievable?* This usually means limiting the aims so they are achievable within the time frame of the lesson, ensuring that the learners are not overloaded and that they have adequate practice of what is taught. A 60-minute lesson for a beginners' class introducing and providing practice of *can* for ability (e.g., *I can speak Italian*) would normally be achievable; a 60-minute lesson which also introduced *can* for other uses such as permission (e.g., *Can*

I leave early?) and deduction (e.g., *That can't be true!)* would not normally be achievable.

- *Are the aims specific?* Good lesson aims tell the reader of the lesson plan – normally the person observing the lesson – what to expect. Using the example of the lesson on *can* above, a statement such as "To teach *can*" would be unsatisfactory. The reader of the lesson plan needs to know (i) what particular use(s) of *can* feature in the lesson, with perhaps some example utterances from the lesson; (ii) whether the lesson is assuming this is new language for the learners or language that is being revised / extended; and (iii) the nature of the practice the learners will receive. So the aim of this particular lesson with a beginners' class might be stated as "To introduce and to provide controlled oral and written practice of *can* for ability, e.g., *I can speak Italian / I can't speak French / Can you speak German?*"

Neil, teacher trainer, Australia

CHAPTER 7

Classroom Observation in Teaching Practice

INTRODUCTION

Observation plays a central role in practice teaching, both observation of your teaching by your cooperating teacher and supervisor, as well as your own observations of your co-operating teacher's class. Other school staff may also wish to observe one of your classes from time to time, such as the principal, the vice-principal, or a senior teacher, so you need to prepare well for every lesson in the event that someone asks to observe your teaching. You may also have the opportunity to observe other teachers in your host school and to review video recordings of your own teaching and that of other student teachers in your teaching practice seminars. The purpose and nature of observation, however, differs according to who participates in the observation process. For example, in observing your cooperating teacher's class your focus will be on *how* the teacher teaches, on such things as how the teacher creates a positive atmosphere for learning, on the strategies and procedures used by the teacher in setting up activities, on the way the teacher gives instructions and explanations, and how he or she gives feedback to learners. As a novice teacher you will not be evaluating your cooperating teacher's teaching. When *you* are being observed by your cooperating teacher or supervisor, however, the focus will often be on *how well* you carried out different aspects of the lesson. In this chapter we deal with both kinds of observations.

THE NATURE OF CLASSROOM OBSERVATION

Although it is an important component of teaching practice, the nature and limitations of observation need to be kept in mind. Teaching is a complex and dynamic activity, and during a lesson many things occur simultaneously, so it is not possible to observe all of them. Thirty students in a class may be responding to the lesson in many different ways. Some may be finding the lesson stimulating and may have a clear sense of what the purposes of activities are and how they are supposed to carry them out. Others may find some of the activities insufficiently challenging or motivating and may be paying minimal attention to the teacher or the lesson. And at the same time the teacher may be struggling mentally to maintain the flow of the lesson and may have realized that he or she set the lesson up in a nonproductive way. None of these aspects of the lesson are directly observable. And even if aspects of classroom behavior are observable – such as the amount of talking students engage in when completing an activity – you may not be able to tell whether this is an indication of confusion or of interest. For all these reasons information you or your cooperating teacher gain during an observation always needs to be clarified through conversation and discussion in order to understand the meaning of what you observed (or thought you observed).

At the same time, the presence of an observer in the classroom sometimes influences the nature of the lesson, making the lesson untypical of the teacher's usual style of teaching. As a student teacher you may "overprepare" for a visit by your supervisor or cooperating teacher in order to show yourself at your best. You may also feel tense knowing that the observer is not only there to assist you in developing your teaching skills, but also to evaluate how well you are doing. However, initially you may find the presence of your cooperating teacher or supervisor distracts you from being able to teach your best. If this is so you should discuss this with the observer both before and after an observation. Experienced teacher trainers are of course well aware of the influence their presence may have on a student teacher, but comments such as the following are not uncommon:

I was so scared the first time I was observed by my cooperating teacher because I knew she was evaluating me as a teacher. Sometimes I looked in her direction and saw her writing something down and I wondered what she was thinking and at those times I lost a bit of my own flow of teaching. Anyway, I was glad when it was over and only wanted to know what she thought of my teaching.

Jae Hee, Korea

I could never be myself when I was being observed by my cooperating teacher, no matter how much she tried to put me at ease before the observation or how much I had prepared before the class. I could not sleep properly the night before each observation. Even my students could see that I was not normal when someone (either my supervisor or my cooperating teacher) was in the back of the room and they always asked me how I was after class, which was sweet.

Catharine, United States

The first time my supervisor just showed up and I froze, literally. He would pick a morning that was after the night before for me because I was still a university student and thus active on campus as I returned each day after teaching practice. I was not fully prepared for the class and I guess it showed because I think the students could feel this too. Needless to say, I was always well prepared after this and I realized that this was a real job and settled down to teaching practice after this.

John, Canada

Last term, I observed three different teachers teaching different classes and different skills. I realized that a teacher's personality has a lot to do with the functioning of a class. This term, I began my practice teaching by observing my cooperating teacher teach the first two classes. I realized that the more experienced a teacher is, the more effortless a class appears to move. After two classes of observation, it was now my turn to be observed. I found it to be a very uncomfortable experience. I felt (and still feel) that I was not myself when I was being observed. I continuously felt the pressure of being observed by the teacher on one end and the students on the other. In trying to be acceptable to both, I seemed to lose all focus on the learning demands of the students.

Vidya, Canada

OBSERVING YOUR COOPERATING TEACHER'S CLASS

Your practice-teaching assignment will often begin with a series of observations of your cooperating teacher's class. These observations will give you a chance to familiarize yourself with such things as the course materials the teacher is using, the teaching methods and strategies the teacher uses, how he or she interacts with students, how the learners respond and interact with the teacher and among themselves, and the kinds of language they understand and produce. These observations will help you prepare yourself for some of issues and problems that you may have to face while teaching the class. You can see what methods and strategies the teacher employs and decide if you will be able to use these yourself when you come to teach the class. You will also learn more about the learners (e.g., their interests, motivations, and learning styles) and this will better prepare you for the time when you will take over teaching the class. As Gaies (1991) has pointed out, "What we see, when we observe teachers and learners in action, is not the mechanical application of methods and techniques, but rather a reflection of how teachers have interpreted these things" (p. 14).

THE FOCUS OF THE OBSERVATION

If observation is to serve a useful purpose it needs to be carefully planned. The purpose of the observation is to collect information that you can later use during a follow-up discussion with the teacher. Before you observe your cooperating teacher's class you will normally have a preobservation meeting to decide on the focus for your observation and the procedures you will use to record your observations. You may suggest aspects of the class you would like to learn more about, such as how the teacher makes use of group work or how he or she deals with classroom management. Your cooperating teacher will also suggest things to look for during an observation. Normally you should focus on only one or two aspects of the lesson since you cannot focus on too many things at the same time. Some aspects of a lesson are relatively easy to observe (such as the kinds of questions students ask), whereas others may not be observable and have to be inferred (such as the degree of interest students had in the topic of the lesson, decisions teachers made during a lesson, or problems that occurred that might not have been visible to an observer). The following are examples of the things your cooperating teacher might ask you to observe during his or her lessons:

Lesson structure
- The way the lesson opens, develops, and closes
- The number of activities that constitute the lesson
- The links and transitions between activities

Classroom management strategies
- Setting up groups
- Maintaining order
- Time management
- Seating arrangements

Types of teaching activities
- Whole-class activities
- Pair and group activities
- Individual activities

Teaching strategies
- Presenting tasks
- Organizing practice
- Teaching techniques

Teacher's use of materials
- Use of the textbook
- Use of other resources

Teacher's use of language
- Use of instructional language
- Use of questions
- Feedback techniques
- Explanations of vocabulary and grammar

Students' use of language
- Use of language in group work
- Use of the mother tongue during class
- Problems with grammar
- Problems with pronunciation

Student interaction
- Time on task
- Questioning behaviors
- Student-to-student talk

The following comments illustrate what different student teachers learned from being observed:

When I started to observe my cooperating teacher she just said to watch the class in general and how she started the class and went through the various activities she had planned – I had a copy of her lesson plan. Then after the class she told me what she thought of it and how it went from her perspective. She said that she was happy that all her students were participating and learning. What really struck me was how she was able to get all her students involved. I was surprised because this was a big class of 30 students and it was fast moving, so I wondered how she took it all in. For the following observations she asked me to focus on classroom management and how she accomplished this because she told me I would have to take over this class and she had wanted me to know how to control them. I found observing my cooperating teacher very useful because I incorporated many of her classroom management techniques when I took over the class and they worked because the students were used to them.

Jin Da, Thailand

After observing my cooperating teacher's class I realized that giving clear, precise, and brief instructions to the class is an important skill as it avoids miscommunication and misunderstanding between the teacher and students in class. In giving out long instructions, I realized I could help the class by writing the instructions down so that time can be used more productively. This would enable the class to clarify any doubts they have and also to ensure that the class is clear on the requirements of the assigned task.

Bernie, Singapore

My cooperating teacher gives me very little feedback about my teaching. So I feel that I don't get to learn much from her. So the fact of being observed just plays as a negative factor rather than anything constructive. But I also realize that half of the problem is my own doing. I have been focusing on the wrong issues. Rather than try and evaluate the needs of the students, I have been trying to be acceptable to the others. I now try to concentrate on the lesson plan and the course material and try to forget that I am being observed (though I am not always successful in this).

Vidya, Canada

OBSERVATION PROCEDURES

In order to make effective use of observation, you will have to decide how to make a record of the information you collect. The procedures you use will depend on the focus of the observation, but the following are often used.

- **Checklists**
  A checklist contains a list of different features of a lesson, which you complete while observing a lesson. Checklists provide a clear focus for observation, however they can only be used for certain aspects of a lesson, such as features that are easy to count, and should focus on only one or two aspects of the lesson. There are several published checklists than can be used in classroom observations (e.g., Wajnryb 1992) but these may need to be adapted to suit your needs. Alternatively, you and your cooperating teacher can develop your own checklists. Examples of checklists are given in Appendix A.

- **Seating charts**
  Seating charts showing the arrangement of desks in the classroom as well as the position the teacher normally teaches from, can also be used to code such things as the number of times students ask the teacher a question or vice versa, and the number of times a student asks other students questions. The seating chart observation record (SCORE) in Figure 7.1 shows a ten-minute segment of a question-and-answer period after a student (speaker) had delivered a thirty-minute speech in English (Farrell 2008d). The teacher (MH) said that she was surprised to find out from this SCORE analysis that she had asked forty-five questions in the ten-minute period as she had thought that she was "a silent participant as a listener in my classes." She continued, "Until now I had no realization about my questioning pattern."

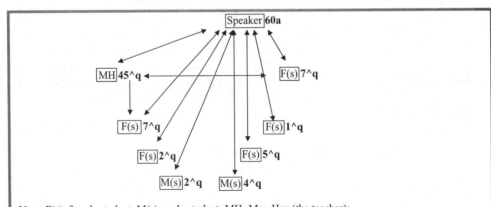

Note: F(s)=female student; M(s)=male student; MH=Mee-Hee (the teacher);
^q=ask; a=answer question. The long arrows show the directional flow of the questions.

Figure 7.1 SCORE Analysis I (Farrell 2008d)

- **Field notes**

These consist of brief descriptions in note form of key events that occurred throughout the lesson. They can provide a summary of the lesson as a whole, or can be time-based (e.g., every five minutes). For example:

8:30 – Class begins.

8:33 – Teacher writes instructions for class on board as students turn on computers.

8:35 – Teacher gives oral instructions for online reading task.

8:40 – Students engage in online reading task with computers.

8:45 – Silence – reading comprehension ensues.

8:50 – Silence

8:55 – Teacher checks with a student about why he's not reading and circulates to see how other students are doing.

9:00 – Silence continues as students read.

9:04 – Students finished with online reading task look up at teacher.

9:05 – Teacher takes up answers for the online reading task students were working on.

9:08 – Teacher tells students to go back to computers to do scanning practice.

9:09 – Teacher assists one student to get online and understand scanning.

9:13 – Teacher helps student scan and then tells whole class what they should be doing when "scanning" and focusing on key words.

9:17 – Teacher circulates room and helps individual students while reading on their computers.

9:20 – Teacher concludes class.

- **Narrative summary**

A narrative summary is a written summary of the lesson that tries to capture the main things that happened during the course of it, such as how the lesson opened, the sequence of activities that occurred, how the teacher introduced each activity, and so on. The account should contain as much information as possible but should not contain any evaluation of the lesson. Here is an example:

The teacher initiated the peer-response session of the writing cycle and started the class by asking the students to move into groups to answer questions on peer-response handouts. The students were asked to fill out these handouts to answer questions about their peer's composition. The students sat in groups of four, read compositions and then wrote at length on the handouts. Next they exchanged the peer-response handouts and talked to each other mostly in Mandarin for the remainder of the class. The class ended and all left the room.

Tom, Singapore

- **The follow-up conversation**

Following an observation, your cooperating teacher will normally find time to discuss your observations with you and to answer any questions you may have. It is important to remember that during the follow-up meeting you should focus on clarifying and interpreting information you obtained from your observation in order to learn more about how the teacher approaches his or her teaching. For example:

○ *Explanations as to why things happened*: e.g., "Why do you think the students found this activity difficult?," "Why did you use group work at this point in the lesson?"
○ *Explanations of how the teacher would respond to events during the lesson*: e.g., "What would you have done, if the students had finished this activity ahead of time?"
○ *Suggestions from the teacher*: e.g., "How should I respond if students tell me an activity like this is too difficult?"

When I observed my cooperating teacher giving instructions to the class I learned that it may not be enough to just tell the students what to do because they may not react until a few minutes later. So when I saw my cooperating teacher also write these instructions on the whiteboard after giving them orally, I noticed a few of the students only seemed to understand at that moment what was required of them.

Tony, Brazil

I really saw the importance of teacher enthusiasm when I observed my cooperating teacher teaching a class on grammar tenses. Seeing the lesson plan on paper is one thing but she magically transformed that plan into a lively and enjoyable lesson with her bubbly personality. I realized at that time that the teacher is the real method when it comes to teaching, and materials or even plans mean nothing if we don't engage our students.

Terry, United States

BEING OBSERVED BY YOUR COOPERATING TEACHER OR SUPERVISOR

As we noted in Observation Procedures, being regularly observed by your cooperating teacher or supervisor during your practice teaching is one of the things you will doubtless find stressful. Knowing that the strengths and weaknesses of your teaching are being assessed naturally causes some degree of anxiety. However, if you have developed a comfortable working relationship with your cooperating teacher, observation can become a positive learning experience. Your cooperating teacher will usually find many good things to comment on about your teaching. And he or she can also help you monitor your own teaching by observing things that it would be difficult for you yourself to observe. As with observation of your cooperating teacher's class, a preobservation and postobservation conversation is usually scheduled to prepare both you and the observer for your lesson and to discuss it afterwards.

There are several purposes for observation by the cooperating teacher or the supervisor:

- to collect information about your lesson that it would be difficult for you to observe: e.g., how members of a group interacted during a group task and how much interaction each group member took part in
- to observe how you are implementing a new teaching strategy or technique that you are trying out: e.g., how you address reading strategies when teaching a reading lesson

- to observe how you implemented specific stages of a lesson: e.g., how you dealt with the opening and closing of the lesson
- to identify those aspects of the lesson that were the most successful
- to identify those aspects of the lesson that could be improved
- to identify techniques and practices you can apply to your own teaching
- to help you gain a better understanding of your own teaching

In addition to these points, if you are being observed by a supervisor, he or she may be interested in issues such as the following:

- to see how you are able to implement strategies and ideas discussed in your training class
- to see if you are making progress in your skills as a teacher
- to identify issues that can be discussed in follow-up sessions with you and other student teachers

Although most research on supervision suggests that the nature of talk between the supervisor and the teacher learner in postobservation conferences is dictated by the supervisor, you nevertheless can take more initiative in these conferences by sharing your reactions to the class, the surprises you encountered, what you would have done differently, what you have learned, and what you think the students have learned. Your supervisor can also help you develop an overall action plan that can help you further develop as a teacher.

Your cooperating teacher may use some of the procedures discussed in this section in observing your lessons, or may simply make brief notes to use in a follow-up discussion. However, you may also find it useful to arrange for some of your lessons to be recorded. Audio and video recordings are relatively easy to make (details on procedures for audio and video recording are given in Chapter 11) and provide a more accurate record of a lesson than checklists or observation forms. If you choose this option you may want to transcribe some or all of the lesson if time permits, or simply replay the recording to focus on particular aspects of the lesson. For example, you may be interested in reflecting on the impact of your verbal instructions in a lesson: In this case, you can listen to and transcribe those parts of the tape that show you giving instructions.

I never realized that I used the word "OK" so many times when I teach until I heard myself teaching from the audiotape of my class. I am not sure I would have even believed my cooperating teacher if she had told me the same but it was all too real for me when I heard it on tape. I now try to catch myself before I say "OK" and this usually works but when I get excited while explaining something to a student, I still use it a lot.

Bob, United States

After watching the video of my class I realized that I usually ignore the right side of the room not only with my gaze, which is usually focused on the left of the room, but also with whom I ask questions to as well, which is also to the left side of the room as well. My whole body language looks as if I am facing left and, of course, I cannot then see the students on the right and especially in the front rows. Even the cooperating teacher did not notice this until we watched the class together.

Bernie, Singapore

THE ETIQUETTE OF SUPERVISORY OBSERVATION

When a teacher learner is being observed for administrative reasons, the observer (this includes the cooperating teacher, the school principal and vice-principal, and the practicum supervisor) should try to make the visit as noninvasive as possible (Master 1983). As Master points out, the observer administrator is a stranger in the room, and in the eyes of a teacher learner a typical observation goes like this:

> The administrator enters the room, often after the class has begun, and quietly takes a seat in the back row. The teacher may introduce the newcomer but cannot, of course, announce why the newcomer is there (i.e., to see how good the teacher is). Scanning the faces of the students, watching for the cues that indicate the attention level of the class, the teacher is suddenly confronted with a critical, non-participating observer. This establishes a new relationship, no longer between the teacher and the students, but between the teacher and the administrator. The students have become secondary. The lesson plan that once lay clearly in the teacher's mind now evaporates, and the teacher must break rhythm and refer to the written lesson plan on the desk. The students become nervous. The teacher, now so intent on appearing to be a good instructor, loses the ability to pick up the essential facial cues of the students. At the end of the lesson, waiting for the administrator's assessment, the teacher feels nervous, knowing that the class has not gone as well as it usually does. (Master 1983: 498)

This "invasive scenario" of classroom observation for administrative purposes can be avoided, as Master suggests, by having the observer follow a certain etiquette in order to bridge the dichotomy between the necessity for observation of teacher learners and this feeling of invasion. Master offers the following guidelines for observation etiquette and his suggestions seem equally relevant today:

- *Deciding When to Visit*: Most teachers prefer that an observer arrive before the class begins rather than at some time during the lesson. This gives teachers the opportunity to establish at least minimal contact and allows them to tell the students that an observer will be visiting the class that day (students are likely to offer spontaneous words of welcome under these circumstances, which can further reduce tension). If the observer can socialize with the students in the immediate vicinity before the lesson, perhaps asking what they have been studying or what they will probably be learning that day, the whole class is likely to feel more comfortable about the observation. There are different opinions regarding whether the visit should be on a pre-announced or a drop-in basis. From the administrative point of view, both have their disadvantages. Pre-announced visits almost always force teachers to put on their best show, giving a somewhat unnatural picture of a normal class period. Drop-in visits run the risk of encountering a quiz or a student report.
- *Choosing the Best Vantage Point:* To avoid the danger of setting up a teacher-observer relationship that excludes the students, the observer should not sit in the back of the room, as is commonly practiced, but rather among the students or facing them from the side in order to have a clear view of the students' faces.

- *Adopting the Best "Bedside Manner":* Some teachers feel more comfortable if they can treat the observer like a student. Others prefer to use the observer as a back-up resource, as the only other native speaker in the room. Still others prefer the observer to be a quiet friendly presence. The observer should be sensitive to the teacher's style, perhaps asking beforehand what the teacher prefers. When the teacher begins the lesson, the observer should appear pleasant and supportive (if the observer feels unable to do this, the visit is best postponed to another day). The eyes of the observer should be not so much on the teacher as on the students, watching how they react to their teacher and how the teacher responds to them. If the students feel themselves to be under scrutiny, they are often stimulated to perform, and this stimulates teachers to behave in a more natural, less threatened manner as they sense the greater response of the students.

- *Taking Notes:* Most observers need to take notes. However, an observer taking notes cannot be a participant in the class at the same time. Hence, an observer who is continuously writing can distract the teacher, just as a student reading a newspaper can. Note taking should therefore be kept to a minimum. A word or a short phrase is usually enough to remember a point found useful or confusing. The observer can embellish the notes later.

- *Giving the Teacher Oral and Written Feedback:* At the end of the lesson, having thanked both teacher and students for the pleasure of visiting the class, the observer should immediately go over the notes taken during the class with the teacher, praising as well as pointing out weaknesses and providing suggestions for improvement. The written report of the observation can take a variety of forms. A desirable format is one in which the observer first describes what the point of the lesson was, then describes the procedures used, and finally comments both specifically and generally on the teacher's handling of the class. This kind of form obliges the observer to be attentive to content as well as to style and enables teachers to challenge the description if they feel the point of the lesson was missed. It also obliges the observer to be a more active participant in the process. This is preferable to the type of observation form in which the observer must simply check appropriate responses like a multiple choice test. Such forms often fail to adequately characterize the unique nature of a single lesson in a single class. Whatever the form used, the teacher should be given a copy and allowed to challenge it, if desired. The teacher should also be given the option of requesting another visit (or another observer when possible) if the class has not gone well, just as the observer, when appropriate, can request a follow-up visit later in the course to see how the teacher has grown with the class and incorporated the suggestions.

(Master 1983: 499–500)

CONVERSATION WITH THE COOPERATING TEACHER AFTER OBSERVATION OF YOUR LESSON

Following an observation of one of your lessons your cooperating teacher will normally want to meet with you as soon as possible after the lesson to discuss his or her observations. Remember, though, that your cooperating teacher may have limited time to discuss your lesson and answer any questions you have, so keep your questions focused. As we saw in Chapter 4, cooperating teachers have different styles of interacting with student teachers, and you and your cooperating teacher will need to establish the kind of supervision style you both feel comfortable with. The following vignette shows the approach used by one teacher trainer:

When talking about their teaching, and particularly when talking about specific lessons they have taught, it is natural for preservice language teachers to focus on their success, or lack of it, in experimenting with the new classroom procedures and techniques they are exposed to in the methodology part of their teacher education course. In the postlesson conversation with a teacher after observing their lesson, it is important for the teacher educator to acknowledge such experimentation, praise success, and give clear and specific methodological direction when there have been complications. However, as a teacher educator, I am always impressed when a teacher starts the self-evaluation of their lesson not with talk about what they did or didn't do, but rather with comment on the learners and learning; that is, if the pitch of the lesson seemed right, if the aims were achieved, what activities they thought the learners most benefited from, what activities and what particular points of language they thought the learners had trouble with, how learning could have been better promoted. The discussion of specific procedures and techniques can, and indeed should, emerge from discussion of these broader issues.

Neil, teacher trainer, Australia

Normally the postlesson conversation will follow the following format:

1. You give your account of the lesson, focusing on what worked well, what didn't work so well, and what you might do differently next time.
2. If you have asked your cooperating teacher to focus on specific aspects of the lesson, you can both discuss the information that was collected and its implications.
3. Your cooperating teacher responds to your account of the lesson and adds his or her own observations.
4. Any problem areas of the lesson are discussed and strategies for addressing them are identified.
5. A goal is set for the next observation.

The following comments describe a cooperating teacher's postlesson conversation with a student teacher:

After the lesson I was a bit nervous to speak to my cooperating teacher because I wondered what she would say about the lesson. I felt the lesson had gone well, but you never know what another more experienced teacher will say about it. To my relief she told me that she was happy with the lesson in general and that it was delivered clearly with a specific direction that was in the lesson plan. She said that she noticed that I attempted to provide more learning opportunities for the students than when she had observed me the previous time and I agreed because the last time, I felt that I had difficulty putting myself in the shoes of learners of that age and of course little did I expect that I had overestimated their learning capacity. I guess this has something to do with my own experience when I was a student – my classmates and I understood what my English teacher was saying most of the time when I was a student. I suppose our better command of English helped. Now I told her that I intend to teach slowly whenever I introduce a new topic in order for students to build a strong foundation for the basics of the topic. I was very pleased that she noticed this change because she had written this on my observation sheet before and now she could see that I was following her suggestions. This time, however, she did suggest that I should try to liven up the lessons a bit as she said I seemed a bit tight. That is true, I guess, but I always feel a bit scared when she observes me and I think I am different and more relaxed when

I teach the class by myself. She also suggested that I try to set more of a nonthreatening learning environment for the class, and I should try to inject more humor into the lessons. I think this too is related to my nervousness of being observed by my cooperating teacher. Anyway, I will try to relax in my next observed lesson.

Tung, Singapore

Table 7.1 summarizes some of the issues teachers may want to consider for classroom observations.

1. The nature of classroom observation	• Teacher discusses nature and limitations of observations with cooperating teacher.
2. Observing your cooperating teacher's class	• Teacher learns about current course materials and strategies used, interactions with students, how learners respond and interact with the teacher and among themselves, and kinds of language they understand and produce.
3. The etiquette of supervisory observation	• Observer and teacher negotiate when to visit, the best vantage point, the best "bedside manner" to adopt, when and how to take notes, and the giving of feedback.
4. Focus of observation	• Cooperating teacher can suggest focus and / or teacher can suggest aspects of class on which to focus observation.
5. Observation procedures	• Depending on observation purpose, teacher can choose from checklists, seating charts, field notes, and / or narrative summaries.

Table 7.1 Classroom observation

SUMMARY AND CONCLUSIONS

Learning through observation plays an important part in practice teaching. In order to make the most of opportunities to observe classes taught by your cooperating teacher or other teachers, you should have a clear focus for your observations, you should establish suitable procedures to help you describe what you see, and you should remain an observer in the lesson and not an evaluator or a participant. Observing the way the cooperating teacher teaches the class before you begin your practice-teaching sessions in the class will help you anticipate some of the issues involved in teaching the class and help you better prepare for your practice teaching. You may not look forward to having your own lessons observed, but the feedback you get through this process is essential to your development as a teacher.

The number of observations you take part in will depend on the practice-teaching arrangements in your host school. However, you may also find other opportunities for observation experiences that you can initiate yourself. Other teachers in your host school may be willing to let you observe their classes from time to time to enable you to see classes containing different types of learners and being taught by other teachers. And you and your fellow student teachers can also arrange to observe each other's classes. In this way you can learn from watching others solve the problems you also have to solve during your practice-teaching classes and from observing the teaching strategies employed by other teachers.

Further reading

Bailey, K. M. (2006). *Language teacher supervision: A case-based approach*. New York: Cambridge University Press.

Gebhard, J. (1984). Models of Supervision: Choices! *TESOL Quarterly 18*, 501–13.

Oprandy, R. (1999). Exploring with a supervisor. In J. Gebhard and R. Oprandy (Eds.), *Language teacher awareness* (99–121). New York: Cambridge University Press.

Wajnryb, R. (1992). *Classroom observation tasks*. Cambridge: Cambridge University Press.

Discussion questions

1. Have you ever been observed by others while you were teaching? Who observed you and why? How did you feel about it?

2. What are some important aspects of teaching than cannot be observed?

3. What can you learn from observing another student teacher teach a class?

4. How can you best prepare for observing another teacher's class?

5. What is the difference between being observed by your students – which happens every time you teach – and being observed by your cooperating teacher?

6. How best can you deal with the tension or nervousness that the presence of an observer in your class may have?

7. Discuss the suggestions for the etiquette of observation on pages 98–99 and comment on them.

8. Several procedures for classroom observations are outlined in this chapter. Discuss the advantages and disadvantages of each procedure. Which procedure would you be most / least comfortable with? Why?

9. What do you expect your cooperating teacher to include in your preobservation and postobservation conversations?

10. Read what Tung wrote in her teaching journal about her postobservation discussion with her cooperating teacher (see pages 100–101). What do you think of the type of feedback she received?

Follow-up activities

1. Develop an observation form or instrument that could be used to observe any of the issues discussed in the section on "The Focus of the Observation" (see pages 92–94). With your cooperating teacher's permission, try it out when observing a lesson. How useful was it?

2. Read Jacob's reflections of his first observation as a teacher by his cooperating teacher (see Appendix B page 105). Do you think Jacob benefited from the visit? Do you think any other kind of feedback on the lesson would have been useful?

Appendix A: Examples of observation checklists

1. *Observation checklist used in a Mexican teacher-training program*

Observation Checklist

Benemérita Universidad Autónoma de Puebla
Facultad de Lenguas / Licenciatura en Lenguas Modernas
Práctica Docente II
Formato de Observación

Student's Name_____ School:_____

Teacher's Name_____ Level:_____

Number of students:_____ Schedule_____ Date:_____

INSTRUCTIONS: Check (√) the statement that you consider appropriate according to your criteria.

Good ☺   Needs Improvement 💡

		☺	💡	And this is why…..
	Preparation			
1.	Lesson plans according to number of students and language level.			
2.	Clear and specific objectives for lesson.			
3.	Selection of equipment and materials according to the objectives of the lesson.			
4.	Time planning according to the objectives of the lesson and the activity(s) presented.			
	Teaching			
5.	Use of teaching techniques according to the objectives (e.g. error correction, instructions, explanations, feedback and evaluation, etc.)			
6.	Use and promotion of meaningful communication			
7.	Learners actively involved in the class.			
	Class Management			
8.	Student groupings according to activities.			
9.	Use of equipment needed for the class. (e.g. neat and organized use of the board).			
10.	Use of materials needed for the class.			
11.	Pace and time management through the development of the class.			
12.	Ability to deal with occasional classroom management problems.			
	Self Management			
15.	Punctuality			
16.	Friendly and respectful to students			
17.	Use of body language, gestures and teaching space as needed			
	Language Use			
18.	According to student's level.			
19.	Tone and volume of voice as needed			

Table 7.2   Observation checklist from a Mexican teacher-training program [(Brenes-Carvajal, M. 2009: 190). Initial development of language teachers in Mexico. Dissertation for Macquarie University].

2. *Grammar correction: Observing how the teacher provides grammatical feedback on students' writing*

Method	Number of responses
Teacher writes symbols such as "sp" for spelling and "T" for tense near the errors to tell students the error types.	
Teacher explains orally students' common grammatical errors in class.	
Teacher writes down the correct form of the error after it is identified.	
Teacher writes down grammatical explanations.	
Teacher explains orally to individual students.	
Teacher rewrites the sentence(s) completely.	
Teacher only underlines or strikes off the grammatical errors.	
Other (such as Teacher writes in the margins the number of errors in each line, without telling students what the errors are or where in the line they are located).	

3. *Observing group interaction*

This checklist helps the observer determine how the group uses its time when completing a task. The observer marks at 10 to 15 second intervals to note what the group is doing at that moment.

Task	Frequency
Reading some text	_____
Discussion in target language	_____
Discussion in native language	_____
Task discussion: General group	_____
Task discussion: One / two dominate	_____
Procedural discussion	_____
Off-task discussion	_____
Dispute: Procedural (roles, etc.)	_____
Dispute: Task relevant (answer content)	_____
Group silence (confusion)	_____

4. Questioning strategies

This checklist can be used to describe the kinds of questions a teacher uses during a lesson.

Type of question asked	Frequency
Factual: Teacher asks a question that students can answer by looking for factual answers.	_____
Opinion: Teacher asks a question that students can answer by using their own knowledge.	_____
Type of response required	
Display: Student must provide teacher's required answer	_____
Referential: Student must provide answer that involves own thought and reasoning.	_____
Selection of student	
Calls student's name directly before asking question.	_____
Calls student's name directly after asking question.	_____
Calls for student volunteers after asking question.	_____
Allows students to self-select when to answer.	_____

Table 7.3 Checklist for types of questions used by teacher

Appendix B: Being observed – how did it feel?

I remember in my TESOL class during university that one part of the class was to be observed by our TESOL instructor. Since I had never been observed before as a teacher, I didn't really know what to expect. All I knew was that my TESOL instructor would come in, sit in my class, and observe how I teach, interact with the students, and maintain control of the class. I knew I wouldn't be nervous when the instructor came because I typically don't get nervous in these types of situations. I also felt very confident that my instructor would not find much negative to criticize or comment on because that week I had planned a very good lesson as we were covering a great topic. The only thing I did not like about being observed was that when the instructor came, she was late and the only seat that was left was in the very center of the classroom. So much for trying to pretend she wasn't there! During the observation, I felt very confident that what I was doing seemed very professional and well organized. Also, my students were being "extra good" that day as everyone actively participated in the lesson and listened to my instructions the first time. After the lesson was finished, I felt very confident that my instructor liked what I did and that I really was capable of being an ESL teacher. Later on that week I went to my instructor's office to talk to her about my lesson and sure enough, she enjoyed observing my lesson and thought I did a very good job and had what it takes to be an ESL teacher. The whole experience of being observed really made me reflect on how I teach and also gave me the confidence to know that I am good at what I do.

Jacob, Canada

CHAPTER 8

Creating an Effective Classroom Learning Environment

INTRODUCTION

One of the key transitions that occur when you move from being a graduate student in a TESOL program to being a student teacher on your teaching practice assignment is that as a student teacher, you now have to assume a new role and identity. You now have to assume and enact the social and cultural roles expected of a language teacher and your students need to accept you in this new role. However, your students know that you are a student teacher and that you are in the class to learn the art and skills of teaching. They do not expect you to have the same depth of knowledge, skill, and expertise of the regular class teacher. Establishing the students' trust, respect, and confidence in you will happen gradually. But you can lay the groundwork for this process by being open and frank with your students and by raising relevant issues early on in your teaching experience. For example, you might have a brief group discussion activity in which students debate questions such as:

- What are some of the qualities you like to see in an English teacher?
- How do you think the teacher can best help you achieve your goals in this class?
- What are you most worried about with your student teacher taking over your usual teacher's class?
- What are you most excited about with your student teacher taking over your usual teacher's class?
- What are some of the difficulties your student teacher will face in teaching your class?
- How can you help him or her overcome these difficulties?
- What would you like your student teacher to focus on most while teaching you?

Activities of this kind can help you establish a sense of your professional identity within the social context of the classroom and to respect and understand the identities of your students so that together you can create a community of learners that maximizes the learning potential of the classroom. Here a supervisor describes some of the qualities she expects in a student teacher:

My expectations of student teaching are high. I expect the candidates that I work with to have carefully planned their lessons with knowledge of their learners, the content area they are working with, and the types of English language skills they are building in their learners. When I observe a lesson, careful planning is evident. I also expect nervousness, some false starts, and some moments that truly cause the candidates to rethink their decisions . . . cognitive dissonance leads to deeper understanding.

Margo, teaching practice supervisor, United States

CREATING THE RIGHT CLASSROOM CLIMATE

Classroom climate refers to the "affective" side of the classroom, that is, the feelings the students have toward the lesson, to the teacher and other students, and the learning atmosphere of the classroom. As a teacher you will need to find ways of helping your students develop a positive view of you and of their class so that they have positive expectations for you and your lessons. Senior, citing Ormrod, suggests that in order to create an effective classroom climate teachers need to do the following:

- communicate acceptance or respect for and caring about students as human beings;
- establish a businesslike, yet nonthreatening atmosphere;
- communicate appropriate messages about school subject matter;
- give students some sense of control with regard to classroom activities; and
- create a sense of community among the students.

(Senior 2006: 81, citing Ormrod 2000: 601)

Senior (2006) suggests a number of ways in which a positive classroom climate can be created, such as by using humor to create an informal class atmosphere, by building rapport with the students through discussing common interests and concerns, and by teachers showing that they are friendly and approachable and are there to help their students:

I work very hard at trying to make myself a person who can be interrupted, or who makes you feel you won't be regarded as a prat for asking a question. I think I try to create an atmosphere in the classroom where it's okay to ask questions, it's okay to catch the teacher's eye – not stick your hand right up, but wave a finger to indicate "what" or "Can you say that again, please?"

(teacher cited by Senior 2006: 90)

Other factors Senior discusses include creating a safe learning environment for students where they are not afraid to take risks or make mistakes, establishing professional credibility and a sense of purpose in lessons, as well as establishing appropriate norms of classroom behavior. The content of a lesson can also have an influence on classroom climate. If the lesson is too difficult, students may become bored and distracted. If the lesson is too easy on the other hand, students may feel insufficiently challenged. In both situations, the results can be an unmotivated class. The following comment illustrates how a student teacher is trying to create an effective classroom climate:

Last term, as a part of my 30 hours of observation, I saw three different teachers handle their classes in different ways. Whereas one of them conducted the class activities by a combination of group, pair, or individual activities, the other two seemed more comfortable with either individual or with pair work. In each class, however, I sensed a really good feeling about the class among the students. Now as a student teacher myself, I realize that I too feel comfortable with individual or pair work and I think it helps the students better connect with each other as a class too. My mentor teacher gives me a lesson plan to teach every week. As almost everything she asks me to do is based on a textbook and has to do with doing either question-and-answer exercises or some other related exercise, I find it convenient to make the students work individually or as pairs. Moreover, I find that the classrooms are not big enough to make the students move about and divide them into groups. Apart from this, at this moment, I feel I am still new to the class and fear I may not be able to handle the class if something goes wrong, though I sense that I have got the students on my side. However, I have noticed that the lack of any group activities in my class has not really affected the smooth flow in the classroom activities. To make up for a lack of group activities, I sometimes try to involve the whole class in class discussions and judging by their participation, the students seem to enjoy them.

Vidya, Canada

ARRANGING THE CLASS TO PROMOTE EFFECTIVE LEARNING

Whereas lesson plans represent a map of the territory you want to cover in a lesson and the route you want to take to get you there, a successful lesson also depends on the kinds of interaction you provide for during the lesson. This will include opportunities for interactions between you and the class as well as interactions among the students themselves. There are four possible ways of arranging a class, and each offers different learning potentials: whole-class teaching, individual work, pair work, and group work.

WHOLE-CLASS TEACHING

This mode of teaching involves you teaching all the students together, and the extent to which you arrange your lesson in this way will depend on the type of lesson you are teaching and the particular stage of the lesson. A lesson may begin with a whole-class activity, and then move to pair, group, or individual work. Whole-class teacher-fronted teaching can serve to focus students' attention quickly on a learning task. When carefully carried out, it can lead to the achievement of lesson objectives quickly and effectively, since time management is maximally under the teacher's control. Additionally, although whole-class teaching has often been criticized for reflecting a teacher-dominated teaching style, if teaching is viewed as a jointly constructed activity in which the teacher mediates, assists, and "scaffolds" learning tasks for students, we can identify a more positive role for whole-class teaching. Scaffolding means providing the temporary support students need as they develop their language skills, support that can gradually be reduced as their language learning progresses. When used appropriately the scaffolding and support provided by whole-class teaching can serve to enrich the learning opportunities provided in the lesson. For example, Verplaetse analyzed teacher-fronted discussions in a high-school science class which:

> . . . encouraged high levels of interaction from both native and non-native English speaking students. His initiation strategies of *wondering out loud, questioning*, and *drafting student participation*, feedback strategies of *acceptance and / or echo of student comments*, and *non-judgmental accepting paraphrasing strategies* all worked to create multiple opportunities for students to be full participants in the reconstruction of knowledge in the classroom. (Verplaetse, cited in Johnson 2009: 72)

While you are planning your teaching you will need to consider when whole-class teaching is appropriate and when you will make the transition to other types of learning in order to promote student-to-student interaction and to allow students to work on tasks at their own pace.

When I first observed my cooperating teacher in class I noticed she used a lot of activities that were teacher fronted in that she expected choral answers and also individual answers from the class. The students all seemed comfortable with this and so I decided to do the same when I took over her class. Another reason I did whole-group activities with the class was because I was a bit scared of losing control of the class as I had not established any real rapport with them and I did not want to look like I was not a teacher in control. My teacher never used group work while I was a student and so I am not always comfortable doing it even if it worked in my microteaching lessons with my peers. When I used whole-group activities the students responded well and I felt good after the class, not to mention that my cooperating teacher was pleased with the outcome too.

Kim, Korea

INDIVIDUAL WORK

There will also be points in a lesson where students will best work individually, such as when they are reading or listening to a text or completing exercises in a textbook or workbook. Individual work allows students to work at their own pace and to work on activities suited to their proficiency level or interests, and it allows you to provide individual support or assistance to learners. "In terms of effective use of time, individual work also allows students to be on-task quickly, especially if the teacher's instructions are clear and precise. Individual work often presents fewer discipline problems since social interaction is temporarily suspended. It also allows for personal reflection and for individual students to set targets for their own learning" (Anthony Seow, personal communication).

In planning individual work you will need to consider how well students understand what is expected of them and whether the task provides adequate challenge, support, and motivation to sustain their interest. Here a student teacher describes how he tries to achieve a task focus in lessons:

I feel that I am at my best when I let my students work by themselves at their computers during my writing classes because they do not need me lecturing them about how to write all the time. What is most important is that they get as much experience as possible writing.

So a writing class to me is just that: My students will be writing. I usually move around the room and assist when I am asked although I usually initiate this process with students whom I know are not strong writers because this saves me time in the long run when I have to mark their papers. In fact, I do the same in my reading classes because, again, they must get as much experience reading as possible and I fear that not many of them read a lot of English texts or even newspapers outside my classes. Of course, I must lay the law down sometimes when the students do not focus on their writing or reading and this is my most difficult moment as I am not experienced in how to keep them focused and only working individually.

John, United Kingdom

PAIR WORK

Pair work provides opportunities for sustained interaction and has long been advocated as a key means of promoting both linguistic and communicative competence. Grouping students in pairs can take into consideration ability level, language and cultural background, and other factors that will facilitate a positive approach to learning, although students who are not familiar with this learning arrangement may need careful orientation and preparation for pair-work activities.

GROUP WORK

Group-based learning is widely used in all forms of teaching and significantly changes the interactional dynamics of the classroom. In language classes it can help promote self-esteem, it increases student talking time, and it can also increase student motivation by providing a risk-free environment for language practice. However, setting up group activities poses a number of challenges. These include:

- *Time*: The logistics of putting students into groups can be time consuming.
- *Cliques*: Students often seat themselves in cliques by age, language group, friendship, and so on.
- *Limited language proficiency*: Low-level students may have difficulty following instructions and be intimidated if working in a group with stronger students, leading them to remain silent.
- *Control*: Some teachers may feel that they are no longer in control of the class.

Successful implementation of group work involves the following considerations:

- *Group size:* Groups of four are best for ease of classroom management, especially for teacher learners.
- *Group formation:* You or your cooperating teacher should select group members initially to achieve more of a heterogeneous mix that promotes peer tutoring and keeps the members focused on the task at hand.
- *Mixed proficiency levels:* One way is to mix the groups with learners of different proficiency levels, as they can help each other with different tasks. Higher-proficiency students can be given more challenging tasks, such as acting as the group reporter or by taking notes about the group's discussion.
- *Noise levels:* One student in each group can be appointed as a noise monitor to keep the noise at acceptable levels.

- *Nonparticipants:* Students who are unfamiliar with group work may not value group-based learning work. In this case gentle persuasion may be needed.
- *Unequal completion times:* Have a back-up plan (e.g., an additional task to complete) to limit the amount of disruption from groups who may finish early.
- *Monitoring group performance:* Silver (2008) suggests that teachers:
   - Pause regularly to visually survey the class as a whole, each group, and individual students.
   - Keep visits to each group short so you can continuously observe all in class.
   - Give students feedback to note when they are on track as well as off track.
   - When students seem to be going in the wrong direction, look and listen to see what they are doing before jumping in.
   - When you do intervene, comments should be intended to guide students back to the point at which they could do the work themselves.

In the following comments, student teachers describe decisions they made concerning grouping:

On Thursday I had a vocabulary lesson, partly because it was scheduled in the scheme of work, but also because I believed it would be beneficial for the students to be exposed to the use of the thesaurus and learn that there are many more words they can learn to use to replace the simple vocabulary that they tend to use every time they write. The lesson's objective was for students to be able to distinguish emotive words from their supposed "neutral" counterparts, for example, consume your food as opposed to wolf down your food. Students also had to demonstrate the ability to construct sentences with the emotive words they found on the online thesaurus. I broke the students up into groups of four and each group member had a specific role to play in the allotted time for this activity. I gave each group a thesaurus and the worksheet and let them at it. The groups had great fun and found it easier to tell apart that "wolf" is definitely more emotive compared to "consume" when they saw the word "wolf" listed on the thesaurus. So not only did the students appear more interested and engaged, they also asked several questions which proved that their attention was caught and their genuine interest to learn about the subject was present. After the lesson my cooperating teacher noted that I probably should have planned for time to go through at least some of the sentences to see that they are really getting the concept right and are able to do sentence construction with the words they pick up. However, she noted that they have definitely learned how to use a thesaurus and believed that this would come in useful for them in her future classes.

Zhez Zu, Singapore

Another lesson that I conducted this week was one that sought to help students generate more extended similes in their writing. I had suspected that, although most students knew what a simile was, most did not venture beyond the usual fixed "dull as dishwater" kind of similes. At the beginning of the lesson, I sought to establish what students knew about similes. And I was proven right. In order to stimulate students to generate their own interesting similes, I first distributed a worksheet that had unconventional similes, but used in a somewhat awkward manner. The students were required to work in pairs to replace the awkward similes with their own. In the second part of the lesson in order to engage the students, I took the bold step of proclaiming that day "Insult Student Teacher Day," a day where students could insult me all they wanted, subject to certain guidelines to ensure decency. Hence, after evaluating some similes that students had generated in pairs on their worksheets, and praising the more creative and adventurous ones, they were instructed to write a passage in their groups of four, describing and insulting the student teacher. I must say that when I submitted the lesson plan to my cooperating teacher before the lesson, she had serious doubts about the lesson but nevertheless let me go ahead with it. She agreed at the end that it turned out to be a really enjoyable lesson, both for the students and myself. On top of this, in terms of instructional value, I felt that the lesson had also succeeded; some of the similes generated were the most creative and sardonic I had ever come across. This has strengthened my resolve that once we as teachers are able to engage students in pair work and groups, learning will be much enhanced.

Carl, Hong Kong

When using a particular grouping arrangement, such as pair work or group work, it is important to make the purpose of the grouping arrangement clear to the students. Having students work in pairs or groups does not serve any useful purpose if the teacher continues to teach to the whole class despite the fact that students are in pairs or groups.

MANAGING YOUR USE OF CLASS TIME

Your lessons may last from 40 to 50 minutes, but not all of that time is available for teaching and learning, since you will often have procedural issues to attend to, such as returning assignments, discussing an activity you have prepared and how it is to be carried out, and so on. Some lessons have a good sense of pace and movement and maintain their momentum – an important part of retaining students' interest and motivation in the lesson. Other lessons progress too slowly. Richards and Lockhart cite a number of strategies teachers can use to maintain the pace of a lesson:

- Avoiding needless or over-lengthy explanations and instructions, and letting students get on with the job of learning
- Using a variety of activities within a lesson, rather than spending the whole lesson on one activity
- Avoiding predictable and repetitive activities, where possible
- Selecting activities of the right level of difficulty
- Setting a goal and time for activities: activities that have no obvious goal or conclusion or in which no time frame is set tend to have little momentum
- Monitoring students' performance on activities so that they have had sufficient time to complete them but not too much time

(Richards and Lockhart 1994: 123)

As a novice student teacher, one of the major problems I had (and to a certain extent still have) is with time management. I found it difficult to know how much time to give to a particular activity. I also noticed that I find it difficult to make appropriate transitions from one part to another. With practice, I have been getting a little bit better than before. Now in my lesson plan, I give special importance to these two areas. Somehow putting every detail in black and white in the form of a lesson plan has helped me focus better on these issues. I do agree with the fact that students get restless when they are bored and it is up to the teacher to keep them occupied in a creative and fruitful manner.

Vidya, Canada

A helpful way of thinking about the use of time in a lesson is through thinking of classroom time as consisting of four different categories:

1. *Allocated time* is the time allotted for teaching a class in the timetable, such as the typical 40- or 50-minute class period.

2. *Instructional time* is the time actually available for teaching after you have completed noninstructional activities such as taking attendance, returning homework, and so on. Perhaps in a 40-minute class period, 30 minutes of instructional time might be available.

3. *Engaged time* is that portion of time in which the students are actively involved in learning activities (also known as *time on task*). Perhaps it took a while for students to start assigned activities since they spent some time chatting, organizing their desk or computer, and so on. Perhaps 25 minutes of the instructional time was actually engaged time.

4. *Academic learning time* is the amount of time during which students are actively engaged and participating in an activity and learning successfully from it. If an activity was too difficult or not well set up, students may spend some time on ineffective learning routines and strategies before they finally find a successful way of completing the activity.

In observing your cooperating teacher's class and in reviewing your own lesson it will be useful to find out what strategies are effective in providing for the maximum amount of academic learning time during a lesson. Timing is an issue described by a student teacher as follows:

The second part of the lesson was a follow-up activity on a previous lesson dealing with the present continuous tense. Since the previous lesson sought only to touch on a basic level of understanding of the tense, this lesson aimed to build upon the previously acquired foundation of the students, helping them to create text using the present continuous tense in a well-defined context. The activity required students to describe the ongoing activities in a picture. As expected, without realizing it, students made extensive use of the present continuous tense in describing the activities in progress, as shown in the picture. This activity was also conducted in the form of a game where different groups competed against one another to see which group could come up with the most sentences to describe the picture. The real intent of the activity was only made known at the end, where students realized that they had actually made use of the target structure unconsciously. One regret I had for the lesson was perhaps the fact that I was overly ambitious and tried to cover too much ground within thirty-five minutes. As a result, the second part of the lesson, involving the present continuous tense, was at times a little rushed and I think the students also felt rushed. Perhaps what I should have done was to begin the lesson with the game of picture description, and following that, instruct students to individually create a story each, based on what each has observed in the picture. I think it is easier to put the plan on paper than carry it out because I still do not have an appropriate grasp of the time element with my lessons. My cooperating teacher noted the same and told me that this will come with experience in the classroom. She also mentioned that I should not be afraid to change my lesson plan during the class if I see it is too time consuming or if it is going too fast.

Günter, Germany

MAINTAINING APPROPRIATE CLASSROOM BEHAVIOR

In order to teach a successful lesson there needs to be an atmosphere of respect and trust between teachers and students and a shared understanding of appropriate forms of classroom behavior. The class needs to develop a sense of community, of people working together cooperatively to achieve shared goals. This will not happen if students do not take the class seriously, if some students are allowed to disrupt the class with inappropriate talk or behavior, to use their mobile phones, or send text messages during lessons, if students choose when it suits them to come to class, to start work on an assignment, and so on. A challenge for you as a student teacher is to establish norms for appropriate classroom behavior as soon as you start your teaching practice so that the students develop a sense of responsible and cooperative behavior during lessons. Your cooperating teacher will hopefully have done much of the groundwork for you but you cannot assume that the norms of conduct he or she has established will also work for you, since once you assume responsibility for the class a different set of factors comes into effect, depending on the relations you establish with your students and how you and the students come to regard each other. Rather than adopting the role of discipline master, your challenge will be to work with your students to establish an acceptable set of class rules that will allow for productive teaching and learning. This can be done in several ways. For example:

- You can ask the students to discuss what they feel appropriate rules for classroom behavior should be.
- You can propose different ways of dealing with classroom issues and ask students to discuss them.

Of course the rules you establish should apply both to you and the students, if you expect them to take you seriously. In one class the teacher and students agreed that the door of the classroom would be locked once the lesson started. A few days later the teacher arrived late for class and found that the students had locked the classroom door! Dörnyei (2001: 46) gives the following example of a set of class rules.

For the students:
- Always write your homework.
- Once a term you can "pass," i.e., say that you have not prepared.
- In small group work only the L2 can be used.
- If you miss a class, make up for it and ask for the homework.

For the teacher
- The class should finish on time.
- Homework and tests should be marked within a week.
- Always give advance notice of a test.

For everybody
- Let's not be late for class.
- Let's try and listen to each other.
- Let's help each other.
- Let's respect each other's ideas and values.

- It's OK to make mistakes; they are learning points.
- Let's not make fun of each other's weaknesses.
- We must avoid hurting each other, verbally or physically.

Dörnyei (2001: 46)

In the following comments a student teacher describes how an activity helped to minimize classroom management issues:

For the informal-letter-writing lesson, I got the students to read an article about a hen in trouble writing to an "Animal Agony" column in a magazine. I chose this article because I wanted the students to get started on writing and expressing a problem because this will be what they will do for the formal letter writing about their neighborhood. For the activity leading to informal writing, the students enjoyed it very much. They were amused by some of the problems that the animals faced and some of them actually identified with the notion of freedom. This made writing more enjoyable for the students and they seemed to like the fact that they took on a different persona from the usual human ones. They had fun making up their own address and expanding on the existing problems stated on their slips of paper and they enjoyed putting in their own personal feelings to it. So the lesson went very well indeed. The students enjoyed the activity. This activity did not pose any problem for class management because it was an individual activity and each person had a different assignment. As my cooperating teacher told me, if we keep the students suitably motivated and busy, we will not have any disruption and it is usually when they are bored that they become restless. She is correct.

Carl, Malaysia

CREATING A CULTURALLY SENSITIVE CLASSROOM

Second language classrooms by their nature contain students with diverse cultural and educational backgrounds. Teaching students with different cultural backgrounds requires particular levels of sensitivity and awareness. Some of the characteristics of what can be called a culturally responsive classroom include the following:

Legitimizing students' cultures and experiences. This can be achieved by inviting students to share information about their cultures and traditions and by showing a genuine interest in finding out more about them.

Including significant and comprehensive information about different cultures and their contributions in lessons. This may involve adapting or supplementing topics from the textbook or curriculum to include information from the learners' cultures.

Using the cultural legacies, traits, and orientations of diverse students as filters through which they learn academic knowledge. This may involve adapting teaching methods to accommodate the preferred learning styles of the students you teach. (Gay 2006, cited in Taylor and Sobel 2008: 2)

Although the class that I practice teach is a culturally diverse class, so far I have not faced any problems arising out of this diversity. In fact, I have found that a class can be made interesting because of the diverse backgrounds and different ranges of experience. Recently, we had a class discussion about different education systems around the world and the class got to learn a lot because of students coming from different countries. I feel if the teacher demonstrates a proper respect for different cultures, the students will follow the lead. So all in all it is the responsibility of a teacher to create and maintain a harmonious learning atmosphere.

Vidya, Canada

In culturally sensitive classrooms the goal is to shape the learning environment in such a way that it can accommodate a wide range of native languages, cultures, racial-ethnic backgrounds, religions, learning styles, and abilities in their classroom. Dörnyei offers a number of ways in which this can be accomplished, and activities like the ones below can also focus on the cultures represented in your classroom:

- Familiarize learners with interesting / relevant aspects of the students' cultures.
- Develop learners' cross-cultural awareness systematically by focusing on cross-cultural similarities (and not just differences) and by using analogies to make the strange familiar.
- Collect common stereotypes and prejudices about the second language speakers and discuss how valid these are.
- Share your own positive cross-cultural experiences in class.
- Collect quotations and statements by well-known public figures about the significance of language learning and share these with your students.
- Ask students to bring various cultural products to class (e.g., magazines, music, TV recordings, videos).
- Supplement the coursebook with authentic materials.
- Encourage learners to share interesting information about their cultures and to prepare a presentation.
- Arrange meetings with speakers from different cultures and invite some interesting guests to class.
- Organize class trips to different culturally distinct neighborhoods.

(adapted from Dörnyei 2001: 55)

Cultural sensitivity is an issue written about by a student teacher as follows:

When I was placed in the campus-based language school for my teaching practice I did not know what kind of students to expect nor did I know where they would be from. I was surprised the first day that the class I was assigned to observe was like a mini-United Nations with so many students from all over the world. When I observed my cooperating teacher teach the class I noticed that he spent a lot of time explaining the cultural aspects of life in the United States and that some of the culture may be strange for the students. When I took over teaching of that class I was careful to try not to offend anyone with the way I corrected mistakes so the students would not lose any face and also with the lessons that were covered in the textbook. I made sure to ask as many students as possible in this speaking class to explain what would be the case of X (a topic from the textbook) in their country. This was a real challenge because we can offend people from different cultures in our classes without even knowing it.

Frank, United States

Table 8.1 summarizes how teachers can create an effective classroom environment.

1. Create the right classroom climate.	• Teacher examines the feelings the students have toward the lesson, the teacher and other students, and the learning atmosphere of the classroom.
2. Arrange the class to promote effective learning.	• Teacher considers four possible ways of arranging a class, and each offers different learning potentials: Whole-class teaching, individual work, group work, and pair work.
3. Manage your use of class time.	• Teacher considers different strategies that maintain a good sense of pace, movement, and momentum.
4. Maintain appropriate classroom behavior.	• Teacher needs to ensure that the class develops a sense of community, and of people working together cooperatively to achieve shared goals.
5. Create a culturally sensitive classroom.	• Teacher develops cultural sensitivity and awareness by legitimizing students' cultures and experiences.

Table 8.1 Creating an effective classroom environment

SUMMARY AND CONCLUSIONS

Teaching a successful language lesson involves not only knowing what you plan to teach and how to teach it, but also creating the right kind of classroom environment for a successful lesson. An excellent lesson plan can fall flat if the teacher has not succeeded in creating the right classroom learning environment. How teachers do so, however, is often a question of the teacher's personal teaching style, the kind of students in the class, and the nature of the lesson itself. Your students need to have a positive expectation for the lesson and for you as the teacher, as well as a willingness to work cooperatively with other students to create a sense of community with shared goals and concerns. These are aspects of the classroom climate, which depends upon your rapport with your students, the students' relationship with each other, and your ability to manage the class effectively.

Different options for teaching, such as whole-class, group-based, and individual work, present different opportunities for teaching and need to be used according to their appropriateness for different kinds of learning tasks. Anticipating the kinds of classroom arrangements you will need for a lesson, the roles and expectations you have planned for students during the lesson, as well as issues raised by the content of the lesson, can help you deliver a lesson that both you and your students feel creates a positive environment for learning. ESL classrooms are culturally diverse classrooms and acknowledging the cultural richness of your students' backgrounds can provide important support for teaching.

Further reading

Farrell, T. S. C. (Ed.). (2008e). *Classroom management*. Alexandria, VA: TESOL Publications.

Hadfield, J. (1992). *Classroom dynamics*. Oxford: Oxford University Press.

Tudor, I. (2001). *The dynamics of the language classroom*. Cambridge: Cambridge University Press.

Wright, A. (2005). *Classroom management in language education*. Basingstoke: Palgrave.

Discussion questions

1. What are some ways in which you can establish a positive rapport with students in your practice-teaching class?

2. What are some circumstances in which whole-class teaching is likely to be more effective than other classroom arrangements?

3. How do you think you can best monitor students' performance during group work?

4. Students sometimes feel that group activities are not real teaching activities. How can you provide a suitable orientation for your learners to group-based learning?

5. What are some ways in which you can get the maximum amount of academic learning time out of a lesson? Is use of time the most important criterion for judging the success of a lesson?

6. Have you observed any discipline or behavior problems in your cooperating teacher's class? How did he or she deal with them?

7. What are some issues that might arise in a culturally diverse classroom? How can you respond to them?

8. Read Tiffany's journal entry for one of her classes in the Appendix and discuss what you would do if you encountered a situation like this.

Follow-up activities

1. Interview an experienced teacher and find out what kinds of classroom management problems the teacher sometimes encounters. How does he or she deal with them?

2. Examine a unit from a textbook and discuss different ways of using whole-class teaching, group work, pair work, and individual work when teaching the unit.

3. Observe your cooperating teacher's class or another teacher's class and note how the teacher does the following:

O uses humor
O establishes rapport with students
O keeps students on task
O maintains appropriate classroom behavior
O acknowledges the students' cultural or linguistic backgrounds

Appendix: A student teacher's account of a difficult lesson

Oh, my goodness, what a class. I spent a lot of time planning for this class but as with the prewriting lesson last week, I was really pressed for time. I feel though it was not my fault because the class had a Math test before my lesson and the students were all really in a bad mood because I heard that the test was very difficult and that they really do not like their Math teacher because he apparently keeps them back after school if they do not do well on their tests. Now because this Math teacher did not let them out on time to come to my English class, I only had 20 minutes left to go through the lesson with them. I felt rushed all throughout and it did not help either that I was not feeling well that day. Anyway I went through the questions for peer conferencing quickly and I realized that I should not have done so as some students did not understand what I wanted them to do with some of the questions.

But I was pressurized by my cooperating teacher to ensure that their essays are submitted by Monday, which means to say I must complete the peer conference by this lesson. The students, however, were still caught up in trying to edit their friends' grammar mistakes and they were meandering around the room and some of them were making too much noise and talking about their previous Math test and not doing what I had asked them to do. I had to then shout at the class to make them look through their friends' ideas and provide suggestions to them but it never really happened during the lesson. I really wished that I had time to go through a sample paragraph and work out the improvements together with the students. In this way, the students would be able to better understand how to improve their friends' drafts. I know I never really had control over this class or this particular lesson and I did not know what to do because I was left on my own to teach and the cooperating teacher trusted me to get the material covered. I do not know what I should tell her because I do not want to look bad.

Tiffany, United States

CHAPTER 9

Developing Learner-Centered Teaching

INTRODUCTION

When you begin your practice-teaching experience you will naturally be concerned with how well your students respond to you as a teacher and to your lessons. You will want to make a good impression on your students and to communicate the sense that you know what you are doing and that your lessons have been carefully planned. You will doubtless be somewhat critical of your own performance, evaluating your lessons on the basis of how successful they were in realizing your goals as well as how well they reflected the principles you have studied in your teacher education course.

But teaching is much more than a performance by the teacher. Above all, a successful lesson makes the learners – rather than the teacher – the focus of the lesson. Was the lesson content something students could relate to and that was relevant to their needs? Were the activities students took part in during the lesson sufficiently challenging to engage them but not so challenging that they became frustrated and lost interest? Were the students motivated during the lesson? Did the lesson provide opportunities for active participation by all the students in the class or was it dominated by one or two students who monopolized questions and discussion? In this chapter we will explore how you can move from a teacher-centered approach to teaching to a learner-centered one, that is, one in which students' needs, interests, and preferences take priority in teaching.

DEVELOPING THE ABILITY TO MAKE YOUR LEARNERS THE FOCUS OF YOUR TEACHING

An important skill in teaching is the ability to make your learners the focus of your teaching. This involves understanding your learners' needs and goals, communicating trust and respect for them, acknowledging diversity of needs and learning styles, giving feedback on their learning in ways that help develop their confidence and self-esteem and minimize loss of face, and using strategies that help develop an atmosphere of collaboration and mutual support among learners (Dörnyei 2001; Lamb 2003). In some lessons, the focus is more on teacher performance than learner engagement, as is reflected in the following aspects of the lesson:

- the amount of talking the teacher does during the lesson
- the extent to which input from learners directs the shape and direction of the lesson
- the extent to which the teacher's primary preoccupation during the lesson is with such things as classroom management, control, and order
- the way the teacher presents information and explains tasks
- the extent to which the lesson reflects the teacher's lesson plan

Some teachers, however, achieve a more learner-focused approach to teaching, as is reflected in features such as these:

- the degree of engagement learners have with the lesson
- the quantity of student participation and interaction that occurs
- the learning outcomes the lesson produces
- the ability to present subject matter from a learner's perspective
- how well the lesson addresses learners' needs
- how the teacher reshapes the lesson based on learner feedback
- how the teacher responds to learners' difficulties

Experienced teachers are often better able than novice teachers to create learner-centered teaching because they are familiar with typical student behaviors, they use their knowledge of learners to make predictions about what might happen in the classroom, they build their lessons around students' difficulties, and they are able to maintain active student involvement in lessons (Lynch 2001). They recognize that language learning is not necessarily a direct consequence of good teaching but depends on understanding the different ways in which learners learn, the role of individual learning styles, motivations, backgrounds, and purposes in learning, and the understanding that teaching needs to be adapted to both their students' individual as well as their collective needs (Benson 2005; Tarone and Yule 1989). Observing how your cooperating teacher achieves these characteristics in his or her lessons will be an important focus of your classroom observations. The following comments describe a supervisor's emphasis on learner-centeredness in teaching:

I usually tell my student teachers that the focal point of their teaching should always be their students. The focus should not be on how they teach the lesson, but on how they can help their students learn optimally from their lesson. The first thing they need to do is to create a learning-friendly classroom atmosphere, which includes drawing the students' attention to the goal and purpose of the lesson and getting students interested and motivated in the lesson by connecting it to their past learning experiences and by helping them see the relevance of the lesson for their future learning. Once the students are sufficiently motivated, they will become more willing to participate more actively in the lesson.

Of course, the activities that follow should be equally motivating from both a cognitive and affective point of view. That is to say that the tasks should be sufficiently challenging from a cognitive point of view so that the students know that if they put in enough effort they will succeed in completing the tasks. The tasks should also be sufficiently motivating so that the students are willing to put in extra effort and sustain their interest in doing the tasks. Another thing I tell my student teachers is that learning should be fun and if students associate learning with fun things, they will enjoy learning at school.

Willy, practicum supervisor, Singapore

Benson (in press) argues that learner-centered teaching is more effective than other modes of teaching for several reasons:

- It is sensitive to individual needs and preferences.
- It encourages construction of knowledge and meaning.
- It draws on and integrates language learning with students' life experiences.
- It generates more student participation and target language output.
- It encourages authentic communication.
- It breaks down barriers between in-class and out-of-class learning.
- It opens up spaces for discussion of motivations, learning preferences, and styles.
- It encourages students to take more personal responsibility for their learning.
- It challenges the view that learning is equivalent to being taught.

We will now explore several ways in which learners can become the focus of your teaching.

UNDERSTANDING YOUR LEARNERS' NEEDS AND GOALS

ESOL classes consist of many different kinds of learners, some with similar needs and goals, and some with a great diversity of needs. The students in your practice-teaching class may be fairly homogeneous in nature, with students of a similar age, educational background, and goals – such as a class of students preparing for college or university study. Conversely you might find yourself teaching a class of a very different kind, with students of different ages, interests, nationalities, cultural and educational backgrounds, and needs. You may have already developed a comprehensive profile of your students' needs. This may include the following kinds of information:

- reasons they are taking the English course
- occupations
- current learning goals
- longer-term goals
- attitudes toward learning English
- interests
- cultural backgrounds
- current proficiency level
- out-of-class use of English
- skills needed
- main language difficulties

An example of part of a class profile is given in Appendix A. Where this sort of information is not available, you can use a variety of means to get an understanding of your learners' needs and goals, including conversations with your students, classroom activities in which students discuss issues related to needs and goals, questionnaires, journal writing, and other forms of writing. Here is an example of what a student teacher learned from a learner profile:

When I did a learner profile of my students I was interested in finding out about their family backgrounds, their language backgrounds, their motivational cues, their learning preferences, their personal interests, and their overall perspective in learning English. When I put all these together I learned a lot about my students before I stood in front of them and the information helped me to better prepare my lessons. For example, for one student (Jin Hai) I discovered that he is from a working-class family and they all speak Mandarin Chinese at home together. In fact, the only time he speaks English is in this English class. He is not fully motivated to study English and is only here because his parents made him attend. He likes activities that keep him active, like games, in lessons. On the other hand, my learner profile of Lai Shan is different. She is from a middle-class family and although they speak Mandarin Chinese at home like Jin Hai, her siblings try to speak English to each other. She normally pays attention in class and appreciates visual stimulus. If she is bored, she will stare at the whiteboard. She likes pair work and group work.

Khoo Wee, Singapore

UNDERSTANDING YOUR STUDENTS' CLASSROOM PARTICIPATION STYLES

Any language class will contain a mix of students with different dispositions toward learning. For example, Good and Power (1976) identify six different types of students, each of which favor a different style of classroom interaction and participation:

1. *Task-oriented students*: They are generally highly competent and successful in completing tasks. They enjoy learning, are active learners, aim for high levels of performance, are cooperative, and create few discipline problems.

2. *Social students*: They place a high value on personal interaction, and although competent in accomplishing tasks, tend to place a higher value on socializing. They enjoy working with others, may be talkative and outgoing, and do not hesitate to ask for assistance from the teacher or others when needed.

3. *Dependent students*: These students need constant support and guidance to complete tasks. They tend not to favor group work and often depend on the teacher or other students to tell them if their learning has been successful.

4. *Phantom students*: These students do not draw attention to themselves although they generally work steadily on tasks. They rarely initiate conversation or ask for help. Because they do not disrupt the class or other students, the teacher may not know them well.

5. *Isolated students:* They set themselves apart from others and withdraw from classroom interactions. They may avoid learning by turning away from activities such as peer or group work. They are reluctant to share their work with others.

6. *Alienated students*: They react against teaching and learning and may be hostile and aggressive. They create discipline problems and make it difficult for those around them to work. They require close supervision and their learning problems may be related to personal problems.

Hopefully the class you have been assigned for your teaching practice will contain a majority of students who have a positive attitude toward learning. Your cooperating teacher will also have developed an awareness of the kinds of learners who make up the class and will be able to advise you how to interact with students who may pose difficulties. Here are some problems student teachers encountered during teaching practice, and how they developed successful ways of responding to them:

The back-row distracter
I had a student who always sits at the back and tries to distract other students. I decided to talk to him after class to discuss the problem. And I moved him closer to the front of the class for the rest of the course.

Tersesa, Singapore

The nonparticipant
I had one or two students who did not want to participate in activities. I decided to ask the class to draw up some rules for classroom behavior and for responding to students who preferred to sleep during class rather than participate.

Richard, Canada

The overexuberant student
I have a student who always shouts out answers without waiting for others to participate and who generally tries to dominate the class. I tried to deal with her in a fun way, by making a gentle joke to remind her that others also needed to practice their English in class.

Simone, Hong Kong

UNDERSTANDING YOUR STUDENTS' COGNITIVE STYLES

Your class will also represent students who approach language learning in different ways and whose educational background and language-learning experience has established a particular set of beliefs and preferences about how best to learn a language. This may be reflected in different ways. For example:

- preferences for particular kinds of classroom activities
- preferences for particular styles of teaching
- preferences for particular classroom arrangements
- preferences for studying particular aspects of language
- preferences for a particular mode of learning

These are referred to as differences in cognitive style (also known as learning style). So whereas some students enjoy games and role plays, others may feel that such activities do not have a real teaching goal. Some students may like the teacher to correct any mistakes in their pronunciation, while others may feel pronunciation is less important than fluency. Some students may feel more comfortable when the teacher is engaging in whole-class teaching, while others may prefer group-based learning. And some students may prefer learning from technology and media-based resources to learning from books and other print-based materials. So, as a teacher, it is important to recognize that you have convictions about the best teaching principles, techniques, and learning approaches, and so do your students.

The following cognitive styles have often been referred to in discussing learning-style preferences, and you may begin to recognize these in some of your learners. They may also lead to different styles of classroom participation:

- *Visual learners*: These learners respond to new information in a visual fashion and prefer visual, pictorial, and graphic representations of experience. They benefit most from reading and learn well by seeing words in books, workbooks, and on the board. They can often learn on their own with a book, and they take notes of lectures to remember the new information.
- *Auditory learners*: These learners learn best from oral explanation and from hearing words spoken. They benefit from listening to recordings, teaching other students, and by conversing with their classmates and teachers.
- *Kinesthetic learners*: Learners of this type learn best when they are physically involved in the experience. They remember new information when they actively participate in activities, such as through field trips or role play.
- *Tactile learners:* These learners learn best when engaged in "hands-on" activities. They like to manipulate materials and like to build, fix, or make things, or put things together.
- *Group learners:* These learners prefer group interaction and class work with other students and learn best when working with others. Group interaction helps them to learn and understand new material better.
- *Individual learners*: Learners of this type prefer to work on their own. They are capable of learning new information by themselves, and remember the material better if they learned it alone.

(Richards and Lockhart 1994: 68–69)

Activities in which students write about or discuss their successful and less successful language-learning experiences can help you learn about your students' preferred cognitive styles and their preferences for the kinds of teaching they expect or prefer. At times they may have very different understandings from yours. You can avoid misunderstanding by sharing with your students your reasons for using the kinds of activities and teaching approach that you use, rather than imposing it on your students without explanation. Here are some comments from student teachers on their students' learning preferences:

I found that most of my students organize their thoughts in their native languages first before trying to verbalize them in English. This usually results in some incoherent expressions of ideas and if I correct them too much, they will just clam up. So I try to give them enough time to listen in English, translate into their native language, think in their native language, translate back into English, and then speak in English.

Phil, Canada

I noticed that one of my students is very spontaneous in class and I think this is because of his extroverted personality. So he is less inhibited in the use of English even though his pronunciation is unclear at times. He always tries to express his opinions to his group and only becomes shy if people try to correct him a lot.

Wei Ming, Hong Kong

Because I know that the classroom is the only place my students (they are all Korean and all hang around together during the day speaking Korean and live in one house too) use

English all day and as such is the only real place they have full exposure to English, I try to design activities that encourage them to speak in English and in a low-anxiety environment so that they will not be too self-conscious. For this, too, I try not to correct them too often for fear they will not participate.

Melanie, United States

CREATING A COMMUNITY OF LEARNERS

Although learner-centered teaching involves understanding your learners as individuals and finding ways of addressing their individual needs and differences, a language class can also be thought of as a community of learners, that is, a group of people with shared goals, needs, and concerns. A student in a British classroom captured this sense of community when she said: "When I arrived to start English classes it was like being in a big family. They help each other and try to understand" (Cooke and Simpson 2008: 36). Thinking of a class as a community means seeing it as a place where the individual members of the class cooperate and collaborate to achieve their common goals. This leads to more productive learning. Senior (2006: 201) comments: "The unique character of each language class is based on shared understandings about how individuals (including the teacher) typically behave, react, and interact with one another within the confines of the communicative classroom." Arends states this forcefully:

> Making one's classroom a learning community is one of the most important things a teacher can do, even more important perhaps than the practices used in the more formal aspects of instruction. The classroom learning community influences student engagement and achievement, and it determines how a teacher's class will evolve from a collection of individuals into a cohesive group characterized by high expectations, caring relationships, and productive inquiry. (Arends 2004: 137)

One student teacher in Canada reflected on this and on his membership in the community of ESL teachers:

I feel very proud and I feel that I want to give something to the community, both inside the classroom and outside the class. Inside the classroom, I want to move from just teaching in a room with fee-paying students who are all from different parts of the world to developing this into a community of learners where my students' past and ethnicity do not matter and where we are all equal with equal learning opportunities. Outside the class, I want to be able to learn more from the community of teachers that I now feel I belong to.

Frank, Canada

Effective teachers build a sense of community in their classroom in different ways (Dörnyei 2001; Senior 2006). These include:

- by using their students' names
- by recognizing their students' different cognitive styles
- by helping students find learning partners and groups they are comfortable with
- by encouraging interaction within the class

- by encouraging a sense of friendship among the students
- by regularly using small-group tasks
- by using activities that require cooperation and collaboration
- by encouraging students to share interesting experiences and stories
- by treating students fairly
- by seeking consensus on ways of dealing with classroom management problems

You may find that your practice-teaching class has already developed a sense of community. If so, this will make your teaching experience more productive and enjoyable. If not, you will need to think carefully about how best you can create a socially cohesive group among your students. The following are comments from teaching practice students in Mexico that focus on interactions with students:

I realized that I had never introduced myself (oops!). Then I introduced myself and gave them all my personal information. I told them to ask if there was something else they wanted to know from me, and I was surprised when they started asking a lot of questions about my life, school, and many other things. I think it helped to make them feel more confident toward me. It helped me too.

Hada

I feel that as I get to know the students more, I have more confidence with them, and this helps me to carry out better the lesson.

Anita

You need to be friends with the students, you need to be part of the group and that is very interesting, and you enjoy being a part of them.

Reina

It is quite a challenge to deal with a big class for a long time, but it's even more difficult when they are teenagers and getting their attention is not easy. The first two minutes of the class I did not yet know how to create a nice classroom environment, but as the class went by, I felt very comfortable.

Hada

PERSONALIZING YOUR TEACHING

By personalizing teaching we mean trying to center your teaching wherever possible on your students and their lives, concerns, goals, and interests. This can be achieved by linking the content of your lessons to the students' lives and by involving your students in developing or choosing the content of lessons. For example, in teaching narratives, whereas the textbook you are using will provide examples of what narratives are and describe their linguistic and textual features, sharing personal stories among themselves can be a powerful way of promoting genuine communication. In sharing accounts of their childhoods and discussing significant events or experiences in their lives, students will be prompted to practice and develop their communicative resources by asking questions, asking for clarification, responding with their experiences, and so on. However, it is also important to recognize that cultures have different perceptions of information that is considered suitable for public disclosure and that which is considered private. Age, income, marital status, and family might be considered suitable for public discussion in some cultures but not in others, so particularly with adult learners, you need to be careful not to raise issues that might cause discomfort or embarrassment for some learners.

Students can also be involved in generating lesson content. For example, they can work in groups to choose suitable topics for essay writing. Instead of using examples from the textbook to present a lesson on idioms, students can compile lists of idioms they have encountered out of class and bring these to class. They can also be encouraged to bring in books they would like to read for extensive reading exercises rather than having the teacher decide these (Cooke and Simpson 2008). For listening activities the students can be encouraged to move away from audio recordings provided with books and listen to their favorite songs, watch TV shows or DVDs. You may be able to assign specific TV shows for students to watch and then discuss these in listening class later. Here is an example of how a student teacher attempted to personalize his teaching:

For my speaking class I ask my students to bring things they would like to talk about to class. These can be photos from magazines, news stories from the newspaper, or even things they have bought recently. I put them in groups and each group member first presents his or her item, then the others discuss it or ask questions. Later students take turns talking about their item to the whole class. This is when I help them more with accuracy and vocabulary.

Steven, United States

Another way of personalizing your teaching is to try to make links with the real-life situations where your students use English. Will they have a chance to use English in job interviews, in sending e-mail messages, in shopping, in talking to their neighbors, at the medical clinic, and so on? Try to find out in what situations and for what purposes your students need English and bring these situations into the classroom through role play, through bringing realia (e.g., catalogs, brochures, advertisements) to class and using them as the basis for activities, through dialogues and other activities that reflect the students' language use in the real world. Here is an example of how a student teacher in a Korean setting tried to get her students to use real English outside the classroom:

I decided to try and get my students to use their current language skills and practice with real people; so after getting my cooperating teacher's permission I gave them all a task for homework: to go out and interview a native English-speaking person (adult or child) about their life and leisure. I told them to go out in pairs (for safety's sake) and to make up a list of questions before they started but also to not be afraid to change these questions once they had some interviews completed. Well, the following week they were all really excited with what they had not only learned from interviewing the people but also from what they realized about English as a live language because for many of them, this was the first time they used English outside the textbook.

Marie, Korea

BUILDING MOTIVATION INTO YOUR LESSONS

An important question to ask of every lesson you teach is, "Was it worth my students' time to come to class today?" There are a number of features of lessons that contribute to a student's opinion of the value of a lesson. For example:

- The lesson was interesting.
- Students enjoyed the lesson.

(ctd.)

(ctd.)
- Students were involved and engaged during the lesson.
- The lesson and the activities in it had a purpose.
- Students came away feeling that they had learned something.
- Activities were at the right level.
- Activities gave a sense of success rather than of failure.

A common feature of all of these lesson characteristics is that they relate to how well the teacher is able to motivate the students during a lesson. And this depends on how the teacher addressed the following kinds of questions:

- Was the content of the lesson suitable for the class?
- Were there opportunities for fun, for humor, and for pleasure?
- Was the pacing of the lesson right or did the lesson become boring because too much time was spent on one activity?
- Did the activities connect to the students' interests and did they involve inter-action, collaboration, and sharing of information?
- Did the students feel pleased with what they had achieved, and did the teacher provide the support they needed to complete tasks and praise them for success?

Here are examples of how student teachers tried to make their lessons more motivating:

I decided to teach my writing lesson with activities that would get my students out of their seats. And so I asked them to go up to the board and pin up their story line under the genre that they chose to write it in as homework from the previous class. I was hoping that under each genre there would be more than two students contributing so that they can share their ideas so that they have more story lines to write. This seemed to work well and the students all seemed more alive, especially in the hot afternoons here, because they were up and doing something rather than listening to me talk!

Serene, Singapore

Students seemed to enjoy the group activity in my reading lesson and they seemed to be able to concentrate better while working in a group where peers take turns to read one paragraph aloud to the others, rather than when I read to the whole class. Many of them mentioned specifically that they prefer to do reading comprehension this way rather than having to read the whole passage by themselves. Indeed, after the group activity, most of the students were able to provide the correct answers to the comprehension questions, which exemplified their understanding of the passage.

Martin, Hong Kong

BUILDING LEARNER-CENTERED OUTCOMES INTO YOUR LESSONS

In your teacher-training course you probably studied ways of setting goals in teaching. You may have been introduced to the use of objectives or competencies as planning devices in teaching. These typically describe what the teacher seeks to accomplish in a lesson or unit. For example, a reading lesson may address outcomes such as the following:

- Students will learn how to recognize and interpret formal cohesive devices for linking different parts of a text.
- Students will recognize the function of discourse markers in texts.

Whereas describing outcomes like this can be a useful way of organizing the content of a lesson, lessons can also be thought of in terms of what the learners take away from a lesson and the outcomes they perceived for themselves. Dörnyei suggests a number of ways in which learning outcomes can acknowledge learners' concerns:

- By including tasks which involve the public display or performance of the outcome: Activities such as role play or presenting a poster that students have designed allow students to publicly display what they have learned.
- By making results tangible: Visual or written summaries of what has been learned such as in the form of a wall chart or a mention in a class newsletter can remind students of what they have learned.
- By celebrating success: Find different ways of praising and rewarding students for successes in learning.

(Dörnyei 2001: 126)

Here are some examples of these kinds of learning outcomes from student teachers' lesson plans:

At the end of the lesson, students will design and write a travel brochure for their hometown that includes interesting information, interesting places to visit, and any other relevant information. This will be a nice wind-up to the lesson.

Jerry, United States

The lesson will end with each group of students acting out the role play they have written. Then I will ask the class to vote on which one was the best. It should be a lot of fun.

Jung Hee, Korea

SUMMARY AND CONCLUSIONS

Learner-centered teaching means teaching that reflects learners' individual differences in cognitive styles, motivations, needs, and interests. Developing a learner-centered focus to your teaching involves drawing on students' life experiences, creating opportunities for students to interact and cooperate, and to develop a sense of shared interests and concerns. Acknowledging the diversity of classroom participation and cognitive styles among students in your class reminds us that learning is not simply a mirror image of teaching. A goal of learner-centered teaching is to create a sense of community among learners and to personalize your teaching to engage learners more actively in lessons. Building motivation into lessons depends not only on the kinds of activities you use but by setting goals that address the affective and social aspects of learning.

Keeping your students' needs and interests at the forefront of your teaching is not always easy, since managing the processes and routines of teaching can sometimes distract you from the real point of teaching, which is to facilitate learning on the part of your students. Whenever possible think through your lessons and the teaching activities you make use of from the point of view of your learners and use the focus points discussed in this chapter to help make your teaching more learner centered. Table 9.1 summarizes how you can develop learner-centered teaching.

1. Develop the ability to make your learners the focus of your teaching.	• Teacher develops understanding of learners' needs and goals, communicates trust and respect, acknowledges diversity of needs and learning styles, gives effective feedback, and uses effective strategies.
2. Understand your learners' needs and goals.	• Teacher develops understanding of different kinds of learners, some having similar needs / goals, and some with great diversity of needs / goals.
3. Understand your students' classroom participation styles.	• Teacher develops understanding of learners who make up the class and listens to advice from the cooperating teacher on how to interact with students who may pose difficulties.
4. Understand your students' cognitive styles.	• Teacher develops understanding of students who approach language learning in different ways and whose educational background and language-learning experience has established a particular set of beliefs and preferences about how best to learn a language.
5. Create a community of learners.	• Teacher develops an understanding of a language class as a group of people with shared goals, needs, and concerns.
6. Build learner-centered outcomes into your lessons.	• Teacher develops an understanding of lessons in terms of what learners take away from it and outcomes perceived.

Table 9.1   Developing learner-centered teaching

Further reading

Benson, P. (2001). *Teaching and researching autonomy in language learning*. London: Longman.

Benson, P. (2003). Learner autonomy in the classroom. In D. Nunan (Ed.), *Practical English language teaching* (289–308). New York: McGraw Hill.

Scharle, Á., & Szabó, A. (2000). *Learner autonomy: A guide to developing learner responsibility*. Cambridge: Cambridge University Press.

Discussion questions

1. What are some ways in which you can find out more about your learners' needs? How can you use the information that you obtain?

2. What classroom participation styles have you observed in your cooperating teacher's class? How does the teacher deal with students' different classroom participation styles?

3. Have you noticed examples of language-learning preferences among students you have observed or taught?

4. Do you think you have a preferred cognitive style? If so, how does it influence the way you study or learn?

5. What are some ways in which your cooperating teacher builds motivation into his or her classes? What strategies have you used to build motivation into your lessons?

6. Do you feel that your practice-teaching class functions well as a community of learners? What activities do you use to help maintain a sense of community?

7. Read and compare the student teachers' reports on learner-centered teaching in Appendix B. What principle did each teacher learn from the experience they describe?

Follow-up activities

1. Examine a lesson from a textbook and suggest ways in which you could personalize the lesson to make it more interesting to your learners.

2. Look at the example of part of a class profile in Appendix A for an elementary-level class in a school in Canada. What features would you include in a profile of students in your practice-teaching class?

Appendix A: Example of part of a class profile of an elementary-level ESL class in a language school in North America

Name	Background information	English proficiency	Interests	Learning style	Implications for teaching
Jae Hee	Korean; female; 18; full-time student	Intermediate reading & elementary writing; basic speaking; intermediate grammar	Enjoys computer games; movies	Auditory & visual	Provide supportive environment; encourage independence but don't make her speak in public yet; encourage interaction with other students
Abdullah	UAE; male; 22; full-time student	Basic writing; intermediate speaking; elementary reading; basic grammar	Likes movies, fast cars; likes reading	Kinesthetic; easily distracted; dislikes tests	Develop positive attitudes toward classroom activities and homework; develop writing skills slowly; encourage cooperation to let others speak
Franco	Italy; male; 22; full-time student	Elementary reading & writing; intermediate speaking; poor grammar	Enjoys physical activities; likes watching movies and listening to stories	Kinesthetic; auditory	Encourage small group interaction; encourage cooperation to let others speak; give him job as monitor to see who does not speak enough

Table 9.2   Example of part of a class profile

Appendix B: Lesson accounts by student teachers in Indonesia

The first week was probably the worst for me intensity-wise. In the second week I started to enjoy the relationships forming with my students and felt that I was creating a "safe" working environment where we all supported and helped each other to learn. I had a couple of very good lessons in the second week too and my confidence was definitely boosted.

Hannah

When I first started my teaching practice I felt completely overwhelmed. I felt like I had to perform well or I would fail. I completely forgot the whole reason I decided to become a teacher, which was because of my students. They motivated me to want to do my best for them. Later on I realized that teaching practice is not about how much you already know, but about the progress you make and the initiative you take to improve.

Michelle

During the teaching practice I have become increasingly aware of the need to plan the lesson from the students' point of view and think through all the lesson activities before I use them. The importance of pitching the lesson right and choosing engaging topics and activities has also become clear to me.

Eldri

During the first few lessons I discovered that most of the students were the same age as me, or even older. As a result, I tried very hard to build a rapport with them as equals and use similar interests as the basis for my teaching.

Bryony

I am now aware that language skills can develop incredibly quickly in the right learning environment with a student-centered, low-TTT teaching approach. I am aware that I need much more exposure to the student-centered, minimal-TTT approach and much more observation of a broad range of teachers in order to internalize this.

Linda

I have learned that the main focus is the student, and providing them with the materials and means for a productive learning experience. This can be achieved by choosing appropriate material and exploiting it in a number of ways to sufficiently challenge and sustain the interest of the students and should also optimize student talking time.

Claire

I have consciously tried to reduce teacher talking time in my lessons and increase opportunities for students to talk in situations that are as authentic as a classroom environment can provide. This is a challenge and I'm not yet satisfied that I am achieving the right balance, but am optimistic that my skill in this area will develop with more experience.

Cheryl

CHAPTER 10

Classroom Discourse and Communication

INTRODUCTION

Language is used in many different ways in second language classrooms since it is both the means and the end of learning. A crucial aspect of language classes, therefore, is the way in which teachers use language to support and manage the processes of language learning. The language input learners receive during a lesson and the opportunities it opens up for language practice and use are provided by the teacher, by the teaching resources he or she makes use of, and by the students' interactions with each other. Many observers of language classrooms have commented that in many classrooms, students have only restricted opportunities to participate in the communicative and interactive uses of language and hence have restricted opportunities for language learning (Thornbury 2005). In this chapter we want to explore the kinds of communication, interaction, and discourse that occur during the instructional phase of a lesson (rather than when the teacher is engaged in noninstructional activities, such as classroom management) and how they can be used to effectively support and guide second language learning.

THE NATURE OF INSTRUCTIONAL DISCOURSE

The nature of verbal interaction in second language classrooms shares some of the characteristics of verbal interaction in classrooms where other subjects are being taught. Both teachers of English as well as teachers of other subjects have to find ways of presenting new learning content in ways which engage learners, which make connections with previous learning, which present content at a comprehensible and learnable rate, and which provide opportunities for learners to master lesson content through processes such as analysis, reflection, application, and practice. A common interactional structure that emerges during the teaching of many school subjects follows this pattern: initiation by the teacher (I), the response (R) by a student (or students), and the teacher's evaluation (E) of the response – the IRE sequence. Johnson (1995: 9) suggests that in the classroom, the teacher, "being the one with the authority to control, is the one who dominantly carries out the initiation and evaluation acts as a way of controlling classroom discourses." In contrast, the students act mainly as respondents to the teacher's questions in the talk. This IRE sequence is termed the "unmarked" or "default" pattern of classroom lessons (Cazden 1988: 53). The following example is from an intermediate EFL class from a secondary school in Malaysia (Johnson 1995). The lesson is a vocabulary exercise from the class textbook and is based on an advertisement for a clearance sale. The teacher (T) is addressing a series of questions to the students:

Turns 1–34
1. T: What is this advertisement about?
2. Peersak: Radio . . . sale.
3. Milo: Cheap sale . . .
4. T: What is the word that is used there?
5. Suchada: Clearance sale.
6. T: Clearance sale. OK, in the first place, do you know the meaning of "clearance sale"?
7. Suchada: Clearance sale.
8. T: Clearance sale. Let's look at the word "clearance." What word does it come from?
9. Peersak: Clear.
10. T: Therefore, "clearance" sale will mean what?
11. Suchada: To clear up.
12. T: To clear up, that's right. To clear up all the goods in the store. OK, let's look at the items which are for sale. Where is the photographic department? Peersak, look at the advertisement and tell me, where is the photographic department?
13. Peersak: Ground floor.
14. T: Yes, on the ground floor. Now, if you go to the photo – you get there?
15. Peersak: Camera.
16. T: A camera. Can you be more specific? What kind of camera?
17. Peersak: A Kodak . . . Instamatic 76X camera.
18. T: OK, a Kodak Instamatic camera. What is the usual price of the camera?
19. Peersak: Twenty-seven and forty cents.
20. T: Twenty-seven dollars, forty cents. And what is its price after the sale?
21. Peersak: Twenty-three dollars, seventy-five cents.
22. T: Twenty-three dollars, seventy-five cents. Now, if you buy that camera, what free gift will you get?
23. Peersak: . . . Ball.
24. T: A ball. Now, let's move on to some other department in the store. Milo.
25. Milo: First floor.
26. T: What can you buy there?
27. Milo: Stainless steel kettles.
28. T: How many sizes of kettles?
29. Milo: Five.

(ctd.)

(ctd.)

30. T: OK, these stainless steel kettles come in five sizes. And what is the special feature of this kettle?
31. Milo: Imported.
32. T: What other special features?
33. Milo: Movable handle.
34. T: Yes they have movable handles in addition to being stainless steel. OK, now . . .

(Johnson 1995: 94–96)

The underlying communication sequence in this example is the unmarked IRE sequence where the teacher initiates, the students respond and the teacher evaluates. Within this IRE sequence the students wait to be nominated by the teacher before speaking. Thus, the teacher retains control over all initiations and evaluations. If the student's answer is correct, the teacher will affirm this before making the next initiation (Turn 5). We can also see the patterns in Turns 1 to 6 where the teacher ignores a student's answer if it is incorrect and instead initiates another question. This initiation acts as an evaluation (I acting as E) where the teacher reformulates to get a correct response (Turn 4). It is only after Turn 25 that we see a change where the teacher withdraws positive evaluations to a student's correct responses.

Lessons and lesson sequences generally reflect an *opening phase* to orient students, an *instructional phase,* and a *closing phase.* The opening and closing phases vary from teacher to teacher. The instructional phase, however, can be viewed as a joint production between the teacher and the students in the form of an *initiation, response / reply,* and an *evaluation / feedback.* For the instructional phase of classroom events Mehan (1979) maintains that in content classes, academic information is exchanged between teachers and students during the lessons. For this to occur, interactional sequences, also known as elicitation sequences, are organized around topics and are a joint production between the teacher and the students in the form of an initiation, response / reply, and an evaluation. Language teachers use different ways of introducing these phases of a lesson and in observing your cooperating teacher's lessons you will be able to notice some of the strategies he or she uses (see Appendix A).

Researchers of second language classroom use have pointed out that in too many second language classrooms interaction is dominated by patterns of IRE discourse as described in this section. Consequently interaction is teacher-dominated and questions too often serve merely to elicit or display grammatical knowledge rather than to initiate communicative language use (Nunan 1987; Thornbury 2005). More useful to language learning is interaction that supports learning through the use of what has been termed "dialogic interaction" (Aljaafreh and Lantolf 1994) or "collaborative dialogue" (Swain 2000). This process involves the joint construction of knowledge through the activity of assisted performance, sometimes referred to as "scaffolded learning" (Lantolf and Thorne 2006). The teacher assists the learners in completing learning activities by observing what they are capable of, providing a series of guided stages through the task, and through collaborative dialogue, scaffolding the learning process by initially providing support (the "scaffold") and gradually removing support as learning develops. Learning is initially mediated and directed by the teacher or other more advanced learners and is gradually appropriated by the individual learner. Throughout, the teacher provides opportunities for noticing how language is used, experimenting with language use, practicing new modes of discourse and restructuring existing language knowledge. This process of dialogic interaction is reflected in the following example, where the teacher supports and extends the students' contributions. The lesson is from a class in Barcelona, and the students are discussing suggestions for an activity in the mountains.

S1:   What about go to mountains?

T: What about . . . ?

S1:   What about going to mountains, we can do "barrancking."

[Ss laugh]

T: What's "barrancking"?

S2:   It's a sport.

T: Yes, but what do you do exactly?

S3:   You have a river, a small river and [gestures]

T: Goes down?

S3:   Yes, as a cataract.

T: OK, a waterfall [writes it on the board]. What's a waterfall, Manuel?

S1:   Like Niagara?

T: OK. So what do you do with the waterfall?

S4:   You go down.

T: What? In a boat?

S: No, no, with a . . . como se dice "cuerda"?

S3:   Cord.

T: No, rope, a cord is smaller, like at the window, look [points].

S4:   Rope, rope, you go down rope in a waterfall.

S2:   You wear . . . "black clothes" [mispronounced]

T: Black clothes. Repeat [student repeats] . . . [. . .] This sounds dangerous. Is it dangerous?

Ss: No no.

S3:   Is in summer, no much water.

T: Sorry?

S3:   Poco . . . poco . . . little water, river is not strong.

T: OK . . . and you have done this? What's it called in Spanish?

S4:   Barranquismo. In English?

T: I don't know. I'll have to ask somebody.

S2:   It is good, you come? Com ed diu? Let's go together.

T: I don't think so [laughs]

S4:   Yes, yes, you come, we can go in summer.

T: Well, in the summer, not now, it's too cold.

Ss: No no

                                                    (Thornbury 2005: 127–143)

Another example of how this process takes place is given in Lantolf and Thorne in which the interactions between an ESL tutor in a U.S. college program and a student during feedback sessions on the student's essay writing are described. The strategies the tutor used in responding to grammatical errors in the student's composition are summarized as follows and arranged according to whether they reflect independent functioning on the part of the learner (0) or different degrees of collaborative interaction between the tutor and the learners (Stages 1–12):

0   Tutor asks the learner to read, find the errors, and correct them independently prior to the tutorial.

1   Construction of a 'collaborative frame' prompted by the presence of the tutor as a potential dialogic partner.

2   Prompted or focused reading of the sentence that contains the error by the learner or the tutor.

3   Tutor indicates that something may be wrong in the segment (for example, sentence, clause, line) – 'Is there anything wrong in this sentence?'

(ctd.)

(ctd.)

4   Tutor rejects unsuccessful attempts at recognizing the error.

5   Tutor narrows down the location of the error (for example, tutor repeats or points to the specific segment which contains the error).

6   Tutor indicates the nature of the error, but does not identify the error (for example, 'There is something wrong with the tense here.').

7   Tutor identifies error ('You can't use an auxiliary here.').

8   Tutor rejects learner's unsuccessful attempts at correcting error.

9   Tutor provides clues to help the learner arrive at the correct form (for example, 'It is not really past but something that is still going on.').

10   Tutor provides the correct form.

11   Tutor provides some explanation for the use of the correct form.

12   Tutor provides examples of the correct pattern when other forms of help fail to produce an appropriate responsive action.

(Lantolf and Thorne 2006: 278–280)

Language learning is facilitated by interactions like the ones described in this section in which the interaction proceeds as a kind of joint problem solving between teacher and student. During the process the teacher assists the learner in using more complex language through a type of assisted performance, and this is central to language development.

MODELING LANGUAGE USE

Whereas in the teaching of other school subjects language and discourse are means to an end (the understanding of content), in the case of language classrooms language is both a means and an end. By this we mean that while the teachers' language and discourse serve to support, direct, guide, and shape the processes of learning, they also serve to model the kind of language the students are learning. As Lantolf and Thorne observe:

> The situation regarding foreign-language learning in the school setting is quite different [i.e., from naturalistic language learning outside of class-rooms – authors' comment]. Unlike the native language, foreign languages are learned consciously and intentionally, and generally entail extensive pro-duction and consumption of written texts. This means that the more comp-lex, conscious, and intentional forms and uses of the foreign language are learned from the outset in the classroom setting.
> (Lantolf and Thorne 2006: 294)

One approach in language teaching, for example, often referred to as genre or text-based teaching, focuses on developing understanding and use of the text types students need to master in their different contexts of learning, whether these be workplace or school related. These might include a variety of spoken and written texts such as conversations, interviews, and discussions, as well as essays, letters, and narratives. In teaching students to understand and use different text types the teacher first provides models of appropriate texts then engages in collaborative analysis, shared construction, and finally individual construction of texts. During this process the teacher guides the learners through the processes of text awareness and text construction to the stage where the learners can create texts independently. Here a teacher comments on using this approach:

In teaching practice I planned my lessons via the genre approach. The unit of work I was given by my cooperating teacher stipulates that I teach understanding of different text structures and these must be covered within three weeks. Within each lesson, students are required to perform reading, comprehension, and writing tasks. There is little emphasis on the grammatical aspect of the text structure. I found myself experimenting with different ways to bring a particular text structure and its characteristics across to the students but generally I was required by my cooperating teacher to plan specific activities to cover particular aspects of a particular text structure, such as a lesson on "compare and contrast." I also had to plan and teach a couple of IT (information technology) lessons for every text type during my teaching practice. However, I could not manage to locate any multimedia resources that aid in the teaching of text types. I had to create Web sites to help students go through various characteristics of the text types and despite my general competence, it still takes me a lot of time to create these Web sites when time could be better spent on planning other activities.

Lance, Singapore

Ko, Schallert, and Walters (2003) describe how a teacher provides language support during a story-telling task. The teacher listened for places in the story where key information had been omitted and prompted the speakers to provide it. She reminded the learners to clarify cultural assumptions that the story depended upon, she encouraged other listeners to ask for clarification, and she corrected pronunciation and helped provide needed vocabulary. In this case the teacher modeled the story structure indirectly as the activity unfolded.

The following example shows how a teacher uses transcriptions of authentic conversations to model conversational language and interaction.

In teaching my students spoken English I give my students transcriptions of short authentic conversations, which we studied in one of my classes. We look at such things as turn taking, ways listeners respond or show interest in what the other person is saying, ways of using small talk, and so on. Then I give them examples of dialogues in which I have removed some of the features that they have studied and I ask them to work in pairs to see how they can reconstruct the dialogues. This leads on to role-play activities where they practice using the features of authentic conversational interaction.

Anna, United States

MAKING DISCOURSE COMPREHENSIBLE

One of the skills you need to master as a language teacher is learning how to use language that is comprehensible to your students and at an appropriate level to support assisted learning. The type of language you use outside of an instructional setting may not provide the best input for language learning if it is too complex or idiomatic for the learners. Experienced teachers have often – perhaps unconsciously – developed ways of making their language more comprehensible to second language learners. For example, Saville-Troike (2006: 107) reports that when a survey was conducted at a U.S. university to find out which professors international students found easiest to understand, it was found that faculty who had extensive teaching experience in L2 contexts (and who were hence more practiced in making appropriate modifications in their speech) were rated as being more comprehensible.

There are a number of strategies you can use as a student teacher to make your discourse comprehensible. For example:

- *Repeating requests and instructions* – T: What's the subject of the sentence? (pause two seconds) The subject. . . . What is the subject of the sentence?
- *Speaking more slowly*

(ctd.)

(ctd.)

- *Using pauses, giving learners more time to process your speech* – T: OK now. What I want you to do . . . is to get into groups. . . . Find your group partners. . . . Tony, what's your group called . . . ?
- *Modifying your pronunciation toward a more standard speech style*
- *Modifying your vocabulary, replacing infrequent words with more commonly used words* – T: What can we say when we meet someone for the first time . . . like at a party . . . and you meet someone and you don't know them . . . what do you say to them (teacher avoids using "introduce")?
- *Modifying your grammar, for example, avoiding using complex syntax when simpler syntax can be used* – T: So Maria forgot to leave a tip in the restaurant and the waiter was angry . . . Normally you should . . . leave a small tip . . . and she didn't . . . (teacher avoids "she should have left a tip").
- *Avoiding the use of colloquialisms and idioms*
- *Modifying your discourse, for example, by making meanings more explicit* – T: Can anyone give me the answer to Question 1? [No response] T: Look at Question 1. Who has the answer?
- *Nominating a specific student to provide the answer. In this way the teacher "conducts" the discourse* – T: So what's the answer? Maria can you tell us the answer?

A useful focus for your classroom observations is how your cooperating teacher modifies his or her classroom discourse to make it comprehensible to the learners.

RESHAPING AND EXTENDING LEARNERS' LANGUAGE RESOURCES

As a teacher you also serve as a language informant and model, providing examples of how language is used and assisting learners in refining and expanding their language abilities. This can be achieved in the ways you give feedback to learners on their language use and also by the way you help them expand and develop their language resources. Swain (2000) proposed that successful language acquisition requires not only receiving comprehensible input, but also practicing the production of comprehensible output, that is, language that can be understood by other speakers of the language. Swain suggested that when learners have to make efforts to ensure that their messages are communicated (*pushed output*), this puts them in a better position to notice the gap between their productions and those of proficient speakers, thus fostering second language development. Carefully structured and managed output (the *output hypothesis*) is essential if learners are to acquire new language. *Managed output* here refers to tasks and activities that require the use of certain target-language forms, that is, those that "stretch" the learner's language knowledge and that consequently require a "restructuring" of that knowledge. In the following extract the teacher leads the students toward producing a sentence with the present continuous:

T: Look at the picture at the top of the page. What's that?
S1: Mobile phone.
T: A mobile phone. It's a mobile phone. Say after me, it's a mobile phone.
SS: It's a mobile phone.
T: OK. So the man . . . what's he doing?
S2: Talking . . . the phone.
T: Yes, he's talking on the phone.
S2: Talking on the phone.
T: Say together, the man is talking on the mobile phone.
SS: The man is talking on the mobile phone.

The ways in which you provide feedback to your learners on their language use also plays an important role in facilitating their language development. As we saw in the extract, the dialogic interaction between teachers and learners includes both direct and indirect feedback on the learner's language use. Other strategies that teachers use are:

- Asking the student to repeat what he or she said to see if the student notices the error
- Repeating the student's discourse but correcting the error
- Asking other students to correct the error
- Suggesting that the sentence contains an error
- Indicating the error the student made
- Pointing to the board, where an example of the needed language is provided
- Pointing to a phonetic chart to help students with their pronunciation

The following framework of feedback strategies may be useful, especially when the feedback is in written form (adapted from Lewis 2002):

Agree / disagree: "I agree / disagree with the point you made about . . . "

Ask a question: "Did you say . . . or . . . ?"

Express feelings: "I am delighted to see that you . . . "

Generalize: "Generally, your work is very good."

Provide examples: "For example, your . . . "

Give reasons: "I have marked your math in red because you need to . . . "

Provide comparisons: "By the end of your speech you were really expressing yourself much better."

Make an offer: "Would you like to discuss your speech?"

Make a prediction: "From this speech I can see that you will have no trouble with . . . "

State a plan: "Next week we will . . . "

Make a suggestion: "I would suggest that you . . . "

(See Appendix B for an example of how the teacher gives feedback on students' attempts to produce the past tense.)

It's important to carefully consider the kind of feedback you give so that it serves both to encourage students but also to guide and develop their language learning.

Kramsch (1985, summarized in Thornbury 2005: 138–139) emphasizes the importance of teachers modifying their use of language in the classroom to maximize learning opportunities for learners. She makes the following recommendations:

Turns-at-talk

In group-oriented interaction the teacher should systematically encourage the students to take control of the turn-taking mechanism, by following the five rules of natural turn-taking:

1. tolerate silences: refrain from filling the gaps between turns. This will put pressure on students to initiate turns.

2. direct your gaze to any potential addressee of a student's utterance: do not assume that you are the next speaker and the student's exclusive addressee.

3. teach the students floor-taking gambits; do not always grant the floor.

(ctd.)

(ctd.)

4. encourage students to sustain their speech beyond one or two sentences and to take longer turns; do not use a student's short utterance as a springboard for your own lengthy turn.

5. extend your exchanges with individual students to include clarification of the speaker's intentions and a negotiation of meanings; do not cut off an exchange too soon to pass on to another student.

Topic management

If students are to take an active part in interactions, they must be shown how to control the way topics are established, built and sustained, and how to participate in the teaching and learning of lessons. The following rules of natural discourse can be useful here.

1. use English not only to deal with the subject matter, but also to regulate the interaction in the classroom. You will thus offer a model of how to use interactional gambits in natural discourse.

2. keep the number of display questions to a minimum. The more genuine the requests for information, the more natural the discourse.

3. build the topic at hand together with the students: assume that whatever they say contributes to the topic. Do not cut off arbitrarily a student's utterance because you perceive it to be irrelevant. It might be very relevant to the student's perception of the topic.

Repair tasks

Natural forms of interaction in the classroom would . . . require that the teacher frequently observe the following rules of natural repair.

1. pay attention to the message of students' utterances rather than the form in which they are cast. . . . Keep your comments for later.

2. treat the correction of linguistic errors as a pragmatic or interactional adjustment, not as a normative form of redress.

3. leave students a choice in the linguistic form of their utterances, e.g., if they are not sure of the subjunctive, allow them to avoid this form and to find alternatives.

4. make extensive use of natural feedback ("hmm / interesting / I thought so too") rather than evaluating and judging every student utterance following its delivery ("fine / good"). Do not overpraise.

5. give students explicit credit by quoting them ("just as X said"); do not take credit for what students contributed by giving the impression that you had thought about it before.

(Kramsch 1985, summarized in Thornbury 2005: 138–139)

The following example from a lesson in Spain shows a teacher disregarding the content of a message (the student's marriage) in order to move on with the teacher's lesson plan:

[after taking the register the teacher starts chatting to students]
T: Well then, Jorge, did you have a good weekend?
S: Yes.
T: What did you do?
S: I got married.

T: [smiling] You got married. You certainly had a good weekend then. [laughter and buzz of conversation]

T: Now turn to page 56 in your books. You remember last time we were talking about biographies. [T checks book and lesson plan while students talk to Jorge in Spanish about his nuptials]

(cited in Thornbury 2005: 130)

USING EFFECTIVE QUESTIONING TECHNIQUES

In both content classes and second language classes, asking questions is one of the commonest ways in which teachers direct and structure their teaching. The kinds of questions teachers ask can influence the kind of thinking that occurs during a lesson. In ESL classes questions serve to guide learners through new lesson content, making connections with previous learning and with the students' background knowledge, checking their understanding, encouraging interaction, and eliciting production and practice of new language. Questioning plays a key role in the processes of scaffolding, providing a basis for assisted understanding and use of language. With second language learners, particularly those with limited L2 proficiency, questions provide the means by which teachers mediate between the students' current level of performance and the level they need in order to understand and carry out instructional tasks.

The following are examples of some of the questioning strategies you might observe in your cooperating teacher's class:

- *Concept questions*: Questions used to check understanding of the meaning of a new learning item, e.g., "Does this sentence refer to something that happened in the present or the past?"
- *Comprehension checks:* e.g., "All right? OK?"
- *Confirmation checks:* e.g., "Do you mean it happened to you?"
- *Clarification requests:* e.g., "Can you try to explain what you mean?"
- *Lead-in questions*: These guide the students toward a learning activity by checking background knowledge and previous learning, e.g., before students read a review of a new movie the teacher asks questions such as, "Do you like movies?," "How often do you see a movie?," and "What kinds of movies do you like?"
- *Challenge questions*: These try to promote extended student participation and discussion and require students to come up with their own opinions and ideas, e.g., "What else? Give me another reason."
- *Structuring questions:* These break down a teaching item into a series of stages, e.g., a teacher can say, "Now that we have identified the main properties of language, which do you think chimpanzees use to communicate to each other? Do they communicate in the same way as humans? Do they communicate in the same way as birds? Do birds communicate in the same way as humans?"
- *Form-focused questions*: These serve to elicit particular uses of language in order for the teacher to be able to assess language accuracy, e.g., "What's a good way to introduce yourself to someone you have never met before?"

UNDERSTANDING NONVERBAL CLASSROOM COMMUNICATION

Teachers communicate not only with words, but also with actions and nonverbal signals they make use of to send out different kinds of messages. Two aspects of nonverbal behavior that affect classroom interaction are *kinesis* and *proxemics*. *Kinesis* deals with behaviors such as facial expressions, eye contact and eye expression, body movement, gesture and posture, and body shape and touch, and aspects of these behaviors may differ from one culture to another. A teacher's hand on the shoulder of a student while he or she watches the student at work on a task may be acceptable in one culture, but totally unacceptable in another. *Proxemics* refers to the general use of space and peoples' attitudes toward space in public places. For example, in some cultures people stand closer to each other when talking than they do in other cultures. Space arrangements can play an important role in the interactional dynamics of the language classroom. This is especially true when teachers are trying to arrange classroom space to encourage an optimal learning environment for their students.

It is important also for students to be able to understand a teacher's nonverbal communications; they must to be able to "read" what teachers require from them from the teachers' nonverbal cues as well as their verbal expressions. These nonverbal cues include the teachers' pitch, facial expressions, and body postures. Students must also be able to accurately interpret teachers' use of praise so that they can gauge the extent they are doing what is required from them. For example, Johnson (1995) has suggested that students of high ability perceive a teacher's praise as a reward and will participate more in class as a result of receiving this praise. On the other hand, students of low ability see a teacher's praise in terms of obtaining information about being on the right track rather than as a reward. So, in order for students to participate successfully in classroom events, they must be able to recognize a teacher's expectations.

Closely connected to the arrangement of classroom space is the teacher's own use of space in the classroom and its influence on classroom participation. Duncan and Biddle (1974) use the term the teacher's "action zone" to describe the interactional space a teacher uses. It is defined as the classroom space where specific students get the full focus of a teacher's attention through such nonverbal behaviors as eye contact and gaze and verbal behaviors, such as questioning and nomination. Richards and Lockhart (1994) maintain that how narrow or wide a given teacher's action zone is may depend on the physical layout of the classroom – how the desks are placed (rows, semicircular, etc.). The teacher's action zone may also depend on how mobile a teacher is and on an individual teacher's preferences (personal action zone) and predispositions to look at one side of the class more than the other, or to call on one gender, ethnic group, or skilled learner over another. Figure 10.1 shows an example of a teacher's action zone during a lesson. It indicates clearly how many students in the class were outside it and hence unable to participate actively in the lesson.

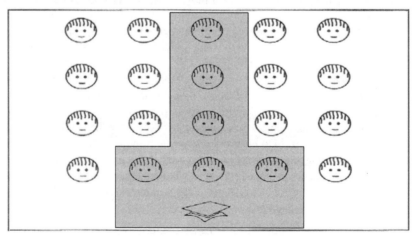

Front

Figure 10.1   A teacher's action zone – The grey area represents students who are inside the teacher's action zone. Students not included in the grey area are outside the teacher's action zone

Table 10.1 summarizes how teachers can develop an understanding of classroom discourse and communication.

1. Understand nature of instructional discourse.	• Teacher finds ways of presenting new learning content in ways which engage learners, make connections with previous learning, present content at a comprehensible and learnable rate, and provide opportunities for learners to master lesson content through processes such as analysis, reflection, application, and practice.
2. Model language use.	• Teacher's uses of language and discourse serve to support, direct, guide, and shape the processes of learning, and also serve to model language the students are learning.
3. Make discourse comprehensible.	• Teacher learns how to use language that is comprehensible to students and at an appropriate level to support assisted learning.
4. Reshape and extend learners' language resources.	• Teacher provides examples of how language is used and assists learners in refining and expanding their language abilities.
5. Use effective questioning techniques.	• Teacher understands that questions serve to guide learners through new lesson content, make connections with previous learning and with the students' background knowledge, check their understanding, encourage interaction, and elicit production and practice of new language.
6. Understand nonverbal classroom communication.	• Teacher understands the two main aspects of nonverbal behavior that affect classroom interaction: kinesis and proxemics.

Table 10.1   Understanding classroom discourse and communication

SUMMARY AND CONCLUSIONS

An important goal in language teaching is to create opportunities for students to participate in authentic uses of language in order to facilitate their language learning. Instructional discourse however is often teacher dominated and may provide insufficient opportunities for communicative language use. The role of the teacher is crucial in modifying his or her use of language in the classroom to maximize its learning potential for learners. This can be done through modeling language use, through providing comprehensible discourse, through appropriate use of questions, as well as by giving feedback which can further shape the learners' language development. The process of dialogic interaction provides support for learning through the process of scaffolding, which guides and assists learners toward more complex and accurate language use.

During this interaction, language meanings are clarified and learners' linguistic resources are expanded through modeling, through feedback, and through the use of activities that consolidate and develop their linguistic and communicative competence. For a language teacher, using classroom discourse to achieve these goals constitutes a core dimension of the art and skill of teaching.

Further reading

Allwright, D., & Bailey, K. M. (1991). *Focus on the language classroom: An introduction to classroom research for language teachers*. Cambridge: Cambridge University Press.

Johnson, K. E. (1995). *Understanding communication in second language classrooms*. New York: Cambridge University Press.

Lewis, M. (2002). *Giving feedback in language classes*. Singapore: RELC.

Discussion questions

1. In observing your cooperating teacher's class, note some of the ways in which he or she deals with these phases of the lesson:

O   the opening
O   the initiation of an activity
O   the closing

2. What are some ways in which your cooperating teacher helps students "notice" features of language that they need to learn? What other ways might be appropriate?

3. List some ways in which your cooperating teacher provides models of language use to his or her learners.

4. What are several ways of modeling language use that are mentioned in the chapter? What are other ways that you can think of?

5. Give some examples of how your cooperating teacher modifies his or her language and discourse to make it more comprehensible to the learners.

6. What strategies do you think are helpful in giving students feedback on the accuracy of their spoken language?

7. Does your cooperating teacher correct students' spoken language? How? Do you find the teacher's correction techniques helpful?

Follow-up activities

1. Observe a class by your cooperating teacher and note examples of the different kinds of questions he or she uses.

2. Review an audio or video of one of your lessons and note how you did some of the following things:

O   provided an opening and closing
O   modeled language use
O   helped students notice features of language

○ made your discourse more comprehensible
○ gave learners feedback on their language use
○ used questions

3. Appendices A and B contain short transcripts of a class on "compare and contrast." Which of the features of classroom discourse discussed in this chapter do you see reflected in these transcripts?

4. In Appendix C, try to code the classroom communication by the IRE sequence. What can you say about the sequence you notice?

Appendix A: Transcript from a lesson segment on compare and contrast

T:	Today, we're going to read a passage that is pretty much related to all of us. Okay, it is basically about a student describing his school life. Okay? We'll just take three short minutes. Read through everything first and then after that we will carry out a short activity.
	Everyone clear? Okay. Very good, start reading.
	(*3 minutes later*)
T:	Finished?
Ss:	Finished.
T:	Okay, good.
	Can someone tell me what the passage you've just read is all about?
Ss:	Teachers.
T:	Okay, very good. Talking about teachers.
	Now look at the Compare and Contrast organizer that I have just given to you.
	Okay, this is what we're going to do. In the passage, look at how similar or how different the two teachers are.
	Okay. Hee Soon, who are the two teachers we have?
Hee Soon:	Miss Foo and Mr. Lee.
T:	Okay. Miss Foo and Mr. Lee, right?
	Let's go back to the passage again.
	Can I direct you to Paragraph 3 of the passage? Starting from this line onwards, we're going to look at the lines that actually describe how Mr. Lee and Miss Foo are alike. Okay, Sang Ho, can you read from Line 2 to Line 4 and then tell us whether there is anything that tells us if Mr. Lee and Miss Foo are alike?
Sang Ho:	Read or what?
T:	Yah. Of course.
Sang Ho:	Two of them who taught me in high school really stick out in my mind. Mr. Lee and Miss Foo. I admire these two the most out of all the teachers I have come across.
T:	Okay. Right, is there anything in these three lines that tells us how Mr. Lee and Miss Foo are alike?
	Yes, no? Bung Soon, would you like to help Sang Ho out?
Bung Soon:	They are alike because they are admired by the writer.
T:	Okay, very good. So the writer admires the two of them.
	So in your Compare and Contrast organizer, under how alike, we should have:
	Both are admired by the author.

	Okay, everyone clear how to do this?
	Okay, good. Let's carry on.
	Now we're going to take a look at one difference which they might have.
	Pam, do you mind reading for us from Line 5? They both . . .
Pam:	They both possess many similarities and differences. For instance, Miss Foo is young and hip and modern. Mr. Lee is more the fatherly type that will be concerned over his students.
T:	Okay, good. Thank you, Pam.
	Marlyn, can you tell any difference or similarity?
Marlyn:	Mr. Lee is definitely older than Miss Foo.
T:	Very good. So probably the difference is with regards to age: Mr. Lee is much older and Miss Foo is much younger. Why is that so, Marlyn?
Marlyn:	Because in the context, Mr. Lee has been described as *fatherly*.
T:	Mr. Lee is fatherly. Miss Foo is young and hip.
	Very good, Marlyn.
	Okay, this is what I'm going to do next.
	In your groups, you're going to come up with the complete chart.

Appendix B: A form-focused lesson sequence

[In this lesson, two students are looking at material, which has phonetic spellings of two characters, Benny and Penny, and drawings of two objects, shirts and shorts]

T:	OK . . . who can make the first sentence here? . . . Who wants to make a sentence about Penny . . . or about. . . . Abdullah, make a sentence about Benny please.
S1:	What does Benny . . .
T:	No, not questions yet . . . just make a sentence.
S2:	Which one?
T:	No . . . not questions.
S2:	Ah, it's Benny?
T:	Yes, tell me something about Benny.
S2:	Benny washing.
T:	IS washing. Benny IS washing.
S2:	Uh, shirt . . . er . . . on the last day . . . the last day . . . on the last day . . . no.
T:	Yesterday.
S2:	Yes.
T:	OK . . . What did he wash yesterday?
S2:	He was wash . . . er He washing.
T:	Mohammed, can you help him?
S3:	Benny washED his short . . . shirt
T:	Mmmm . . . we don't say washED though do we?
S3:	WashED
T:	No, just one syllable. We say washt.
S4:	Wash.
S3:	Washt:
S2:	Washt.
T:	Yes, good, now Khalid, what did Benny do yesterday?
S2:	He washt his shirt.
T:	Good. Mohammed, can you make a sentence about Benny?
S3:	He washed his shirt.

T: No, look at the picture.

S3:   Oh, shorts, shorts, he washed his shorts.

T: That's right. Good

Appendix C: A Korean English class on fact and opinion

The following transcript is from an English language class from a university language program in South Korea. The class consists of 26 students, 17 female and 9 male students, with mixed proficiency levels in the English language. This is a required English language class and the teacher is a Korean female university teacher who is fluent in the English language. According to the teacher, the topic of the class discussion is having the students make "fact and opinion" statements. The teacher said before the class that she wants her students to practice speaking in English regardless of the number of mistakes. She said she herself had a hard time learning English and so she "knows what it takes to speak English." She said that she hopes to teach students how to speak English fluently rather than to get them to speak accurately in terms of correct grammar. The transcript excerpt shows the opening turns of the class.

Turns 1–21

1. T: Today we are going to practice speaking factual statements and opinion statements in English. Let's start with Brendan. What do you know about a fact statement?

2. Brendan: A fact is true.

3. T: True. A true statement is a fact statement. Anyone else would like to add on to that explanation? Susan?

4. Susan: Will happen.

5. T: Will happen, hmm. Fact means something that is true. Anyone else? Peter?

6. Peter: Are they things that have happened before?

7. T: Things that have happened before. OK. How about opinion? Who knows what the meaning of opinion is? John?

8. John: To ask about your thinking on something.

9. T: To ask about your thinking on something? Hmm . . . How about Paul? What do you . . . what do you understand?

10. Paul: What you think about something is an opinion?

11. T: What you think about something is an opinion? How about Sally?

12. Sally: Things that is not true.

13. T: Opinion means things that are not true. Sally, can you give me an example?

14. Sally: I think American movies not good.

15. T: You think that American movies are not good. OK. But do you mean the opposite. What I want to know is . . . is this your real opinion or do you like American movies?

16. Sally: No, I like. I like.

17. T: So, Sally, you say you like watching American movies. This is your opinion, yes?

18. Sally: Yes, I like American movies . . . good action scene.

19. T: You like American movies because there is good action in them?

20. Sally: Yes.

21. T: OK. Any other opinions on American movies?

CHAPTER 11

Exploring Your Own Teaching

INTRODUCTION

At various times during your teaching practice you will be observed by others – by your supervisor, by your cooperating teacher, and perhaps by other student teachers. Listening to their observations of your teaching and discussing issues that arise during practice-teaching sessions will be an important part of your teaching practice experience. However, you can also collect information about your own teaching experiences and use this information to review different aspects of your teaching. Collecting information about your teaching can serve several purposes. It can provide a record of your lessons. It can provide information that you can use to assess your own performance. It can document your progress on goals that you set for yourself. It can also facilitate a deeper understanding of teaching and of your own teaching approach. In this chapter we will examine a number of ways in which this process of self-review can be carried out.

In Chapter 7 we briefly outlined various methods you can consider when collecting information about lessons you observe, such as using checklists, doing seating chart observation records (SCORE) of a lesson, writing detailed field notes and narrative summaries, and making audio and video recordings of a lesson. We will now look at these procedures more closely and describe how they can be used to assess your own lessons.

AUDIO- OR VIDEO-RECORDING A LESSON

An audio or video recording of your lessons can provide insights into your teaching style that you may be unaware of. Often when we teach we are unaware of some aspects of our performance that may be perfectly obvious to others – and that will be revealed when we review a recording of the lesson. On listening to a recording of your lesson, for example, you may learn to your surprise that you dominate too much of the lesson, that you answer your own questions, or perhaps that you give inconsistent feedback to learners when they make errors. You may also be pleasantly surprised to learn that your explanations and instructions are clear and to the point and that your manner comes across as friendly and supportive. Making an audio recording usually involves placing a recording device in a central place in the classroom and trying to make sure you do not stand too far out of range of the recorder during the lesson. The recorder will not capture everything that goes on in the lesson but will nevertheless provide useful information for you to review.

A video recording of a lesson will provide a much richer record of the lesson, and you can ask a colleague or one of the students to help video your lesson or a segment of it. For a video recording, you need to think about what aspects of the lesson to focus on. Will you try to capture a sense of the lesson as a whole, focus mainly on you as the teacher, or focus on the students or individual students? Although the presence of the video recorder may affect you and your students' performance in some ways, usually students soon get used to it and the lesson can proceed relatively naturally. Both audio and video recordings can be used to examine many different aspects of your teaching. For example:

- the amount of talking you and your students engage in
- how you give instructions
- the quality and clarity of the language you use
- how you elicit student practice and production
- how you give feedback to students

In the following comments, student teachers describe some of the things they learned from recording their own teaching:

The first time I played the video recording of my class was a real eye-opener for me because I saw and heard things I never imagined had taken place. The first thing that struck me was my voice – the way I speak – as I had never heard myself before on tape. In fact, the sense of the sound of my voice pretty much dominated my first impressions as well as my appearance. I am not sure I moved on to analyzing my students' learning until I watched the tape for a second time and then I began to notice more about the room and the interactions. But it was that first time that has left a lasting impression with me.

Bruce, Korea

When I played the video of my speaking class it confirmed what I had suspected: That only a few people were dominating the discussions and too many were simply answering my questions with one-word answers. What I was surprised to notice was where the dominance was coming from in the room. Yes, one male student at the back right corner was very vocal but I knew about him. What I did not realize while I was teaching was that in the front right of my class a girl and boy were also dominant and I think they were out of my zone most of the time, or at least I did not notice them. I think I noticed the lack of participation in the back left corner of the room though.

Yuko, Japan

I mainly teach intermediate-level students in a private institute. Recently I was interested in finding out what my response to students' errors was, so I arranged to have two of my classes videotaped. I later looked over the videos to see whether there were any patterns to my error correction. The first thing that surprised me was that I ignored 80 percent of the errors students made. I also found that I tended to correct during controlled practice activities but hardly at all during open-ended fluency activities, such as when students were taking part in group discussions. I discovered that the usual strategy I employed to correct a student was simply to interrupt and provide the correct word or grammatical form. But about half the time I did that, the student did not repeat the correct form or try to correct the error.

Sergio, Argentina

WRITTEN ACCOUNTS OF LESSONS

Many things happen during a lesson. Some things are observable and relatively easy to recall, such as whether you were able (or needed) to keep to your lesson plan and were able to make use of the teaching resources you had planned to use during the lesson. Other things may be less easy for you to observe or write about, such as the extent to which individual students had difficulty with an activity or came away from a lesson with a sense of having learned something useful. Making a written report of your lessons seeks to provide a record of aspects of your teaching that are relatively easy to recall and that you might otherwise forget. The primary audience for your writing will be yourself but may also include your cooperating teacher, your supervisor, and other student teachers you may wish to share your comments with during a seminar. If so, you should not use students' actual names but use pseudonyms, to preserve students' right to privacy.

A convenient way of making a written record of a lesson is to make notes on your lesson plan after you have taught the lesson. These may include unanticipated problems learners had with pronunciation, grammar, or vocabulary, comments on the ordering of the activities in the lesson and any difficulties particular activities posed, whether better preparation or follow-up to a particular activity was needed, or whether a different classroom arrangement might have worked for an activity. These notes can later be used as a discussion point with your cooperating teacher or supervisor.

CHECKLISTS

A checklist contains a list of lesson features that you can complete as soon as possible after teaching a lesson. It could be a simple list such as the following:

Things that worked well:	_____
Things that didn't work so well:	_____
Unexpected problems:	_____
Things to do differently next time:	_____

Alternatively, the checklist could focus on a specific aspect of the lesson, such as vocabulary teaching and the kinds of problems students had with vocabulary during the lesson, for example:

Key words that the students learned in the lesson:	_____
Idioms and collocations I practiced:	_____
Vocabulary errors they made:	_____
Words they still need to practice:	_____

LESSON NARRATIVE

A narrative is a written account of a lesson that serves both as a summary of how the lesson proceeded and a reflection of the overall strengths and weaknesses of the lesson. Generally narratives begin with a description of the overall sequence of the lesson, followed by evaluative comments. The narrative could also conclude with reflections on things you learned from the lesson, issues that the lesson posed, or questions that you would like to discuss with your supervisor, your cooperating teacher, or other student teachers. Here is a written narrative from a student teacher:

Today I taught a listening lesson, using the book we are using for the listening strand of the course. Each unit contains three kinds of activities – a prelistening, a while-listening, and a postlistening. The unit was on relationships, so the students were really interested in it. As a lead-in I asked students to come up with factors they thought were important in friendships. I then went through the activities more or less following the book. I found that the activities took less time than I had planned so I had some time to fill in at the end of the lesson. So I went back to the recordings they had been listening to and used them as a kind of dictation, stopping the tape so they could write down the conversations. Then we looked at some of the features of the language that was on the tape. On reflection I think it's good to go back and work with the language the students have heard in a listening. After they have focused on getting the meaning, they can go back and look more closely at the actual language and maybe pick up some features of it that they can use. I will take this idea up with my cooperating teacher.

Yoko, Japan

Teaching Journal

A teaching journal is an ongoing account of teaching experiences, recorded in a notebook, a book, or electronically. It can be used for a variety of written accounts of lessons and incidents from lessons, including narratives, accounts of successes or problems, as well as summaries of what happened during lessons. Writing about teaching experiences can serve as a record of them, provide the basis for subsequent review and reflection, and can serve as a source of theorizing about teaching and learning. Journal entries may be brief or extended, depending on the amount of time devoted to them, and may be purely descriptive, both descriptive and evaluative, or problem oriented focusing on a problematic issue or incident, the nature of the problem, and possible causes and remedies. They may also be goal-oriented accounts, describing a goal you have set for yourself, measures you have taken to achieve the goal, and the outcomes you have achieved. For example, you may be trying to implement an unfamiliar teaching strategy or technique and write about this in your journal. As with other written lesson accounts the audience may be you, your cooperating teacher and supervisor, and your fellow student teachers.

Here are two examples of journals by a student teacher while on teaching practice in Hong Kong; the first one was written after about two weeks into teaching practice just before she taught a class, and the second one was written after the teacher had had some experience teaching the class.

Journal 1

I have been assigned the highest-level class and I have to work very closely with my cooperating teacher to coordinate the lessons I will teach. This is proving to be a real challenge for me on teaching practice. She said she would focus on oral and structured writing while I am to focus on narrative writing, comprehension, grammar, and perhaps listening comprehension. Not sure why she split the lessons this way but I am not too thrilled to have to teach grammar. We were told in the teacher education course that the focus is now off overt teaching of grammar in most English language schools. But now I am asked to teach the rules of grammar to the students and they have to memorize these and fill in the blanks in mindless worksheets. She said also that I am allowed to use resources other than the textbook whenever I feel appropriate.

Journal 2

Well, I have tried to follow what my cooperating teacher wants but I am having problems because she does things that I think are from the Middle Ages. She does not know anything about genre theory and how to teach this approach but we focused on this in our teacher education courses. When she observed me teach a class in which I attempted to use this approach she said that it was "not focused" because she could not understand it herself and she noticed that the students were asking too many questions about the class indicating to her that they too did not understand it. Another time I was told to teach a reading class or a comprehension class, as it is called by my cooperating teacher. In this lesson, I was supposed to go through the answers with the students while they marked their answers on the spot. This to me is just testing their reading comprehension ability so I decided to do more as I heard the cooperating teacher would not be able to observe me that day. The reading passage is based on dialogues so I asked different students to play the main leads and read the passage in a type of role-play situation. Then we had a short discussion about the passage before finally going through the answers. I had the students provide the answers and I reinforced the answers when necessary. The passage was a simple one and the questions were mainly reference questions and word meaning questions. As such, the students did not have many problems with the questions and this class progressed smoothly. The students all seemed pleased that I was actually teaching them reading comprehension because they told me that their teacher (my cooperating teacher) always just had them read the passage and answer the ten questions after it without telling them or showing them how to find the answers.

Sze, Hong Kong

CASE REPORTS

A case report is an account of a teaching incident or experience collected over a period of time. The purpose of compiling a case report is to focus on how an incident or situation develops over time. The topic for the case report is chosen because it is of special significance or because it is problematic in some way, and collecting information about it over time through the case report process can serve to clarify and better understand it. For example, you may decide to monitor a high-performing and a low-performing student over a period of time to try to identify what learning strategies each student seems to be employing in relation to specific classroom tasks. Or you may focus on your own attempts to implement a particular teaching technique or classroom management strategy over time. Your case report will normally describe the teaching context you are working in, the particular issue you are writing about and why, and a series of observations or descriptions recorded over the observation period, followed by your conclusions. Here is an example:

When I started my student teaching in the United Kingdom, I had some issues maintaining control in my classes while teaching. Although I tried to win the students over by being as friendly as possible to them both inside and outside class, they still realize that I am still only a student teacher and so they don't want to take me very seriously. When I give them activities to complete in class, my students will only do them if the cooperating teacher, their usual teacher, is there in the room as well. I am afraid, however, to tell my cooperating teacher about these problems in case I will be seen as a weak student teacher and not able to control my own students and thus I might get a low or even failing grade for teaching practice. So when I heard that the school usually has outings with the students, I signed up even though I did not have to, and said I would take the class to a local site of historical significance. When I got on the bus, the students were their usual noisy selves and I wondered if this was such a good idea. When we arrived at the site it was pouring with rain and the only place they could find to keep out of the rain until the bus came back for them some three hours later, was an expensive café. So I decided to buy them all lunch even though I am still a student with financial difficulties. The class were so delighted with this development that they started to change in their approach to me and started to accept me as a "real" teacher. They all had a great time that day and during the following day's class, all of them listened carefully and carried out the various activities without any of the usual disruptions – what a great investment I made.

Steven, United Kingdom

TEACHING PORTFOLIO

A teaching portfolio is a collection of documents and other items you put together over time and that serve to provide a record of your teaching, to provide a source of information for reflection and review, and that together provide a picture of the kind of teacher you are. The portfolio may focus on what you have done to achieve a certain goal (for example, to make your teaching more varied and interesting for students) or it may seek to show you at your best, that is, to show the range of skills and knowledge you possess. In some practice-teaching courses the teaching portfolio may be used as a component of the evaluation of the student teachers' performance and development.

The contents of your portfolio will depend on your goals in compiling the portfolio. It could include:

- an account of your personal teaching philosophy
- a summary of field experiences
- examples of lesson plans
- materials you have prepared for your classes
- student evaluations of your teaching
- written accounts of lessons
- observers' comments on your lessons

Here is an example of a student teacher reflecting on assembling a teaching portfolio:

When I was on teaching practice my supervisor suggested that I assemble a working teaching portfolio in order to document my growth and development on the practicum. For this we were recommended to include lesson plans, anecdotal records, student projects, class newsletters, videotapes, annual evaluations, and letters of recommendation, and the like. Initially I wondered if all this was just busy work and if it had any real purpose or value for me as a student teacher. When I saw (literally) what I had put together in my teaching portfolio at the end of my teaching practice I was really amazed. For example, for the section on Planning and Delivery of Lessons, I included an outline of my beliefs about teaching and learning, a few sample lesson plans and samples of my students' work and their evaluations of my lessons. I also put in a DVD recording of one of my classes with a written description of what I was teaching that day and my reflection on that class. Because my cooperating teacher observed that same class, I also included her feedback and finally I wrote a reflective essay on my growth in planning, delivery, and assessing instruction (this latter was a requirement from my teacher education institution). When I put all these together I could literally see my development as a teacher while on teaching practice. I now plan to keep this portfolio and use it when I am looking for a full-time teaching job.

Frank, Canada

CRITICAL INCIDENTS

During your teaching practice you will sometimes encounter an unexpected classroom incident that may cause you to stop for a moment and consider its implications, and it may even prompt a rethinking of an assumption or perhaps trigger a deeper understanding of some aspect of teaching. For example, Teresa was planning to use group work for a central part of one of her lessons. To her surprise, one of the students commented, "I hate group work – I'm going to work on my own." Teresa didn't know how to handle the situation and, to avoid embarrassment, decided to abandon her intention to do group work. After discussing the event with her cooperating teacher she decided she needed to talk to the class about the kinds of learning activities they found useful and to make a case for some of the activities she wanted to make use of.

Incidents like these are sometimes called critical incidents. A critical incident is any unplanned event that occurs during class. An incident can appear to be typical rather than critical at first sight, but really only becomes critical through analysis. When you reflect on these incidents and write about them, you can uncover new understandings of the teaching and learning process. Generally when you report on critical incidents you should try to make a detailed written description of what happened and especially what led up to it and what followed it. Then you can ask yourself why you think this happened and think about how the incident led (or could lead) to a change in your understanding of teaching.

The following procedures can be used for writing about critical incidents (Farrell 2008f):

1. When you experience a critical incident, write a brief description of it, detailing who was involved, where it took place, when, and what happened exactly. At this first stage, do not attempt to explain or interpret the incident.

2. On a separate page, you can next attempt to explain and interpret the incident.

3. If you are meeting regularly with other student teachers (or with your cooperating teacher or supervisor) you can share your incidents and interpretations and see if you have the same understanding of them.

The following critical incident report describes an incident that occurred in a grammar lesson:

I was teaching a class in a high school that was considered to have above average English language proficiency skills. The class consisted of forty students, and I prepared sentence examples on subject–verb agreement on an overhead transparency before the class. Then as I was going through the lesson and was answering questions I had set for the students because they could not answer them, I suddenly realized to my horror that I really was confused about grammar teaching and wondered there and then if I should give the grammar rule or not or should I just keep going with the lesson. I decided to just keep going but as the lesson progressed I became less focused because I also just realized that my lesson objectives were a bit vague statements, and I could not get my students to interact more with each other. In fact, they looked as if they were not following at all. Maybe I should have checked their prior knowledge of subject–verb agreement before I started the lesson, but I did not show my lesson plan to my cooperating teacher beforehand because she was busy.

Jacinta, Malaysia

ACTION RESEARCH

While you are on teaching practice you may also have the opportunity to carry out action research, although this will depend on the duration of your practice-teaching assignment. Action research refers to small-scale teacher-conducted classroom research that seeks to clarify and resolve practical teaching issues and problems. It generally involves identifying an issue or problem you would like to resolve, developing a strategy to address it, implementing the strategy, and observing its effects. The following are examples of the kinds of issues that can be researched during teaching practice:

- Teaching the four skills (issues related to changes in the way aspects of reading, writing, listening, or speaking are taught)
- Classroom dynamics (issues related to the kinds of interaction that occur in the language classroom and how these can be changed)
- Learner language (issues related to the kind of language students use when completing classroom activities and the amount of language they produce)
- Grouping arrangements (issues related to how different grouping arrangements, such as pair, group, or whole class, affect learner motivation and language use)
- Use of materials (issues relating to different ways in which materials can be used and how these affect the lesson)
- Grammar and vocabulary (issues related to the teaching of grammar and vocabulary and the effect of using different teaching strategies)
- Assessment (issues relating to changes in the forms of assessment used)

Action research involves four phases: *planning, action, observation, and reflection.* The planning phase involves identifying an issue you would like to explore (e.g., the effects of using a particular error correction strategy) and developing an action plan to address the issue (e.g., by implementing the strategy over a period of weeks); implementing the plan; observing the results; and reflecting on the action plan. Sometimes the action cycle may be conducted a second time after making some changes in the plan. An example of action research carried out by a Japanese English teacher in Japan is given below:

I realized that I had gotten into the habit of using too much Japanese in my English lessons and I wanted to see if I could do something to increase the amount of English I was using. To do this I first investigated how much Japanese I was using and for what purposes I was using it. I audio-recorded some lessons and checked three tapes recorded at different times over a two-week period. First I listened to them just to determine the proportion of English to Japanese I was using. It was about 70 percent English, 30 percent Japanese. I then listened to the tapes again to find out the purposes for which I was using Japanese. I found I was using Japanese for two main purposes: classroom management and giving feedback. I then drew up a plan to reduce the amount of Japanese I was using for these purposes. I first consulted a guide to the use of English in the classroom (Jane Willis 1981: Teaching English Through English, Longman) and familiarized myself with English expressions that could be used for classroom management and feedback. I wrote out a set of expressions and strategies on 3 by 5 inch cards, and put these in a conspicuous place on my table. These served not only to remind me of my plan but also helped me remember some of the expressions I wanted to use. Each day I would place a different card on top of the pile. I then continued recording my lessons and after a few weeks checked the tapes. My use of Japanese had declined considerably.

Satoshi, Japan

STUDENT TEACHER SUPPORT GROUPS

An activity that can provide support throughout the period of your teaching practice is to form a student teacher support group – a group of fellow student teachers who meet regularly to share their practice-teaching experiences, to discuss goals, problems, and concerns, and to collaborate on projects of interest to the group. Among the activities the group may wish to focus on are:

- *Trying out teaching strategies:* One group member may volunteer to try out a teaching strategy (e.g., jigsaw reading) and report on how it worked to the group.
- *Peer observation*: Group members can take turns observing each other's lessons.
- *Observing videotapes*: The group may watch teacher-training videos or other classroom videos and discuss them.
- *Action research*: The group may plan and implement action research projects.
- *Lesson planning and materials development*: The group may plan lessons and materials collaboratively, teach them, and then discuss the results.

The following is a report of a student teacher support group:

We decided to form a student teacher support group for the period of our practice teaching. During the period of the group we decided that the main reason for our collaborating was to practice our teaching with each other in minilessons on grammar, writing, and reading so that we would be ready for our teaching practice. This gave us the opportunity to exchange our prepared lesson plans and teaching resources, and so it removed some pressure while we were teaching as we knew we could rely on each other for support and resources at a moment's notice. We held many group discussions and we evaluated each member's lesson on the grammar and writing components because we were all placed in the same school district and thus using similar curricula and in some cases two of us were placed in the same school. For me, the experience with my support group during the practicum was a real lifesaver not to mention the start of my professional development as a teacher.

Bearnie, United States

Table 11.1 summarizes how teachers can explore their teaching.

1. Audio- or video-record a lesson	• Record of lesson to examine different aspects of teaching
2. Written accounts of lessons	• Writing account of lesson using checklists and narratives
3. Teaching journal	• Written ongoing account of teaching experiences in notebook, book, or electronic form
4. Case reports	• Account of a teaching incident or experience collected over a period of time
5. Teaching portfolio	• Collection of documents over time to provide record of teaching, a source of information for reflection and review, and a picture of the kind of teacher you are
6. Critical incidents	• Written accounts of any unplanned event that occurs during class
7. Action research	• Small-scale teacher-conducted classroom research that seeks to clarify and resolve practical teaching issues and problems
8. Student teacher support groups	• Group of fellow student teachers who meet regularly to share their practice teaching experiences; to discuss goals, problems, and concerns; and to collaborate on projects of interest to the group

Table 11.1 Exploring teaching

SUMMARY AND CONCLUSIONS

As a student teacher you will receive feedback on your teaching from your cooperating teacher and supervisor. However, you can also monitor your own teaching and use the information you obtain to review the progress you are making in your teacher learning. Different review processes all involve collecting information about your teaching in one way or another, through recording lessons, writing about lessons and lesson incidents, compiling a teaching portfolio or teaching journal, or forming a support group with other student teachers. You may also have the chance to carry out small-scale action research.

Reviewing your own teaching is an important part of your practice-teaching experience, since it may reveal aspects of your teaching that you were unaware of. The results may offer a different perspective on your teaching from that offered by your cooperating teacher and can provide a basis for discussion and reflection. Exploring your own teaching is also part of the process of theorizing from your own practice and developing understandings and principles that will give you greater confidence as a teacher. We recommend that you start with procedures that are simple to implement, such as journal writing and audio-recording lessons, and depending on what you learned from these, then move on to trying some of the other procedures discussed in this chapter.

Further reading

Bowens, T., & Marks, J. (1994). *Inside teaching*. Oxford: Macmillan.

Burns, A. (2010). *Doing action research in English language teaching. A guide for practitioners*. New York: Routledge.

Gebhard, J., & Oprandy, R. (Eds.) (1999). *Language teaching awareness*. New York: Cambridge University Press.

Wallace, M. (1998). *Action research for language teachers*. Cambridge: Cambridge University Press.

Discussion questions

1. Review the case report by Steven (see pages 154–155) and discuss how he solved his problem with getting his students to recognize him as a real teacher. What are other ways you could go about helping your students to see you as a real teacher?

2. Discuss the items you think it would be useful to include in a teaching portfolio and what each item would reveal about you as a teacher.

3. Which of the different ways of exploring your teaching explained in this chapter do you think are most useful to you and why?

4. If you plan to set up a student teacher support group, discuss how you could go about it, what the focus of the group would be, and how it would function.

Follow-up activities

1. Make an audio or video recording of one of your lessons and review it. Did you learn anything surprising about your teaching? What else did you learn?

2. Prepare a checklist that could be used to document either a specific aspect of a lesson or the lesson as a whole.

3. Write a narrative account of one or more of your lessons and share them with other student teachers. Discuss any issues that the account raises.

4. Write an account of a critical incident that occurred in your practice teaching. Then share it with other student teachers and discuss.

5. Choose a topic that interests you and that could be the basis for an action research project during your teaching practice, then suggest how you could investigate it.

CHAPTER 12

After Teaching Practice

INTRODUCTION

Your teaching practice course will have provided you with the opportunity to experience the realities of classroom teaching and to experience some of the problems language teachers deal with on a daily basis. It will also have given you the opportunity to put into practice many of the things you learned during your teacher education course or program. Doubtless however you will have found that no amount of reading, study, or listening to experts can fully prepare you for dealing with the full range of issues that language teaching involves. Some of these may arise from working with learners of different cultural, linguistic, and educational backgrounds; some result from the intrinsic difficulties learning a new language entails; and some may be the result of working with learners who have had difficult life experiences or who have pressing educational and other needs. Some of the issues you confronted may not have appeared in your teacher-training courses. Learning how to deal with others may take considerable skill and experience, and practice teaching is only the start of this learning process. In this chapter we will examine some of the challenges you may face once you commence your teaching career and consider some of the options that are available to support your ongoing professional development. Here is a reflection by a student teacher who has just finished teaching practice:

I feel as though I have just started the process of developing my teaching skills. There is still a long way to go, but at least I know in what direction to move. I have been given the theory and I have the experiences and reflections from my teaching practice to use as the basis for further learning and improvement. I feel that I have a strong platform for my future teaching which I didn't have before I started the teaching practice.

Eldri, Indonesia

AFTER COMPLETING TEACHING PRACTICE

When you have finished teaching practice you will want to go over your experiences with your cooperating teacher and your supervisor to review your experience. In these conversations you can discuss what went well, what you felt well prepared for and had not been so well prepared for, what you enjoyed least and most, what you have learned, and what you think you still need to learn. The following comment on his teaching practice is from a student teacher in Canada:

I had a hard time transitioning from one task to another at first, but I slowly learned through experience and advice from my supervising teacher how to effectively and properly do this. I learned that you can't just drop one activity and move to the next, but that you always need to have a spiel about the importance of the first activity and how it relates to the next. Otherwise students seem to forget the first task and possibly become bored of doing one task after the other without seeing any clear purpose. The same goes for ending a class. There needs to be some kind of "conclusion" where the teacher points out what was learned in that class, why it is important and how it fits into the whole picture. All of these aforementioned steps to classroom routine I learned through experience and trial and error. This seems to be the best way of learning this type of thing rather than a professor or teacher telling you how it works. Most of the things I have learned in university about ESL teaching was by a professor explaining or outlining how to do or accomplish a certain task, but in the end I think I learned the most about classroom routine and order by actually experiencing and testing it out during my practice-teaching opportunities.

Ruben, Canada

EXPERIENCES DURING THE INITIAL TEACHING PERIOD

Your initial teaching experience will inevitably involve a period of adjustment, as you try to apply what you learned in your teacher education program to your particular teaching context. As we saw in Chapter 3, the school context and school culture have a major influence on how teaching and learning occur in classrooms, and can provide a sort of filter to some of the innovations and strategies you may wish to implement. The first year of teaching can consequently be an anxiety-provoking experience because it involves a balancing act between learning to teach (i.e., furthering what was started during the teacher education program and the practicum) and also attempting to become a "real" teacher within the established culture and practices of a school (Farrell 2008g). The following comments reflect some of the problems experienced by teachers in their first year of teaching:

I discovered during my first year of teaching that part of the challenge was all about keeping some sense of balance, or indeed, finding my own balance because there are so many issues thrown at you and you do not have the support or protection you had while on teaching practice.

Carla, United States

During my first year I had lots of problems relating to my new colleagues in the school because they thought I was a bit too eager with everything and that I was showing them up.

Vic, Singapore

When I entered my new institution for my full-time job I was just thrown into the class without any formal process of induction beyond an initial meeting with the institution head. In fact, we did not have any staff meeting for the first seven weeks.

Sarah, Canada

Because I am a nonnative-English-speaking ESL teacher, my first year was full of self-doubt and I lacked self-confidence because of my perceived professional competence, and my experiences concerning discrimination in hiring practices that relate directly to language proficiency in that school did not help me settle at all.

Heesung, Korea

During my first year of teaching, I had to completely forget what I learned on teaching practice and the teacher education program because of the complete domination of the culture of examinations that overly influenced teaching approaches in that school.

Yoko, Japan

Like other novice teachers you may experience several stages of development once you begin teaching (Maynard and Furlong 1995): *early idealism, survival, recognizing difficulties, reaching a plateau,* and *moving on*. In the *early idealism* phase you may feel a strong sense of identifying with your students, believing yourself to be different from traditional teachers because of your recent up-to-date training. The *survival* stage is where you may begin to react to the reality of the everyday classroom teaching situation and perhaps sense that the complexity of the teaching environment will overwhelm you. In the next phase you begin to gain more of an awareness of your teaching situation and begin to *recognize the difficulties* of successful teaching and the limitations of what you may be able to achieve. This in turn can lead to a period of self-doubt. Once this is overcome you may sense that you are *reaching a plateau* where you can now cope better with the routines of everyday teaching, but you may also become more focused on successful classroom management rather than on student learning. It may be some time before you *move on* and begin to focus on the quality of student learning in your classes. In the following accounts, novice teachers describe some of their initial teaching experiences:

Oh, my goodness, I feel embarrassed to write this but when I started teaching I was so eager to please everyone and most especially my students because I felt I could make a difference to their lives. I had so much in my head that I was going to transfer and I was not going to be like certain teachers I had when I was growing up: I would be interesting, energetic, and always ready to listen to my students. Well, did this ever change after the first two weeks in which I thought I was put in a storm of activity and I thought I would not make Week 3 what with all the planning, teaching, meetings, developing tests, and organizing sports and the like, all I wanted to do was get through each class. Then sometime after midterm during the first semester and after chatting to some of the experienced teachers I began to settle down more and started to get used to my hectic life as a teacher. Nothing prepared me for these first few weeks though.

Neil, United States

I think it was about the eighth week when real self-doubt began to set in during my first year as a teacher of English. Yes, the first few weeks were hectic but I had help from my mentor throughout but it was after a period of correcting about 80 compositions from two classes that I wondered if I was really suited to be an ESL teacher. I was feeling physically tired all the time and was beginning to dread getting up in the morning and going to school because I wondered what the students were really learning. I think that batch of compositions really took the wind out of my sails because the students continued to make the same mistakes even though I had gone over these things time after time in the lessons. If it were not for my mentor's help and guidance I would have given up already.

Vic, Singapore

Support from other teachers in the school is often crucial in making the transition to full-time teaching as the comments from this teacher illustrate:

It was lovely and I was just learning so much and I've never known such a collegiate atmosphere anywhere before. Someone would look at you and say, "Oh, are you having problems with that?" And they'd all just come around and offer you suggestions and give you different things. And when people did lessons and creative things and made up cards and all the rest of it, it all went in files for everyone to use. And so everyone shared, shared, shared. There was a huge sharing atmosphere in that place, and it was a lovely way to learn about the communicative style of teaching and to develop as a teacher.

Teacher cited by Senior 2006: 66

Schools normally anticipate the difficulties teachers face in their first years of teaching, and have support systems in place to help novice teachers adjust to their new role as classroom teachers. Typically, a well-designed induction program will orient you to the school's norms of practice and the expectations you will be expected to meet. For example, you may be expected to meet the parents of some of your students and the school will have procedures for how such meetings are organized, the kinds of interactions that normally take place in them, and how to deal with issues that may be raised. You may also be assigned a mentor or "buddy" who will help familiarize you with the school routines and to help you establish yourself within the school culture. However, in some situations you may be left more or less on your own, and you may have to take the initiative to network with other more experienced teachers and to use them as a sounding board to discuss issues you encounter.

In the following comment, a novice teacher describes how he tries to accommodate his teaching to the syllabus that the school prescribes:

Now that I am in my first year I realize that the aim of the syllabus I have been given to teach to is to ensure that the students are exposed to the necessary / desired skills. So, if students need more time on a particular set of skills, teachers should plan lessons that also focus on such needs. However, I don't write a lesson plan anymore for English language teaching even though I used to while I was on teaching practice but this was because I was required to by the supervisor. I think English lessons are not linear and I find detailed lesson plans limiting so I have them in my head. Teachers should plan lessons well but not too detailed, as it may be difficult to stick to. So, my lessons are planned to be loosely detailed yet flexible although I make sure I am not departing from the syllabus. This seems to be what other teachers do in the school.

Deng, Hong Kong

WHAT TO DO WHEN PROBLEMS ARISE

When you begin your first teaching position you will be entering the real world of the classroom and the school culture, and typical problems you will encounter could be teaching large classes, dealing with difficult students (and sometimes difficult colleagues!), and coping with the workload of a full-time teacher. Many schools appoint a mentor who can "show you the ropes," introduce you to the many new people and resources available to you, and help you solve problems that may arise. You may also be able to seek out a "buddy" – an experienced teacher who can provide different kinds of advice and support as you find your feet as a teacher. The need for such support is emphasized in this comment from a novice teacher in Canada:

Considering the high attrition rate of first-year teachers of any kind, I presume all novice teachers might initially appreciate some more general, all-round support and encourage-ment from experienced teachers rather than an avalanche of pedagogical advice, however well intentioned.

Martin, Canada

JOINING A COMMUNITY OF PRACTICE

The stages of development you may experience represent a view of teacher learning as an individual activity and suggest that the issues you will face in your initial period of teaching are things you will have to resolve on your own. But once you start teaching in a school you become a member of a community of teachers who have shared goals, values, and interests, and you will be able to capitalize on the potential for learning and growth that comes from participating in such a community. The school or the teaching institution becomes a learning community and its members constitute a *community of practice* (Lave and Wenger 1991). A community of practice has two characteristics:

1. It involves a group of people who have common interests and who relate and interact to achieve shared goals.
2. It focuses on exploring and resolving issues related to the workplace practices that members of the community take part in.

In your work as a language teacher this can take the form of collaboration with other teachers in order to better understand the nature of the teaching and learning that goes on in your classrooms, to share knowledge and skills, to bring about changes in practice when necessary, and to capitalize on the potentials that team work and group collaboration can bring about. When a school is thought of as a community of practice, opportunities need to be found for you and other teachers in the school to work and learn together through participation in group-oriented activities with shared goals and responsibilities, involving joint problem solving. Many forms of professional development can help foster the sense of a community of practice, such as reading groups, action research, team teaching, peer observation, and peer coaching (Richards and Farrell 2005). Collegiality creates new roles for teachers, such as team leader, teacher trainer, mentor, or critical friend. Here is a comment from a teacher who is working in a collegial environment:

At morning tea, if somebody brings up a problem, then the whole group gets very interested and we discuss and support each other, saying "this works" and "that works," and making suggestions, "Why don't you try this?"

Teacher cited by Senior 2006: 65

An example of how this kind of collaboration can happen is with the Lesson Study Approach that has been widely implemented in Japan (Lewis and Tsuchida 1998). Teams of teachers coplan a lesson that focuses on a particular piece of content or a unit of study. Throughout the planning process, they draw on outside resources, including textbooks, research, teaching theories, and engage in extended conversations while focusing on student learning and the development of specific outcomes. Once the plan has been developed, one member of the team volunteers to teach it, while the others observe. (Sometimes outsiders are also invited to observe.) After the lesson, the group discusses its findings in a colloquium or panel discussion. Typically the teachers who planned the lesson focus on their rationale for how they planned the lesson and their evaluation of how it went, particularly focusing on student learning. The planning group then reconvenes to review the lesson, revise it, after which a different teacher teaches it to a different class. The cycle culminates in the team publishing a report that includes lesson plans, observed student behavior, teacher reflections, and a summary of the group discussions. These are then made available to others.

The following vignette describes the advantages of teacher groups:

We decided to meet regularly as a group of ESL teachers not only to share our experiences as teachers but also to share in the hopes, sufferings, and aspirations of those with whom we teach. We started our group to reflect on our teaching and we decided to not only meet weekly for one semester but also to write a diary and, if possible, observe each other's classes. So we met together as a group once a week and brought journals for each other to read. Keeping a journal allowed us to write down our thoughts and feelings about what we had done in the classroom and discussed at the meetings of the whole group.

All the group meetings were supportive and the diverse subjects we talked about included life experiences, inability to deal with large classes, students' responses to questions in class, handling uninvolved students, material for conversation classes, giving feedback, and the concept of what it is to be an ESL teacher. Some of the responses saw the group members encourage students to work in groups, giving clear instructions, keeping questions open-ended, writing up directions on the blackboard, getting more knowledge from studying ESL materials, and getting together regularly. During the semester, all participants were extremely busy, with up to 25-hour-a-week teaching loads, a situation that created some stress and prevented the members putting in the amount of effort they wanted to. Nevertheless, the meetings lasted an average 2.5 hours each, exceeding the time participants had allocated.

At first, I hesitated to join the group because of my tight schedule. But when I realized what we would be doing in it, I felt the need to take part, to talk about our classes, and to find out what was happening in them. I couldn't resist pushing myself into it. The group members were great. I was especially fascinated by their attitude to and enthusiasm about teaching. They didn't mind revealing how they think, prepare, and teach, and they accepted the differences between themselves and me. During the period the group was meeting, I didn't actually realize much of this, just as if I had been journeying through a wood, not being able to see it for the trees. It was a great opportunity for me to find myself as an EFL teacher, to open my mind, to build better relationships with teachers that could allow better ones with my students, and to acquire a self-awareness that I could introduce to my students. The following semester I have tried to share this feeling of self-awareness by getting students to record their own voice letters to me, to listen back to them and sense their ability and the problems they have, and to discuss ideas they want with me. Sharing ideas and experiences makes us grow personally and professionally I believe. I am empowered now as a result of taking part in this group because we did help each other to develop and we did become better teachers.

Greg, Korea

FROM TEACHER TRAINING TO TEACHER DEVELOPMENT

Your practice-teaching time has provided you with experience that can be regarded as "teacher training." This means you have had an opportunity to prepare yourself for a real teaching position by trying out teaching techniques and strategies based on your coursework and lectures under the supervision of a supervisor or cooperating teacher. You have received feedback that has focused on your strengths and limitations in the classroom and been given suggestions as to how to deal with full-time teaching once your practicum experience has finished. Once you begin full-time teaching and develop the confidence, skills, and flexibility that experience brings, you can then consider longer-term goals for your continuing development as a language teacher. This phase of growth is referred to as "teacher development." Teacher development involves your increase in understanding and skill in teaching over time as well as a deeper understanding of yourself as a teacher. Teacher development includes personal and individual reflection on yourself as a teacher but should go beyond this to include the exploration of new trends and theories in language teaching, familiarization with developments in TESOL, and the development of a specialization in your teaching (e.g., testing, blended learning, teacher supervision, materials writing, study skills).

BECOMING A REFLECTIVE PRACTITIONER

A key to long-term professional development is the ability to be able to reflect consciously and systematically on your teaching experiences. By reflection we mean asking questions like these about your teaching:

1. What kind of teacher am I?
2. What am I trying to achieve for myself and for my learners?
3. What are my strengths and limitations as a language teacher?
4. How do my students and colleagues view me?
5. How and why do I teach the way I do?
6. How have I developed as a teacher since I started teaching?
7. What are the gaps in my knowledge?
8. What role do I play in my school and is my role fulfilling?
9. What is my philosophy of teaching and how does it influence my teaching?
10. What is my relationship with my colleagues and how productive is it?
11. How can I mentor less experienced teachers?

There are many ways in which you can engage in a critical and reflective review of your own practices throughout your teaching career (cf. Richards and Farrell 2005; Richards and Lockhart 1994), for example through analyzing critical incidents, teacher support groups, journal writing, discussion groups, action research, portfolios, and other procedures for self-observation described elsewhere in this book (see Chapter 11). Reflection involves both looking back at teaching experiences as well as looking forward and setting goals for new or changed directions. Dewey (1933) suggested three attributes that can facilitate the processes of reflective thinking: *open-mindedness*, *responsibility*, and *wholeheartedness*. Open-mindedness is a desire to listen to more than one side of an issue and to give attention to alternative views. Responsibility means careful consideration of the consequences to which an action leads. And wholeheartedness implies that we can overcome fears and uncertainties to critically evaluate our practice in order to make meaningful change. The comments below are from two student teachers in Indonesia who have just completed their teaching practice:

The act of reflection itself is an invaluable way of improving your teaching skills. It has given me an invaluable insight into many aspects of my teaching and given me an incentive to improve my overall teaching skills.

Mark

For me personally the reflections motivated me; if the reflections were positive it was an incentive to be even better next time. If the reflections weren't so positive it was a guide to improve that particular skill ensuring learning amongst students is stimulating and fun.

Jikke

BECOMING A LANGUAGE TEACHING PROFESSIONAL

Your academic courses as well as your practice-teaching experience are evidence that language teaching is not something that anyone who can speak a language can do. It is a profession, which means that language teaching is seen as a career in a field of educational specialization, it requires a specialized knowledge base obtained through both academic study and practical experience, and it is a field of work where membership is based on entry requirements and standards. Your decision to acquire a professional qualification in language teaching reflects your recognition of these facts. The professionalism of language teaching today is seen in the growth industry devoted to providing language teachers with professional training and qualifications, in continuous attempts to develop standards for language teaching and for language teachers, in the proliferation of professional journals and teacher magazines, conferences, and professional organizations, and in the greater level of sophisticated knowledge of language teaching required of language teachers. Becoming an English language teacher means becoming part of a worldwide community of professionals with shared goals, values, discourse, and practices, but one with a self-critical view of its own practices and a commitment to a transformative approach to its own role.

There are two different dimensions to professionalism (Leung 2009). The first can be called institutionally prescribed professionalism – a managerial approach to professionalism that represents the views of ministries of education, teaching organizations, regulatory bodies, school principals, and so on that specify what teachers are expected to know and what quality teaching practices consist of. There are likely to be procedures for achieving accountability and processes in place to maintain the quality of teaching, and these will have a considerable impact on your work as a language teacher. Such specifications are likely to differ from country to country and from one teaching context to another.

The second dimension to professionalism is independent professionalism, which refers to teachers' own views of teaching and the processes by which teachers engage in reflection on their own values, beliefs, and practices, that is, becoming a *reflective practitioner.*

You will also find that there are many benefits in joining a professional language-teaching organization, such as Teaching English to Speakers of Other Languages (TESOL) or the International Association of Teachers of English as a Foreign Language (IATEFL), in subscribing to one of the many professional publications for language teachers, in participating in online teacher discussion groups, and in participating in workshops and seminars if these are available in your region. We hope that your academic and professional education, as well as your practicum experience, have provided a good foundation with which to commence your careers as language-teaching professionals. Here are some comments from novice teachers in Canada reflecting on their goals for long-term professional development:

I will try to network with other teachers in the area in order to stay connected with what is happening in the field and I will do this by trying to attend local conferences and professional development opportunities whenever offered.

Faith

I would like to have a group meeting regularly with other teachers. Every member, including English teachers and other professionals, even the administrative staff, will share their experiences and discuss problems. With collaboration, teaching is not merely an individual activity without any resources; instead, in a group you own many resources and know how to accommodate the stress, to get the balanced life, and to enjoy teaching. In Taiwan I was a member of National Teachers' Association R.O.C. before coming to Canada. The association provides regular publications to inform the members of significant news, such as changes in educational policy and current issues.

Shiang-Ru

SUMMARY AND CONCLUSIONS

Your teaching experience during teaching practice will have given you a brief introduction to the realities of classroom language teaching. You will now be familiar with many of the issues that language teachers deal with on a daily basis, from planning lessons and designing teaching materials to conducting the different phases of a lesson. At the same time you will have expanded your understanding of learners, of teaching, of the dynamics of the classroom, and of yourself as a teacher. Once you complete your teacher education program, however, and take up full-time work as a language teacher in a school or institute, you will soon realize that there is still a great deal more to learn, and that teaching practice cannot fully prepare you for the reality of full-time language teaching.

Language teachers form a large international community of dedicated teaching professionals, and as you become a member of this community you should capitalize on the opportunities it offers for collegial support and professional development as well as for networking with colleagues locally and internationally through professional organizations and the Internet. In this way you will be able to sustain your career and your ongoing professional development. You will also experience the satisfaction that results from providing people with the means to acquire one of life's most crucial skills – the ability to learn and use a new language.

Further reading

Books

Bailey, K. M., Curtis, A., & Nunan, D. (2001). *Pursuing professional development: The self as source.* Boston, MA: Heinle & Heinle.

Johnson, K., & Golombek, P. (2002). *Teachers' narrative inquiry as professional development.* New York: Cambridge University Press.

Richards, J. C., & Farrell, T. S. C. (2005). *Professional development for language teachers.* New York: Cambridge University Press.

Journals and magazines

English Language Teaching Journal (ELTJ) – http://eltj.oxfordjournals.org

English Teaching Professional – www.etprofessional.com

Humanizing Language Teaching – www.hltmag.co.uk/sep01/idea.htm

TESOL Essential Teacher – www.tesol.org/s_tesol/seccss.asp?CID=206&DID=1676

TESOL Journal – www.tesol.org

The Teacher Trainer Journal – www.tttjournal.co.uk

Discussion questions

1. What advice would you give to a student teacher who is about to commence his or her teaching practice?

2. What are some goals you could set for yourself in terms of your longer-term professional development as a language teacher?

3. What forms of collaboration with other teachers do you think will be useful to you once you commence full-time teaching?

4. What professional organizations for language teachers are you familiar with? What benefits do you think belonging to such organizations could bring?

5. What unique strengths and dispositions do you possess that would make you an asset to a school or language-teaching institution?

6. What kinds of professional development activities do you think would be useful to you to foster your continued development as a language teacher?

Follow-up activities

Look at some of the following Internet sites (we thank David Deubelbeiss for these) and discuss how useful you think some of them could be for your teaching.

1. http://eflclassroom.ning.com – EFL Classroom 2.0: Lots of resources, games, discussion and tips for using technology in the classroom. For both students and teachers.

2. http://breakingnewsenglish.com – BreakingNewsEnglish: For higher-level students or teaching teachers. Articles with exercises and listening.

3. http://mes-english.com – MES English: Flashcards, worksheets for young learners.

4. http://bogglesworldesl.com – Bogglesworld: Lesson plans, activities, for young learners and middle school students / high school students.

5. http://teachingrecipes.com – Teaching Recipes: Short and simple techniques, ideas and resources to help teachers.

6. www.de.mingoville.com/content/view/13/29/lang,en – Mingoville: Online learning suite for young learners. Free, great for practice.

7. http://acacia.pntic.mec.es/agip0002/auro/inicio.html – Click N Learn: Online learning suite for older students. Free. Great practice.

8. www.diigo.com/list/eflclassroom – A list of MANY sites, all categorized and saved by fellow English teachers. A treasure chest!

9. www.voicethread.com – Voicethread: Create an account, put up a picture, and send your students there to practice speaking and to record messages. Really great for speaking practice.

10. http://voxopop.com – Voxopop: Much like Voicethread but no pictures. Only a series of recordings. Ask a question and your students can go there to reply and speak in English. Make your own class group.

11. https://plans.pbworks.com/academic – Wikis: Create a free wiki for your class and students to edit and share ideas.

12. http://writeboard.com – Writeboard: A class writeboard allows all students to work on a class document, add and edit and see the changes. Teacher friendly!

13. http://pageflakes.com – Pageflakes: Quickly make a page for your class that updates all the rss feeds you want of all the content around the world wide web that your students might need.

14. http://quizlet.com – Quizlet: Allows you to make wordlists which your students can use for practice and also quiz themselves.

15. http://tarheelreader.org – Tar Heel Reader: Make books with pictures. The site has a voice which will read them! Also download them as PowerPoint and use in class directly!

16. http://eslvideo.com – ESL Video: Students or teachers can make quizzes using YouTube videos!

17. http://real-english.com – Real English: Watch videos with subtitles, for all levels. Unique!

18. http://englishcentral.com/teachers – English Central: Sign up as a teacher, invite students to record their voice to real videos. Keep track of their progress!

19. http://edu20.org – Edu 2.0: Create a classroom community using this amazingly simple LMS (Learning Management System). Sign up your class and they can chat, blog, share videos and music. All free!

20. http://penzu.com – Penzu: A very attractive and simple place for students to keep an online journal or diary. They can share with the teacher or classmates. Really easy to set up.

REFERENCES

Aljaafreh, A., & Lantolf, J. P. (1994). Negative feedback as regulation and second language learning in the zone of proximal development. *The Modern Language Journal*, 78, 465–483.

Allwright, D., & Bailey, K. M. (1991). *Focus on the language classroom: An introduction to classroom research for language teachers*. Cambridge: Cambridge University Press.

Arends, R. (2004). *Learning to Teach* (6th ed.). Boston: McGraw Hill.

Bailey, K. M. (1996). The best laid plans: Teachers' in-class decisions to depart from their lesson plans. In K. Bailey & D. Nunan (Eds.), *Voices from the language classroom* (15–40). New York: Cambridge University Press.

Bailey, K. M. (2006). *Language teacher supervision: A case-based approach*. New York: Cambridge University Press.

Bailey, K. M., Curtis, A., & Nunan, D. (2001). *Pursuing professional development: The self as source*. Boston, MA: Heinle & Heinle.

Baird, B. (2008). *The internship, practicum and field placement handbook* (5th ed.). New Jersey: Pearson/Prentice Hall.

Bell, D. M. (2007). Do teachers think that methods are dead? *ELT Journal*, 61(2), 135–143.

Benson, P. (2001). *Teaching and researching autonomy in language learning*. London: Longman.

Benson, P. (2003). Learner autonomy in the classroom. In D. Nunan (Ed.), *Practical English language teaching* (289–308). New York: McGraw Hill.

Benson, P. (2005). (Auto)biography and learner diversity. In P. Benson & D. Nunan (Eds.), *Learners' stories: Difference and diversity in language learning* (4–21). Cambridge: Cambridge University Press.

Benson, P. (in press). Learner-centered teaching. In J. C. Richards & A. Burns (Eds.), *The Cambridge guide to pedagogy and practice in language teaching*. New York: Cambridge University Press.

Borg, S. (2006). *Teacher cognition and language education: Research and practice*. London: Continuum.

Bowens, T., & Marks, J. (1994). *Inside teaching*. Oxford: Macmillan.

Brenes-Carvajal, M. G. del C. (2009). *Initial development of English language teachers in Mexico*. Doctorate in Applied Linguistics Thesis, Macquarie University, Sydney, Australia.

Brindley, G. (1984). *Needs analysis and objective setting in the adult migrant education program*. Sydney, N.S.W. Migrant Education Service.

Burns, A. (2010). *Doing action research in English language teaching. A guide for practitioners*. New York: Routledge.

Burns, A., & Richards, J. C. (Eds.). (2009). *The Cambridge guide to second language teacher education.* New York: Cambridge University Press.

Calderhead, J. (1992). Induction: a research perspective on the professional growth of the newly qualified teacher. In J. Calderhead & J. Lambert (Eds.), *The induction of newly appointed teachers.* General Teaching Council for England and Wales, pp. 5–21.

Carvajal (2009).

Cazden, C. (1988). *Classroom discourse: The language of teaching and learning.* Portsmouth, NH: Heineman.

Cooke, M., & Simpson, J. (2008). *ESOL: A critical guide.* Oxford: Oxford University Press.

Crawford. J. (1995). The role of materials in the language classroom: Finding the balance. *TESOL in Context*, 5, 1, 25–33.

Crookes, G. (2003). *The practicum in TESOL: Professional development through teaching practice.* New York: Cambridge University Press.

Dewey, J. (1933). *How we think.* Madison, WI: University of Wisconsin Press.

Dornyei, Z. (2001). *Motivational strategies in the language classroom.* Cambridge: Cambridge University Press.

Doyle, W. (1986). Classroom organization and management. In M. C. Wittrock (Ed.), *Handbook of research on teaching* (3rd ed., pp. 392–431). New York: Macmillan.

Duncan, M., & Biddle, B. (1974). *The study of teaching.* New York: Holt Rinehart, and Winston.

Farrell, T. S. C. (2002). Lesson Planning. In J. C. Richards & W. A. Renandya (Eds.), *Methodology in language teaching: An anthology of current practice* (pp. 30–39). New York: Cambridge University Press.

Farrell, T. S. C. (2007). Failing the practicum: narrowing the gap between expectation and reality with reflective practice. *TESOL Quarterly*, 41(1), 193–201.

Farrell, T. S. C. (2008a). Promoting reflective practice in language teacher education with microteaching. *Asian Journal of English Language Teaching (AJELT)*, 18, 1–15.

Farrell, T. S. C. (2008b). "Here's the book, go teach the class": ELT practicum support. *RELC Journal*, 39(2), 226–241.

Farrell, T. S. C. (2008c). *Teaching reading to English language learners: A reflective approach.* Thousand Oaks, CA: Corwin Press.

Farrell, T. S. C. (2008d). *Reflective language teaching: From research to practice.* London, UK: Continuum Press.

Farrell. T. S. C. (Ed.). (2008e). *Classroom management.* Alexandria, VA: TESOL Publications.

Farrell, T. S. C. (2008f). Critical incidents in ELT initial teacher training. *ELT Journal*, 62(1), 3–10.

Farrell, T. S. C. (Ed.). (2008g). *Novice language teachers.* London: Equinox.

Freeman, D. (1982). Observing teachers: Three approaches to inservice training and development. *TESOL Quarterly*, 16(1), 21–28.

Freeman, D. (1989). Teacher training, development and decision making model: A model of teaching and related strategies for language teacher education. *TESOL Quarterly*, 32, 27–45.

Freeman, D., & Richards, J. C. (Eds.). (1996). *Teacher learning in language teaching.* Cambridge: Cambridge University Press.

Fujiwara, B. (1996). Planning an advanced listening comprehension elective for Japanese college students. In K. Graves (Ed.), *Teachers as course developers* (151–175). New York: Cambridge University Press.

Fuller, F. F., & Brown, O. H. (1975). Becoming a teacher. In K. Ryan (Ed.), *Teacher education: The seventy-fourth yearbook of the National Society for the Study of Education* (pp. 25–51). Chicago: National Society for the Study of Education.

Gaies, S. (1991). ELT in the 1990s. *JALT Journal*, *13*, 7–21.

Gay, G. (2006). Connections between classroom management and culturally responsive teaching. In C. M. Evertson & C. S. Weinstein (Eds.), *Handbook of classroom management: Research, practice, and contemporary issues* (pp. 343–370). Mahwah, NJ: Lawrence Erlbaum Associates.

Gebhard, J. G. (2006). *Teaching English as a Foreign or Second Language: A teacher self-development and methodology guide* (2nd ed.). Ann Arbor: The University of Michigan Press.

Gebhard, J. G. (2009). The practicum. In A. Burns & J. C. Richards (Eds.), *The Cambridge guide to second language teacher education* (252–260). New York: Cambridge University Press.

Gebhard, J., & Oprandy, R. (Eds.) (1999). *Language teaching awareness*. New York: Cambridge University Press.

Good, T. L., & Power, C. (1976). Designing successful classroom environments for different types of students. *Journal of Curriculum Studies*, *8*, 1–16.

Guyton, E., & McIntyre, D. J. (1990). Student teaching and school experiences. In W. R. Houston (Ed.), *Handbook of research in teacher education* (514–534). New York: MacMillan.

Hadfield, J. (1992). *Classroom dynamics*. Oxford: Oxford University Press.

Johnson, K. E. (1995). *Understanding communication in second language classrooms*. New York: Cambridge University Press.

Johnson, K. E. (1996). The vision versus the reality: The tensions of the TESOL practicum. In D. Freeman & J. C. Richards (Eds.), *Teacher learning in language teaching* (30–49). New York: Cambridge University Press.

Johnson, K. E. (2009). *Second language teacher education: A sociocultural perspective*. New York: Routledge.

Johnson, K. E., & Golombek, P. (2002). *Teachers' narrative inquiry as professional development*. New York: Cambridge University Press.

Katz, A., & Snow, M. A. (2009). Standards and second language teacher education. In A. Burns & J. C. Richards (Eds.), *The Cambridge guide to second language teacher education* (pp. 66–76). New York: Cambridge University Press.

Ko, J., Schallert, D., & Walters, K. (2003). Rethinking scaffolding: Negotiation of meaning in an ESL storytelling task. *TESOL Quarterly*, *37*(2), 303–324.

Komblueth, L., & Schoenberg, S. (1990). Through the looking glass: Reflective methods in teacher training. *TESOL Newsletter*, *24*, 17–18.

Kumaravadivelu, B. (1994). The postmethod condition: Emerging strategies for second/foreign language teaching. *TESOL Quarterly*, *28*(1), 27–48.

Lamb, T. E. (2003). Individualising learning: Organising a flexible learning environment. In M. Jiménez Raya & T. Lamb (Eds.), *Differentiation in the modern languages classroom* (177–194). Frankfurt am Main: Peter Lang.

Lantolf, J. P., & Thorne, S. L. (2006). *Sociocultural theory and the genesis of second language development.* Oxford: Oxford University Press.

Lave, J., & Wenger, E. (1991). *Situated learning.* Cambridge: Cambridge University Press.

Leung, C. (2009). Second language teacher professionalism. In A. Burns & J. C. Richards (Eds.), *The Cambridge guide to second language teacher education* (49–58). New York: Cambridge University Press.

Lewis, C., & Tsuchida, I. (1998). A lesson is like a swiftly flowing river: How research lessons improve Japanese education. *American Educator* (Winter), 12–17, 50–52.

Lewis, M. (2002). *Giving feedback in language classes.* Singapore: RELC.

Lynch, T. (2001). Promoting EAP learner autonomy in a second language university context. In J. Flowerdew & M. Peacock (Eds.), *Research perspectives on English for Academic Purposes* (390–403). Cambridge: Cambridge University Press.

MacDonald, R. E. (1991). *A handbook of basic skills and strategies for beginning teachers.* White Plains, NY: Longman.

Master, P. (1983). The etiquette of observing. *TESOL Quarterly*, 17(3), 497–501.

Maynard, T., & Furlong, J. (1995). Learning to teach and models of mentoring. In T. Kerry & A. S. Mayes (Eds.), *Issues in mentoring* (10–24). London: Routledge.

McCombs, B. L., & Pope, J. E. (1994). *Motivating hard to reach students.* Washington, DC: American Psychological Association.

Medgyes, P. (2001). When the teacher is a non-native speaker. In M. Celce-Murcia (Ed.), *Teaching English as a second or foreign language* (3rd ed., pp. 429–442). Boston: Heinle and Heinle.

Mehan, H. (1979). *Learning lessons: Social organization in the classroom.* Cambridge: Cambridge University Press.

Miller, L. (2009). Reflective lesson planning: Promoting learner autonomy in the classroom. In R. Pemberton, S. Toogood, & A. Barfield (Eds.), *Maintaining control. Autonomy and Language Learning* (109–124). Hong Kong: Hong Kong University Press.

Mishra, P., & Koehler, M. J. (2006). Technological pedagogical content knowledge: A new framework for teacher knowledge. *Teachers College Record*, 108(6), 1017–1054.

Morris, P. (1994). *The Hong Kong school curriculum.* Hong Kong: Hong Kong University Press.

Nunan, D. (1987). Communicate language teaching: Making it work. *English Language Teaching Journal*, 41(2), 136–145.

Nunan, D. (1992). The teacher as decision-maker. In J. Flowerdew, M. Brock, & S. Hsia (Eds.), *Perspectives on second language teacher education* (135–165). Hong Kong: City University of Hong Kong.

Nunan, D. (1999). *Second language teaching and learning.* Boston, MA: Heinle and Heinle Publishers.

Nunan, D., & Lamb, C. (1996). *The self-directed teacher: Managing the learning process.* Cambridge: Cambridge University Press.

Oprandy, R. (1999). Exploring with a supervisor. In J. Gebhard & R. Oprandy (Eds.), *Language teacher awareness* (99–121). New York: Cambridge University Press.

Prabhu, N. S. (1992). The dynamics of the language lesson. *TESOL Quarterly*, 26(2), 225–241.

Randal, M., & Thornton, B. (2001). *Advising and supporting teachers.* Cambridge: Cambridge University Press.

Reinders, H. (2009). Technology and second language teacher education. In A. Burns & J. C. Richards (Eds.), *The Cambridge guide to second language teacher education* (230–237). New York: Cambridge University Press.

Reppen, R. (2002). A genre-based approach to content writing instruction. In J. C. Richards & W. Renendya (Eds.), *Methodology in language teaching: An anthology of current practice* (321–327). New York: Cambridge University Press.

Richard-Amato, P. A. (2009). *Making it happen: From interactive to participatory language teaching: Evolving theory and practice* (4th ed.). New York: Pearson.

Richards, J. C. (1998). *Beyond training.* New York: Cambridge University Press.

Richards, J. C. (2001). *Curriculum development in language teaching.* New York: Cambridge University Press.

Richards, J. C., & Crookes, G. (1988). The practicum in TESOL. *TESOL Quarterly*, 22(1), 9–27.

Richards, J. C., & Farrell, T. S. C. (2005). *Professional development for language teachers.* New York: Cambridge University Press.

Richards, J. C., Ho, B., & Giblin, K. (1996). Learning how to teach in the RSA Cert. In D. Freeman & J. C. Richards (Eds.), *Teacher learning in language teaching* (242–259). New York: Cambridge University Press.

Richards, J. C., & Lockhart, C. (1994). *Reflective teaching in second language classrooms.* New York: Cambridge University Press.

Richards, J. C., & Renandya, W. (2002). *Methodology in language teaching: An anthology of current practice.* New York: Cambridge University Press.

Richards, J. C., & Rodgers, T. S. (2001). *Approaches and methods in language teaching* (2nd ed.). Cambridge: Cambridge University Press.

Richards, J. C., & Schmidt, R. (2010). *Longman dictionary of applied linguistics and language teaching* (4th ed.). Harlow: Pearson.

Roberts, J. (1998). *Language teacher education.* London: Arnold.

Saville-Troike, M. (2006). *Introducing second language acquisition.* New York: Cambridge University Press.

Scharle, Á., & Szabó, A. (2000). *Learner autonomy: A guide to developing learner responsibility.* Cambridge: Cambridge University Press.

Senior, R. (2006). *The experience of language teaching.* New York: Cambridge University Press.

Shulman, L. S. (1987). Knowledge and teaching: Foundations of the new reform. *Harvard Educational Review*, 57(1), 1–22.

Silver, R. E. (2008). Monitoring or observing? Managing classroom peer work. In T. S. C. Farrell. (Ed.), (2008e). *Classroom management* (45–55). Alexandria, VA: TESOL Publications.

Stauffer, R. G. (1969). *Directing reading maturity as a cognitive process.* New York: Harper & Row.

Swain, M. (2000). The output hypothesis and beyond: Mediating acquisition through collaborative dialog. In J. P. Lantolf (Ed.), *Sociocultural theory and second language learning* (97–114). Oxford: Oxford University Press.

Tarone, E., & Yule, G. (1989). *Focus on the language learner*. Oxford: Oxford University Press.

Taylor, S. V., & Sobel, D. (2008). Supporting culturally responsive classroom management. In T. S. C. Farrell. (Ed.), (2008e). *Classroom management* (7–18). Alexandria, VA: TESOL Publications.

Thornbury, S. (1991). Watching the whites of their eyes: The use of teaching-practice logs. *ELT Journal*, 45(2), 140–146.

Thornbury, S. (2005). Speaking to learn. In J. Foley (Ed.), *New dimensions in the teaching of oral communication*. Singapore: Regional Language Centre.

Thornbury, S. (2006). *An A–Z of ELT*. Oxford: Macmillan.

Tudor, I. (2001). *The dynamics of the language classroom*. Cambridge: Cambridge University Press.

Ur, P. (1996). *A course in language teaching*. Cambridge: Cambridge University Press.

Wajnryb, R. (1992). *Classroom observation tasks*. Cambridge: Cambridge University Press.

Wallace, M. (1991). *Training foreign language teachers: A reflective approach*. Cambridge: Cambridge University Press.

Wallace, M. (1998). *Action research for language teachers*. Cambridge: Cambridge University Press.

Williams, A., Prestage, S. A., & Bedward, J. (2001). Individualism to collaboration: The significance of teacher culture to the induction of newly qualified teachers. *Journal of Education for Teaching*, 27(3), 253–267.

Wong-Fillmore, L. (1985). When does teacher talk work as input? In S. Gass & C. Madden. (Eds.), *Input in second language acquisition* (17–50). Rowley, Mass: Newbury House.

Woodward, T. (2001). *Planning lessons and courses*. Cambridge: Cambridge University Press.

Wright, A. (2005). *Classroom management in language education*. Basingstoke: Palgrave.

Zeichner, K., & Grant, C. (1981). Biography and social structure in the socialization of student teachers. *Journal of Education for Teaching*, 1, 198–314.

Author Index

Aljaafreh, A., 136
Arends, R., 126

Bailey, K. M., 47–48, 63
Baird, B., 3, 9
Bedward, J., 34
Bell, D. M., 75
Benson, P., 121, 122
Biddle, B., 144
Borg, S., 18, 24
Brenes-Carvajal, M. G. del C., 19
Brindley, G., 37–38
Brown, O. H., 23
Burns, A., 16

Calderhead, J., 32
Carvajal, M., 3, 103
Cazden, C., 135
Cooke, M., 17, 126, 128
Crawford, J., 57
Crookes, G., 15, 31

Dewey, J., 167
Dörnyei, Z., 76, 82, 114–15, 116,
     121, 126–27, 130
Doyle, Z., 80
Duncan, M., 144

Farrell, T. S. C., 3, 4, 8, 15, 38,
     67–69, 94, 156, 162, 165,
     167
Freeman, D., 47
Fujiwara, B., 60
Fuller, F. F., 23
Furlong, J., 163

Gaies, S., 92
Gay, G., 115
Giblin, K., 80
Good, T. L., 123
Grant, C., 31

Guyton, T. L., 43

Ho, B., 80

Johnson, K. E., 109, 135–36, 144

Katz, A., 73
Ko, J., 139
Koehler, M. J., 20
Komblueth, L., 7
Kumaravadivelu, B., 75

Lamb, C., 74
Lamb, T. E., 121
Lantolf, J. P., 136, 137–38
Lave, J., 165
Leung, C., 168
Lewis, C., 165
Lewis, M., 141
Lockhart. C., 79, 112, 125, 144,
     167
Lynch, T., 121

MacDonald, R. E., 59
Master, P., 98
Maynard, T., 163
McCombs, B. L., 84
McIntyre, D. J., 43
Medgyes, P., 72
Mehan, H., 136
Miller, L., 7
Mishra, P., 20
Morris, P., 34

Nunan, D., 62, 74, 80, 136

Pope, J. E., 84
Power, C., 123
Prestage, S. A., 34

Reinders, H., 20
Reppen, R., 69–71
Richard-Amato, P. A., 61
Richards, J. C., 15, 16, 31, 55, 57–58,
     59–60, 75, 79, 80, 112, 125,
     144, 165, 167
Roberts, J., 4, 7
Rodgers, T. S., 75

Saville-Troike, M., 139
Schallert, D., 139
Schoenberg, S., 7
Senior, R., 4, 10, 11, 14, 18, 21, 22,
     24, 37, 47, 57, 58–59, 82,
     107–8, 126–27, 164
Seow, A., 109
Shulman, L. S., 19, 22
Silver, R. E., 111
Simpson, J., 17, 126, 128
Snow, M. A., 73
Sobel, D., 115
Stauffer, R. G., 68
Swain, M., 136, 140

Tarone, E., 121
Taylor, S. V., 115
Thornbury, S., 17, 134, 136, 137,
     141–43
Thorne, S. L., 136, 137–38
Tsuchida I., 165

Wajnryb, R., 94
Wallace, M., 4, 5
Walters, K., 139
Wenger, E., 165
Williams, A., 34
Wong-Fillmore, L., 77
Woodward, T., 80

Yule, G., 121

Zeichner, K., 31

Subject Index